Guarding the
Forbidden City

www.royalcollins.com

Guarding the
Forbidden City
Memoirs of a Palace Museum Director

Shan Jixiang

Translated by Daniel McRyan

RC
Books Beyond Boundaries
ROYAL COLLINS

Guarding the Forbidden City: Memoirs of a Palace Museum Director

Shan Jixiang

Translated by Daniel McRyan

First published in 2023 by Royal Collins Publishing Group Inc.
Groupe Publication Royal Collins Inc.
BKM Royalcollins Publishers Private Limited

Headquarters: 550-555 boul. René-Lévesque O Montréal (Québec) H2Z1B1 Canada
India office: 805 Hemkunt House, 8th Floor, Rajendra Place, New Delhi 110 008

ISBN: 978-1-4878-1012-2

To find out more about our publications, please visit www.royalcollins.com.

I am the "Gatekeeper" of the Forbidden City

I started to work in the Palace Museum in January 2012.

The Palace Museum holds numerous titles of "the world's best," such as the world's largest and most complete ensemble of ancient royal architecture, the world's richest and most precious treasure vault of China's cultural relics, and the museum that receives the most number of visitors annually.

People must be filled with pride and responsibility to be working in this place that wears plenty of "world's best" titles. However, when I became an employee of the Palace Museum, walking among the visitors on a daily basis and putting myself in their shoes, I find it difficult to truly appreciate these "world's bests" because they have not yet been fully presented. There is still huge space for improvement.

The Palace Museum is enormous, but I have noticed that most areas are not open; the Palace Museum holds an abundant collection of cultural relics, but what I see is that 99% of them are sleeping in the storehouse, and less than 1% on display; the Palace Museum receives the most visitors, but they do not enjoy the exhibition they deserve. Many visitors move around in the museum following the guide's flag and listening to unprofessional explanations; their visit merely includes checking where the emperor used to sit and sleep, and where his marriage ceremony was held; a quick browse of the Treasure Gallery and the Gallery of Clocks; and a short break in the Imperial Garden. Next, their tour ends. I believe this kind of visit experience is just "skimming the surface." We have therefore failed to fully present the charm of this museum to the visitors.

Do some of the "the world's best" titles matter that much? They are important, but not the most important. As time rolls forward, people long more for a cultural life with quality. What truly matters may be to what extent the cultural heritage resources of the Palace Museum can contribute to people's real life. For a visitor, what truly matters may be his personal gain from an incredible cultural journey after he leaves the Palace Museum. In a way, what the Palace Museum lacks is the "people-centered" management philosophy. There is the absence of humanistic care. And this must be changed.

President Xi Jinping pointed out, "It is necessary to systematically sort out traditional cultural resources, so that the cultural relics stored in the Forbidden City, the heritage displayed on this vast land, and the words written in the ancient books come back to life." In the past few years, it was precisely the systematic combing of traditional cultural resources and resurrecting of the cultural relics that have enabled us to realize the healthy development of the Palace Museum.

In the past, when we conducted historical research, archaeological research, and museum management, we used to regard the cultural heritage as "something from the past" that is far away from the current society, as objects to be viewed and studied only. But to bring the cultural relics back to life, it is necessary to return them to people's lives. Only when people feel their significance in real life can people truly protect them, and can they truly possess dignity and charm. Consequently, cultural heritage with dignity and charm will positively promote social development. When that happens, they will benefit more people and inspire more people to join the ranks of cultural heritage protection, thus forming a virtuous circle.

In my opinion, a good museum is not defined by building a grand hall, but by digging deep into its cultural resources, gathering cultural energy, holding meaningful exhibitions and activities, and enabling visitors to feel the museum's significance in their real life. A good museum is where people are willing to go into in their spare time;

what they enjoy themselves so much as to forget to leave but linger on; what they bear in mind constantly and come back to.

Inserting the Chinese character "活 (life)" into the Chinese character "门 (gate)" makes "阔 (broad)." This is common knowledge to Chinese. During my seven years of work in the Palace Museum, everything I do as the "gatekeeper" is insert the character "活 (life)" into the gate of the Forbidden City, so that its cultural heritage resources get closer to people's lives and towards a broader space.

SHAN JIXIANG
March 26, 2020

Contents

Preface: I am the "Gatekeeper" of the Forbidden City / v

Chapter 1   Hand the Magnificent Forbidden City Over to the Next 600 Years
             Intact / 1
             An Endless Column of Successors: The Past Efforts / 2
             From "Safe and Sound" to "Light Up": For the Next 600 Years of the Forbidden
                 City / 24

Chapter 2   The Abundance of Precious Cultural Relics / 43
             The Exact Number of Collections in the Forbidden City / 44
             Twenty-Three Categories of Cultural Relics / 49
             Collection Acquisition / 65
             Examples of Precious Collections in the Forbidden City / 67
             The Palace Museum Exhibition Sensation / 74

Chapter 3   The Palace Museum, an Educational Institution / Research
             Institution / 97
             Volunteers—a Beautiful Sight in the Palace Museum / 98
             For the Children / 109
             From "Gugong Studies" to "Palace Museum Academy" / 120

Chapter 4   The Inspirational Artisan Spirit / 137
             Masters in the Forbidden City / 138
             Greenlight the "Century Renovation" / 148
             Masters in the Forbidden City / 162

Chapter 5   Management Reform / 183
             Better Service / 184
             "Closed" and "Open"—Set the Closing Days and Open More Space / 186
             "Divert" and "Limit"—Balance between Peak Off-Seasons / 196
             "Toilet Revolution" under Big Data / 202
             No Entry for Foreign Guests' Cars, Either / 207

Chapter 6   Hundreds of Millions of Visitors / 217
             Always Trending on Social Media / 218
             Popular Apps / 225
             Website Redesign and Digital Showroom / 229
             Diversification of Digital Applications / 238

Chapter 7   Out of the Palace Museum / 243
             More Approachable / 244
             Steps All over China / 251
             "Standard Configuration" for Permanent Member States of the UN Security
                 Council / 261
             Trump Visited the Palace Museum / 267

Chapter 8   More Fun in the Palace Museum / 275
             The Fantastic Cultural and Creative Products / 276
             The Palace Museum Brand / 287

Postscript: The Power of Culture / 293
Index / 305

CHAPTER 1

Hand the Magnificent Forbidden City Over to the Next 600 Years Intact

It has multiple names, which represent different identities.

First, it is called the Forbidden City. It used to be the imperial palace of the Ming and Qing Dynasties. It is the world's largest and most complete ensemble of ancient royal architecture.

The second name is the Imperial Palace ("Gugong" in Chinese which means "old palace"). In February 1912, Emperor Xuantong of the Qing Dynasty abdicated, hence the name. Today, it stores the cultural relics of past dynasties, thus becoming the world's richest and most precious treasure vault of China's cultural relics.

The third name came even later. During the "Beijing Coup" launched by Feng Yuxiang in 1924, the last emperor Puyi was expelled from the palace. From October 10, 1925, a new name was given to it—the Palace Museum, meaning it has become a public cultural facility open to the society. Today, it is the museum that annually receives the most visitors in the world.

Since it was completed in the 18th year of the Yongle Period in the Ming Dynasty (1420), the Forbidden City has undergone 600 years by 2020. "We will hand the magnificent Forbidden City over to the next 600 years intact." This is our solemn promise to the society.

An Endless Column of Successors:
The Past Efforts

———

For a cause to be carried on from generation to generation, each generation ought to lay the foundation for the successor. This is my understanding of how the "endless column of successors" works. The Palace Museum was established in 1925. In the nearly one hundred years of development, it has undergone the vicissitudes of life. And it is the unremitting efforts of every director and all the museum staff that have made it shine so brightly today.

The first director of the Palace Museum was Mr. Yi Peiji.

After emperor Puyi was expelled from the palace in November 1924, the Beiyang government ordered the establishment of the Aftermath Committee of Royal Family of Qing, where Li Shi served as the chairman and Yi Peiji as a committee member to take over the Forbidden City. Mr. Yi led the preparation for the Palace Museum, and was formally appointed by the National Government of the Republic of China as its first director in February 1929.

During his four years of directorship, all affairs of the Palace Museum got on the right track. He adjusted the organizational structure of the Palace Museum, hired prestigious experts and scholars, sorted and divided the museum's cultural relics and non-cultural relics, and proposed the *Complete Palace Museum Custody Plan* for the first time. Various thematic showrooms were opened, ancient buildings were renovated, and new halls of calligraphies and paintings were built. He also founded a printing office to publish books, created the *Forbidden City Weekly*, and successively published periodicals including the *Forbidden City Monthly* and *Forbidden City Every Ten Days*. Under his leadership, outstanding achievements have been made in palace repairs, exhibitions, collections storage and cataloging, document sorting, compilation and publishing, edition identification and cataloging, and classified stacks. As a result, the Palace Museum took a huge leap. In 1933, as the Japanese army captured Shanhaiguan, the relocation of national treasures was put on the agenda. Mr. Yi led and planned the southward relocation of precious cultural relics to avoid the enemy's plunder, thus paving the road for the next director.

The second director of the Palace Museum was Mr. Ma Heng.

Mr. Ma was the pioneer of modern Chinese museums and he laid the foundation for the launching of the Palace Museum. As early as November 1924, hired as a consultant to the Aftermath Committee of Royal Family of Qing, he participated in making the inventory of the items in the Forbidden City and the preparation for the establishment of the Palace Museum. He worked in the Palace Museum for 27 years, during which he had served as its second director for 19 years.

Having witnessed the founding and early development of the Palace Museum, he was a leader with outstanding achievement in the history of the Palace Museum. When it was founded in 1925, he served as a member of the Palace Museum Council and deputy curator of the Hall of Antiquities. With his personal work experience and methods in Peking University, he led the daily operation of the Hall of Antiquities. He drafted the *Detailed Rules for the Administration of the Hall of Antiquities of the Palace Museum* to standardize the cultural relics storage rules and retrieval procedures. Meanwhile, he led the Hall of Antiquities to conduct cultural relic reviews and appraisals, and personally instructed the inspection of bronze cultural relics. This inspection was the first systematic review and appraisal of cultural relics in the museum, and it has played a rather important role in the research and display of related cultural relics. After the Mukden Incident in 1931, the Palace Museum was ordered to move cultural relics to the south. Mr. Ma Heng led everyone from the Hall of Antiquities to devote themselves to packing the cultural relics. From the heavy and precious stone drums to the flimsy and fragile paintings and calligraphies, 13,427 boxes and 64 packs of cultural relics and archives were safely packed in an orderly manner round the clock, and shipped away from Beijing one after another.

His historical achievements are mainly summarized into two points: one is the southward relocation and the return of the cultural relics during the War of Resistance against Japan; the other is the refusal to their relocation during the War of Liberation.

In July 1933, Director Yi Peiji resigned after being framed for the "Forbidden City Treasure Theft Case." At this critical moment, Mr. Ma Heng was appointed as the acting director of the Palace Museum, and was promoted director in April of the following year to take full charge of its affairs. As soon as he took office, he immediately organized the making of the inventory of the cultural relics of the Palace Museum left in Beijing, and the check and acceptance of cultural relics that were to be moved south to Shanghai. At this time, the Palace Museum was challenged with both the external threat from aggressors and the internal relocation of cultural relics. It was a critical moment. Mr. Ma Heng was managing the Palace Museum at this time, and he racked his brain to protect the national treasure in the chaos. Under his leadership, the cultural relics of the Palace Museum left in Beijing and those shipped to Shanghai were properly counted and registered.

After the Marco Polo Bridge Incident in 1937, he organized the Palace Museum's cultural relics that had been relocated southward to be moved westward. He traveled to various destinations to inspect and select the best site, and stationed himself in Chongqing to guide the work of various offices. In the precarious situation of China, he tenaciously guarded the Forbidden City, the precious national cultural treasure. Despite the turmoil and frequent relocation, he still managed to hold and attend exhibitions, such as flying to the UK to attend the Chinese Art International Exhibition in London, and traveling to the Soviet Union for the Chinese Art Exhibition in Moscow, spreading the national spirit and demonstrating China's determination to win the War of Resistance. When China won the War of Resistance, he instructed the eastward return of the Palace Museum to Nanjing. The cultural relics of the Palace Museum were transported back northward one after another. He began to check and accept the scattered cultural relics of the Qing Dynasty, and organize exhibitions, thus gradually resuming the museum business.

In 1948, the Kuomintang was going to transport cultural relics from both the Nanjing Branch of the Palace Museum and the headquarters in Beijing to Taiwan. Regarding the packing, Ma Heng used "careful, don't rush it" as an excuse to stall the transport. Eventually, none of the cultural relics in the headquarters in Beijing were taken to Taiwan.

After the founding of the People's Republic of China, he continued to serve as the director, leading the Palace Museum into a new era.

In 1952, Mr. Ma Heng, who had turned 70 years old, left the Palace Museum. It was also in this year that he donated a private collection of over 400 precious cultural relics, including oracle bones and rubbings from stone inscriptions to the Palace Museum, to which he devoted his life.

What touches me most is that in the last moments of his life, Mr. Ma was still studying the stone inscriptions of the Han and Wei Dynasties. When Guo Moruo (revolutionary writer) sent bronze rubbings, he threw himself completely into the examination of the rubbings, regardless of his disease. This aggravated his illness. After he passed away, his descendants donated over 10,000 rubbings and books to the Palace Museum, honoring his last wish. Although he is no longer with us, his character and mind have been integrated into the spirit of the Forbidden City, becoming a valuable asset for future generations.

The third director of the Palace Museum was Mr. Wu Zhongchao.

Mr. Wu was an experienced revolutionary. During the War of Liberation, he collected and kept a great many precious cultural relics for the Communist Party of China (CPC) and the people. In 1954, the East China Bureau of the CPC was canceled, and he was employed to manage the affairs in the Palace Museum. Thereafter, he blazed a trail for the transformation and development of the Palace Museum in the new times. Whether in the early stage of socialist construction or during the reform and opening up, he made outstanding achievements and withstood the test of history. The Palace Museum staff who worked with him, while breaking new ground for the Palace Museum, created and accumulated abundant spiritual wealth, making a fine tradition with both the common characteristics of the times and the characteristics of the Palace Museum itself.

When he first took office, despite the five years of development soon after the founding of the People's Republic of China, there were many prominent problems. In order to change the "garbage mountain" image of the Palace Museum, he performed a thorough cleanup with the support of the Ministry of Culture and the People's Liberation Army. Statistics show that, during this cleanup, a total of about 250,000 cubic meters of rubbish, soil, and bricks were removed. At the same time, he allocated manpower to dredge the moat of the Forbidden City, repair the river walls, and the environment, therefore making over the appearance of the Palace Museum. When Puyi visited it in the 1960s, he was in awe of the result, proving the necessity and effectiveness of this environmental governance project.

During his 30 years in office, Mr. Wu always prioritized the status quo of the Palace Museum. He insisted on staying realistic. He believed that investigation should come first to expose the prominent problems before discussions to find solutions, and then work could be performed in a planned, step-by-step, and targeted manner. His courageous revolutionary spirit and pragmatic management style are valuable lessons for us to learn. In response to the situation of "too many problems," he targeted the key link of management system reform, first adjusting and improving the institutional settings. On the basis of the original storage department, exhibition department, mass work department, and several special committees, academic, editing and publishing, cultural relic collection, cultural relic review, cultural relic identification, and cultural relic repair committees were added, and some business departments were opened, including the ancient architecture repair department, research office, Forbidden City

Press, etc. At the same time, efforts were made to promote the professionalization of all sorts of tasks of the Palace Museum such as the ancient architecture repair, cultural relic storage, display and exhibition, and academic research. Additionally, in order to cope with the development of the organization, the rules and regulations were constantly revised and improved, and the staffing and talent building constantly strengthened and enhanced.

Mr. Wu's explorations in ancient architecture protection, cultural relic storage, exhibition business, and talent management were groundbreaking. They paved the road for the general development and specific business of the Palace Museum in the future.

Regarding ancient architecture protection, in the 1950s, the Palace Museum clarified the renovation policy of "emphasized maintenance, focused renovation, comprehensive planning, and gradual implementation" and the safety policy of "prevention first, with the focus on fire prevention." At the time of the "Cultural Revolution," a series of major renovation projects had been completed. In the 1970s, the three front halls and the three back halls along the central axis were also repainted on a large scale, which beautified the appearance of the architecture in key areas. In 1974, the State Council greenlighted the *Five-Year Renovation Plan for Ancient Architectures of the Palace Museum*. As planned, the Palace Museum renovated and repainted the Sparrow Wing Towers at the Meridian Gate, the southeast Corner Tower, Hall of Imperial Supremacy, the rear three palaces, Palace of Accumulated Purity, Palace of Great Benevolence, and Area of Six Eastern Palaces, therefore greatly enhancing the architectural style. Thereafter, the protection and renovation of the ancient architecture of the Forbidden City have become routine, with the focus on preservation and maintenance. During the preservation and renovation of ancient architecture, Mr. Wu attached great importance to scientificity and rationality. For example, regarding whether the renovation of ancient architecture should be "totally as the new," or "totally as the old" or "mostly as the old," in addition to organizing seminars among experts and scholars in and out of the museum, he also formulated different plans, performed experimental practices, and gradually sorted out a set of renovation procedures, techniques, and experiences suitable for the ancient architecture of the Forbidden City.

When it comes to the storage of cultural relics, in order to address the problem of an unclear base number of the collections, Mr. Wu, overriding all objections, concentrated all efforts on sorting out the cultural relics. From 1954 to 1957, the *Plan for Sorting Out Historical Dead Stock* and the *Interim Measures for Clearing Non-cultural Relics* were formulated to sort out cultural relics, dispose non-cultural relics, tidy up the warehouses, and establish special inventories; as per the *Inventory Report of Items of the Forbidden City* in 1925 and the *Check and Acceptance List of Cultural Relics in the Palace Museum* in 1945, inventory, appraisal, classification, and coding of cultural relics were performed from palace to palace. This move saved 2,876 pieces of valuable cultural relics, including more than 500 grade-one cultural relics, such as a three-goat square zun (a type of Chinese ritual bronze or ceramic wine vessel) of the Shang Dynasty, *Listening to the Qin* by Emperor Huizong of the Song Dynasty, etc. From 1960 to 1965, as per relevant regulations, the collections were appraised and graded, the general register of cultural relics in the Palace Museum was created and perfected, and the classified cultural relics register of each inventory was verified. This arduous and complicated task spanned more than 10 years, and eventually resulted in the cultural relic register compiled from the "old" collections of the Forbidden City and the general register of the Palace Museum's collections complied from the "new" cultural relics registers that began to be made in 1954, therefore ensuring a basic grasp of the quantity of the cultural relic collections.

In terms of display and exhibition, Mr. Wu has always adhered to the concept of scientific management. Initially, he positioned the Palace Museum as a comprehensive ancient art museum that integrates history, art, ancient architecture, and royal palaces. The clarification of the positioning has basically pointed out the development direction and basic pattern of the preservation and exhibition of the ancient architecture of the Forbidden City in the following 30 years, and it is still working today. The display and exhibition pattern that combines the original display and thematic display fundamentally reflects the positioning of a comprehensive ancient art museum. How to arrange the display well according to the characteristics of the Forbidden City? Mr. Wu believes that it makes perfect sense for the three halls (Hall of Supreme Harmony, Hall of Central Harmony, and Hall of Preserving Harmony), the rear three palaces (Palace of Heavenly Purity, Hall of Union, and Palace of Earthly Tranquility) and the Area of Six Western Palaces on the central axis of the Forbidden City to be displayed in their original historical forms. So does it mean all palaces are going to be displayed in their original forms? He pointed out that the single display layout would be monotonous and less attractive. Therefore, a museum of art of past dynasties was set up on the inner western road, special exhibitions of bronzes were made on the inner eastern road and Hall of Ancestral Worship, and a painting gallery and a treasure hall were built on the outer eastern road. This layout, which has been well received by experts, scholars, and visitors at home and abroad, remains in use today.

Mr. Wu deeply believed the idea of respecting knowledge and talents. He prevailed over all dissenting views and gathered a legion of intellectuals and skilled craftsmen to the Palace Museum. This talent policy of "embracing it all" and "drawing upon the strength from others" has made the diversified pattern of academic thought in the Palace Museum on the one hand, and has formed a tradition of hiring talents in an eclectic style on the other. He fully implemented Premier Zhou Enlai's major instructions on intellectuals, recruiting a large number of them. With deep faith in the idea of well selecting, well using, well training, and well nurturing talents, he promoted experts and scholars, trained business cadres, and hired professionals. In the 1950s, he appointed Tang Lan, Chen Wanli, and Shan Shiyuan to chair the Academic Committee and Ceramic Research Office and the Architectural Research Office respectively, thus laying the foundation for academic studies; he appointed Yang Boda and Li Hongqing as deputy directors of the exhibition department and the storage department, and Zheng Minzhong, Cui Yutang, Ji Zhongrui, Wei Songqing, Huang Tianxiu, and Feng Xianming as professional team leaders; and he transferred cultural relic appraisal experts such as Wang Yikun and Gu Tiefu, Liu Jiu'an, Xu Bangda, Sun Yingzhou, Luo Fuyi, Geng Baochang, Qiao Yousheng, and Wang Wenchang to supplement the talent team. They combined art theories, literature, cultural relics, and palace history, to deepen previous research, to open up new research fields, to develop new research methods, and to improve the academic status and the influence of the Palace Museum in China and around the world.

More importantly, Mr. Wu has always been realistic about the Palace Museum's business. While respecting scholars and experts, whom he put in key positions, he also attached great importance to the introduction and training of technical personnel for cultural relics repair. In the 1950s, he transferred famous scholars and experts in cultural relic repair from all over the country to strengthen the technical capability of the cultural relic repair team of the Palace Museum. One after another, talents of copying calligraphy and painting, such as Zheng Zhuyou and Jin Zhongyu from Shanghai, masters of mounting pictures, such as Yang Wenbin, Zhang Yaoxuan, and Sun Chengzhi from Suzhou and Hangzhou, and bronze repair experts, such as Gu Dewang, Zhao Zhenmao, and Jin Yumin from the Beijing-Tianjin-Hebei area have gathered in the Palace Museum. In order to retain and pass on these precious traditional handicraft arts, he designed a talent training program based on the characteristics of the discipline fields, and a protection and production model of "master-apprentice inheritance" gradually came into being in the field of cultural relics repair. At present, the Palace Museum is in a leading position in the field of cultural relics repair technology in China thanks to the talent strategy of Mr. Wu.

Over the past 30 years, it is well-known that he protects and cherishes intellectuals and technical talents. He once made a witty comparison: "Experts are as precious as pandas." He also pointed out that "It doesn't hurt keeping a few more experts in this grand Palace Museum." Mr. Wu regards them as a national treasure, and treats talents with sincerity and open arms. He has assembled an army of experts, scholars, and technical personnel in the fields of cultural relic research, cultural relic authentication, cultural relic repair, and ancient architecture preservation for the Palace Museum. We are eternally grateful for his contribution to the talent team building.

Mr. Wu had a spontaneous sense of responsibility for the Palace Museum. During his 30 years of guarding the Forbidden City, every year when new employees went through the orientation at the Palace Museum, there was an on-boarding ceremony.

A bus transported the new recruits outside the Gate of Divine Prowess. On the Gate of Divine Prowess Square, they lined up, and Mr. Wu shook hands with them one by one. Then, a welcome party was held there. After reading out the documents specially approved by the State Council, he turned over the documents with the red seal so that everyone present could see it. At the time, everyone would feel the honor to work in the Palace Museum, and with honor came a strong sense of responsibility.

The fourth director of the Palace Museum was Mr. Zhang Zhongpei.

Looking back on his museum management philosophy, policy implementation strategy, and grand ambitions, in awe, I reap no little benefit. Regarding the inevitable questions for the directors of the Palace Museum, like "how to make the characteristics of the Palace Museum stand out," "how to well preserve the architectures and cultural relics of the Forbidden City," "how to well operate the Palace Museum," "how to plan the long-term development of the Palace Museum," his practical actions are the perfect answers. With unremitting effort, he presented the public a complete Forbidden City.

How to make the characteristics of the Palace Museum stand out? This is a core proposition that the director of the Palace Museum must face. Mr. Zhang has deeply pondered this proposition since he assumed office. He expounded the palace history, palace architecture, and ancient art as the three important contents that constitute the characteristics of the Palace Museum, and clarified its development direction.

As early as 1987, Mr. Zhang pinpointed that the advantage of the Palace Museum lies in the fact that it is an ancient royal palace. This advantage is a historical formation, an objective existence, and independent from the public will. Therefore, there are two main tasks for the Palace Museum: one is to preserve the Forbidden City as a whole so that it lasts, which is the prerequisite for all work; the other is to make it special, using the advantages of itself to make the characteristics stand out. He summarized the two core issues in the management of the Palace Museum in the most succinct words "preserve" and "special."

How to well preserve the architectures and cultural relics of the Forbidden City? This is a central task that the director of the Palace Museum must undertake. During his tenure, he has worked scrupulously to fulfill duties. He took protecting the safety

🖻 Visiting Mr. Zhang Zhongpei (January 29, 2014).

of ancient architecture and cultural relics as the heart of the Palace Museum, and maintaining their integrity as its mission. With these goals in mind, he formulated the principles for the complete protection of the Forbidden City and its cultural relics system, and took serious measures to preserve cultural relics. First, destructive opening is prevented by limiting the number of visitors and designing tour routes; second, the protection scope of the Forbidden City is re-determined, re-including "the moats on the east, west, and north sides of the Forbidden City and within their outer edges, and the moats on the east and west sides of the south side of the Forbidden City and within their outer edges"; third, the affairs concerning the cultural relics left in Nanjing during the War of Resistance are actively negotiated; and last but not least, a collection cataloging plan is formulated. Having been in the excavation, sorting, and research of archaeological materials for years, Mr. Zhang deeply believes the idea that "the materials of academic research should be accessible to the public." It is far-sighted to apply it to the management of the cultural relics of the Palace Museum. At present, the compilation of the collections of the Palace Museum and the publication of the collection catalogs all adhere to this idea.

How to well operate the Palace Museum? This is a key issue that the director of the Palace Museum must ponder. During his tenure, he always adhered to the spirit of emancipating the mind and being brave in innovation. He took serious measures to reform the management system. He was the first to propose the implementation of a director responsibility system and the post responsibility system, thus making the management of the Palace Museum scientific and standardized.

How to plan the long-term development of the Palace Museum? This is what the director of the Palace Museum must excel at. He always made it his mission to make the Palace Museum stronger. He focused on talent training and academic research, and emphasized scientific planning. Starting with improving the knowledge structure of talents, he systematically hired a large group of professional talents from colleges and universities. For example, in 1988, the Palace Museum recruited eight postgraduates and four undergraduates from Peking University, Jilin University, Renmin University of China, the Chinese Academy of Social Sciences, and the Central Academy of Fine Arts. They majored in history, archaeology, and art history. After years of training and practice, most of them have now grown into well-known scholars of museology or leaders of museums in China. He started with improvement for the settings of academic institutions, implementing the appointment system for technical positions, and conducted a series of groundbreaking work: setting up the Academic Committee of the Palace Museum, obtaining the qualification to approve the senior and deputy senior positions of the museology system; promoting the function reform of the research offices, integrating the three functions of scientific research, scientific research management, and academic committee offices; strengthening imperial history research, convening international conferences, and connecting business, academic research, and cultural exchanges. He cut in with the preparation of a long-term plan, established the guidelines, principles, and goals of museum operation, and paid sufficient heed to the coordination between the specific plans of each department and the overall plan of the whole museum. *The Seven-Year (1989–1995) Development Plan of the Palace Museum* designed the principal businesses of the Palace Museum from the perspective of the key cultural relics protection units in China and the protection and development of world cultural heritage.

As he long pondered the development direction of the Palace Museum, Mr. Zhang proposed the idea of "a complete Forbidden City, a safe Forbidden City, a historical Forbidden City, and an academic Forbidden City" in the practice of focused protection of national cultural relics, illuminating the path for the long-term development of the Palace Museum.

"Without long-term strategy, short-term achievement is impossible. Without full-scale consideration, simple action is impracticable." With the scientific attitude and rigorousness of an archaeologist, Mr. Zhang had laid out the overall development of the Palace Museum, laying a solid foundation for the prosperity of its various undertakings.

The fifth director of the Palace Museum was Mr. Zheng Xinmiao, my predecessor.

On November 19, 2001, in order to better preserve the Forbidden City, the State Council convened a meeting with the theme "Research on Issues Related to the Maintenance of Ancient Architecture in the Forbidden City and the Preservation of Cultural Relics," where it was decided to "renovate the Forbidden City as a whole," thus giving a new opportunity for the complete protection of ancient architecture in the Forbidden City. Under this circumstance, Mr. Zheng was appointed as Vice-Minister of the Ministry of Culture and Director of the Palace Museum in October 2002, taking full charge of all the affairs of the Palace Museum.

He studied and explained how to understand the value of the Forbidden City and the connotation of the Palace Museum. In March 2003, he gave a speech titled *The Value of the Forbidden City and the Connotation of the Palace Museum* at the International Museum Directors Forum held at the Shanghai Museum. He combed the 80 years of historical experience of the Palace Museum from the awareness of cultural relics, the valuation of ancient architecture, and the excavation of palace culture, and the inheritance of intangible cultural heritage. Based on this, he clarified the position of the Palace Museum: not only the largest cultural and artistic museum in China, but also one of the few museums and cultural heritage in the world, with the characteristics of art museums, architectural museums, history museums, and court culture museums, that conform to the internationally recognized basic principles of "on-site preservation" and "on-site display." This positioning illuminated the path for the development of the Palace Museum with key points highlighted.

From then on, Mr. Zheng continued to ponder and explore the value of the Forbidden City and the connotation of the Palace Museum. On April 24, 2008, *Guangming Daily* published the article *The Value and Status of the Forbidden City*, which was a theoretical summary of the value of the Forbidden City and the connotation of the Palace Museum based on his five-year management of the Palace Museum. He combed the four stages of understanding the value of the Forbidden City from four perspectives: "the Forbidden City as a royal palace," "the Forbidden City as a museum," "the Forbidden City as a world cultural heritage," and "the Forbidden City under the Scrutiny of Gugong Studies." He elaborated the historical value and cultural significance of the cultural relics of the Forbidden City in the following respects: "the meaning of the national treasure collected by the royals," "the national symbol of the Palace Museum," "the national memory of cultural relics moving southward," and "the humanistic pattern of the one Forbidden City but two Palace Museums." And he pointed out the necessity to see the architectural complex, cultural relics collection, and palace historical remains in a holistic view. These ideas and summaries not only help to look at the value of the Palace Museum more comprehensively, but also bridge the exchange and cooperation between the Palace Museum in Beijing and the Palace Museum in Taipei, thus finding an academic home for the old collections of the Qing palace scattered overseas.

In the past decade, effective organizing and implementing the ancient architecture renovation project of the Forbidden City has always been the top priority of the Palace Museum's development. For the smooth running of the ancient architecture restoration project of the Forbidden City, the Palace Museum has overcome difficulty after difficulty, continued the exploration and practices, and eventually made an impressive achievement, which has had a profound impact on the protection of both Chinese and global cultural heritage.

While organizing and implementing the ancient architecture renovation project of the Forbidden City, Mr. Zheng detected the urgency for a massive sorting of the cultural relics of the Palace Museum, because the collection of cultural relics is the basis for the existence and business activities of a museum, and the quality and quantity are the main factors to assess the status and function of a museum. Only by understanding the types and quantities of cultural relics can effective preservation and in-depth research be conducted. This is the first basis for the development of a museum, and also an important task that the Palace Museum must finish well on the road to becoming a world-class museum. Therefore, he went deep into the warehouse, checked the archives, and wrote the 9,000-word *Research Report on the Palace Museum's Thorough Sorting of Cultural Relics*. It systematically combed the four large-scale cultural relics sorting since 1924 when the Aftermath Committee of Royal Family of Qing made inventory of the palace items, objectively analyzed the conditions for a thorough sorting of the cultural relics collections, planned nine tasks for this undertaking, and made four requirements for combining the sorting of cultural relics collections with improving their management.

In October 2004, the Palace Museum prepared the *Palace Museum 2004–2010 Collection Sorting Plan*, intending to perform a comprehensive inventory making and sorting of all collections in all warehouses and palaces within seven years. It listed the work content and schedule of this task. As of 2010, the Palace Museum had completed the three cross-checks of more than 940,000 cultural relics in the register, named them, graded them, counted them, and ran statistics on them; finished the sorting, registration, and cataloging of the materials on the cultural relics in and out of the register, and updated the information of 180,122 pieces of cultural relics. It is worth mentioning that the ancient books, rare books, and book editions in the Palace Museum used to be stored in the way of a library without being graded and being managed as cultural relics as required. During this cultural relic sorting, a total of 603,061 pieces of collections (books, blocks, frames, and packages) in the 19 warehouses managed by

▣ With Mr. Zhang Zhongpei and Mr. Zheng Xinmiao (October 8, 2016).

the library were sorted, including 564,713 pieces of cultural relics and 38,348 pieces of materials. As required, the preparation and entry of the corresponding accounts were completed, including the sorting, verification, grading, cataloging, and registration of nearly 200,000 rare ancient books and 200,000 precious book editions in special collections and museum collections. This is the most comprehensive and thorough inventory-making since the establishment of the Palace Museum Library in 1925.

After seven years of sorting and cross-checking, the Palace Museum has completed the task of grasping the real quantity. Statistics show that it has a total of 1,807,558 pieces (sets) of collections, including 1,684, 490 precious cultural relics (sets), 115,491 general cultural relics (sets), and 7,577 specimens (sets). Among them, precious cultural relics accounts for 93.2% of the total amount of cultural relics in the Palace Museum, and 41.98% of the total amount of precious cultural relics in China. The seven-year cultural relic sorting was the basic work of the Palace Museum on how to improve the storage capacity and the utilization level of the cultural relics. It was another conceptual innovation initiated by the Palace Museum on how to look at cultural heritage and how to recognize the value of the Forbidden City.

In terms of building acreage, quantity of collections, and number of visitors, the Palace Museum is in parallel with the Louvre Museum, British Museum, Metropolitan Museum, and the Moscow Kremlin Museums. But when it comes to international influence, the public is often only familiar with the Forbidden City without knowing the Palace Museum. In order to change this situation, Director Zheng led the Palace Museum to perform lots of creative work: using the "dialogue of civilizations" as a bridge to gradually open up channels for exchanges and cooperation with world-class museums; using "royal culture" as the theme to continuously improve the quality and connotation of the Palace Museum's cultural relics exhibition. Strategic cooperation agreements have been entered into with world-renowned museums, so that there will be exchanges of exhibitions, visits, and projects; national foreign policies and cultural strategies have taken effect on it, allowing the Forbidden City's cultural relics exhibition to promote Chinese culture and art and enhance China's soft power; and unique characteristics of the cultural relics collection have been formed, thus continuing to improve the quality, scale, and influence of the cultural relics exhibition of the Forbidden City.

For historical reasons, the cultural relics of the Forbidden City are stored on both sides of the Taiwan Strait in the two Palace Museums, forming a pattern of "one Forbidden City but two Palace Museums." However, the two Palace Museums have both made unremitting efforts to explore the historical and cultural connotations of the Forbidden City's cultural relics and promote Chinese culture and art, earning themselves prestige in the international museums circle. Based on the Chinese cultural identity, although there are two Palace Museums but only one Forbidden City, and on the fact that the cultural relics of the two Palace Museums come from the same source, he has done extensive work to promote exchanges and cooperation with the Palace Museum in Taipei during his tenure, and has achieved breakthroughs.

As director of the Palace Museum, another groundbreaking task of Mr. Zheng was to popularize "Gugong (the Forbidden City) Studies." For this purpose, he spared no effort to conduct theoretical explorations and practical promotions. "Practice without theoretical guidance is blind, and theory that cannot be applied is no true theory." It is precisely in this spirit that his exploration and construction of Gugong Studies is not limited to pure theories, but based on a deep understanding of the value of the Forbidden City and the connotation of the Palace Museum. Therefore, he believes the Gugong Studies is not only a discipline, a kind of knowledge, but a concept to understand the value of the Forbidden City, an approach to guide its preservation and the development of the Palace Museum. When explaining the academic philosophy of Gugong Studies, constructing its discipline system, and summarizing its theoretical methods, Mr. Zheng actively promoted the construction of its academic platform from multiple levels: setting up research institutions to expand its research platform; founding *Gugong Studies Journal* as its transmission platform; attaching great importance to book publishing to enhance its promotion platform; and cooperating with universities to launch education programs to establish its talent training platform.

During the decade of working in the Palace Museum, with an attitude of historical analysis, Mr. Zheng treated the historical experience of the Palace Museum dialectically, and formed his judgment on the value of the Forbidden City and the connotation of the Palace Museum, as well as the transformation of his museum management philosophy. Based on the basic understanding of the cultural integrity of the Palace Museum, he designed two development paths for it: a) the concept of intact Forbidden City preservation guides the cultural relics preservation and museum management; b) academic research is promoted and a discipline system constructed within the framework of the Gugong Studies.

In a word, as director of the Palace Museum, his long-term exploration and elaboration of the value of the Forbidden City and the connotation of the Palace Museum not only clarify the content and direction of the internal work of the Palace Museum, but also open up horizons and fields for its growth. His keen insight and wise judgment not only came from his rich work experience, but also relied on his persistent research attitude. As a government official in contemporary China, he has been long engaged in cultural undertakings, and has accumulated abundant experience, thus his accurate judgment on the mission and function of the Palace Museum. As a contemporary Chinese cultural scholar, he has never stopped writing and has made considerable research achievements in cultural policy, cultural relics preservation, and museum studies. Most of them are theoretical summaries of his work, which have high theoretical and practical value.

The ten years when he served as the Director of the Palace Museum happened to my years as the Director of National Cultural Heritage Administration. He used to call me back then, complaining that the subordinate unit of the Bureau of National Cultural Heritage Administration had not moved from the Forbidden City. Despite my position, it was difficult for me to make that happen, but I tried my best. Unexpectedly, in the second year after the last subordinate unit moved out of the Forbidden City, I was promoted to be the Director of the Palace Museum. Therefore, my memories are deep and specific. I often joke about it that I was merely trying to lend a hand, but in the end the promotion happened to me. It seems that I should do more good deeds in the future.

In addition to the past directors of the Palace Museum, there is also the most lovely Palace Museum staff.

The Palace Museum gathers all kinds of talents in security service, visitor reception, collection storage, business research, public education, cultural, and creative development. Together, they support and maintain the normal and orderly operation of a museum, so that visitors can enjoy a comfortable tour and service in the museum. And the Palace Museum staff possess a more vigilant sense of safety than ordinary museum employees. They share a strong sense of responsibility and mission to the Palace Museum. More importantly, they all have deep affection for the Palace Museum.

From the establishment of the Palace Museum in 1925 to the present, the Palace Museum staff have gone through wars and chaos as well as peace and prosperity. But regardless, they are committed to the preservation, research, and inheritance of the cultural heritage.

I believe that as a Palace Museum employee, when soaked every day in the culture and history of this living museum, in the nourishment of the everlasting spirit of the Forbidden City, they will naturally start to smell like it. No matter whenever and wherever they are, they will unconsciously give off the unique temperament of Palace Museum staff. This is a wonderful experience that many Palace Museum staff and I have shared. It is what we take pride in, and where our responsibility and mission lie.

It is the responsibility and eternal mission of all Palace Museum staff to take good care of the cultural relics of the Palace Museum, and the ancient architecture and the world cultural heritage of the Forbidden City, and carry forward the "Forbidden City Spirit." The Forbidden City has gone through 600 years, accumulating abundant cultural treasures. In addition to preservation, we hope to be able to display and interpret traditional culture in an approachable way, to interact with the audience, to bring the sleeping cultural relics back to life, to better serve the general public; to share the amazing cultural resources possessed by the Palace Museum to the public, and to leave the fantastic traditional culture contained in and represented by the Palace Museum to the young generation and to the future. Mr. Zheng once summarized the core values of Palace Museum staff, also known as the connotation of the "Forbidden City Spirit," in five aspects: guarding and cherishing, devotion and dedication, excellent service, openness and innovation, and diligence and harmony. The essence is "guarding national treasures as their own life," remembering and passing down the fine traditions of patriotism, diligence, and selfless dedication of the older generations of Palace Museum staff, and calling on all Palace Museum staff to always maintain a strong sense of responsibility and of mission for the protection of the cultural heritage of the Forbidden City and to lay the foundation for the glorious future of the Palace Museum with excellent work styles. Generations of Palace Museum staff have continued to enrich and pass down this "Forbidden City Spirit," thus illuminating the development path of the Palace Museum. They are behind the prosperity of the Palace Museum today.

Director Zheng Xinmiao (first left in the front row), Mr. Zhang Zhongpei (first left in the back row), and I (first right in the first row) attended the groundbreaking ceremony of the renovation project of Hall of High Heaven of the Forbidden City.

The Palace Museum accommodates a collection of cultural relics representing the five thousand years of Chinese civilization, as well as the 600-year-old Forbidden City. It is about to celebrate its 100th anniversary. In front of this museum, we are just toddlers. As mentioned above, our responsibility is to take good care of the cultural relics of the Palace Museum, and the ancient architectures and the world cultural heritage of the Forbidden City, so that they remain beautiful and everlasting. This is the historical duty and honor of every director of the Palace Museum, and of every Palace Museum employee.

From "Safe and Sound" to "Light Up":
For the Next 600 Years of the Forbidden City

————

The fire in 2018 destroyed 90% of the cultural relics of the National Museum of Brazil. The fire in 2019 severely damaged the world cultural heritage site Notre Dame de Paris. These are disasters for human culture. As a public cultural facility, the most important prerequisite for a museum to operate is to ensure the safety, not only of the visitors, but also of the cultural relics.

Fire broke out in both the National Museum of Brazil, a modern building and Notre Dame de Paris, a brick building. The Palace Museum is an ancient architecture with 1,200 wooden structures. The pressure of fire prevention is so overwhelming that no museum in the world is an equal. In 1987, lightning struck Palace of Great Brilliance and burned down part of it. It is eternally painful.

In addition to fire prevention, there is also a rigorous security challenge, guarding against theft. The Forbidden City has suffered six thefts. The most recent was in 2011. Some exhibits were stolen, which provoked a loud social response. And it was because of that thief that I became the "gatekeeper." When I assumed office, I was 58 years old. I thought I would retire in two years according to the regulations. Unexpectedly, I stayed on the position for seven years and three months.

After I took office, we analyzed the hidden dangers in the Forbidden City. We conducted a five-month safety hazard investigation, walked around 9,371 ancient buildings, modern warehouses, and temporary buildings in the Forbidden City. We registered and photographed each of them to find safety hazards, and prepared a manual, "Safe Forbidden City," which details the seven hidden dangers we have found: fire, theft, imperfect anti-seismic facilities, cultural relics corrosion, poor warehousing, malfunctioned municipal infrastructure, and possible stampede. These seven hidden dangers are objective. After they were reported to the State Council, we quickly obtained approval and launched the eight-year "Safe Forbidden City" project.

First, a powerful new security system has been established. There are five central control rooms, in which 65 large screens show the surveillance footage of 3,300 high-definition cameras.

If it is sufficient for a modern museum to be equipped with one central control room and hundreds of cameras, the Forbidden City, whose acreage is much larger and terrain more complicated, requires a stronger security system. We have strengthened the monitoring of the world cultural heritage of the Forbidden City, performing 24-hour dynamic, static, material, non-material, movable, immovable surveillance. Also, anti-seismic facilities are installed under the booths and showcases for stronger shockproof.

In particular, we have boxed all the cultural relics, and put them into dense cabinets to better protect them. At the same time, the location and number of high-pressure fire hydrants have been properly arranged, and the necessary lightning protection facilities have been installed.

In flat and open area, lightning often strikes, so it is necessary to continue to upgrade the lightning protection facilities and increase the frequency of daily monitoring. Firefighting equipment is equally essential. We have developed advanced and large firefighting equipment. Meanwhile, because there are plenty of alleys and small courtyards in the Forbidden City that large firefighting equipment cannot enter, we

Fire drill (October 10, 2016).

have also developed enough special small fire-fighting equipment. Generations of young employees have made up a voluntary fire brigade, which goes through intensive training on a regular basis. All staff must participate in fire drills to learn basic firefighting skills and improve firefighting consciousness.

Annually, we hold major fire drills, training everyone how to rescue the "wounded" and the "cultural relics" in time when a fire breaks out. In addition to firefighters, robots have to go through the fire drills as well to ensure that they can race into the sea of flames and accurately extinguish the open flames first. These drills enable us to stay ready for a fire at all times.

But it is more important to have preventive conservation. We should clean up the Palace Museum and eliminate all potential safety hazards. To achieve this goal, we initiated a three-year environment renovation. After three years of hard work, the employees of the Palace Museum have made 10 indoor improvements and 12 outdoor improvements.

Indoor:

(1) Put in order the cultural relics scattered in different rooms that have not been registered. It was difficult to catalog some of them, and some were not classified. They have been piled up in different rooms for a long time without being included in the collection, so these cultural relics must be put in order.

(2) Put the scattered accessory components of the ancient architecture in order. Some white marble components have been severely weathered, some curtain pendants have become rusted, and some copper doornails and iron door bolts are simply piled together. With no proper protection, they occupied considerable indoor space. This cleanup has packaged the components that should be packaged for storage, and put those that can be used back in use.

(3) Put doors and windows in order. Many of them that were unloaded in the past are stacked in passages and indoors. They are not regarded as cultural relics, but in fact, they are an important part of the ancient architecture. So we have founded the ancient architecture museum to display them after repairing them.

(4) Clean up the boxes. There were large boxes piled up in over 200 rooms. In fact, they were empty boxes because underground warehouses were built in the 1980s and 1990s to accommodate the 970,000 pieces of cultural relics that used to be stored in them. Scattered in the rooms, these boxes, made of camphor wood, red sandalwood, and leather, are also fine cultural relics. They carry historical information and deserve to be well preserved. We built three enormous warehouses to store them, vacating over 200 ancient architecture buildings.

(5) Establish a warehouse for textiles and embroidery. The quilts, beddings, blankets, rugs, and door curtains piled on a kang and on the ground were used by the ancients. They have been left there for too long. Since no collection allows the carrying of germs, we fumigated the textiles and embroidery in dozens of rooms, built a large warehouse for them, and vacated many more rooms.

(6) Clear up the exhibition cabinets and other exhibition equipment. In the past, when some exhibitions were concluded, the exhibition cabinets and equipment were piled in an empty room for storage. As time went by, they were forgotten. With the improvement of the exhibition quality, they could not be used again, but they took up a lot of space. And clearing them up freed a lot of rooms.

(7) Clean up miscellaneous items. With the idea that all his geese are swans, staff were reluctant to dispose some stools, chairs, tables, sofas, and sports equipment that had been used. They occupied a lot of space and gradually lost their value over time. But after all, they were state-owned assets, and thus not to be discarded at will. So, they were gathered in the courtyard on the north side of Hall of Flower, free to be picked up by all units after registration. As a result, none were selected, so we underwent the formalities, cleaned them up, and vacated more space.

(8) Clean up the rooms that have been closed for years. Thick dust accumulated on the ground in these rooms, which posed a serious safety hazard. Meanwhile, it was unfavorable for the preservation of ancient architecture, especially the ground preservation. Now we have cleaned up all the rooms for opening or other rational use.

(9) Repair the non-movable furniture. These pieces of furniture are connected to ancient architecture. Most of them are the kangs where ancient people slept. Left

alone for years, they have rotted. Some of the kangs still have old bedding but lack maintenance. We have repaired them for display in their original form when conditions permit.

(10) Sort out the hanging panels and paste-downs. There were calligraphies and paintings with precious historical and artistic value on the walls in many rooms, but they were not taken down for special storage in order to keep them in their original condition. In fact, they have a short life span and should not be kept this way for long. Therefore, we have repaired them, and display their high imitation copies to the public.

After three years of massive cleanup, thousands of buildings were tidied up, paving the road for the 80% opening of the Forbidden City.

Compared with cleaning up indoors, the work outdoors was trickier. We have made 12 improvements:

(1) Eliminate fire hazards. Branches, leaves, and odds and ends were piled up in some spots in the closed area. They made serious fire hazards. They have been eliminated after the thorough cleanup by all the staff.

(2) Pull up the weeds. The senior employees of the Palace Museum are experienced. Before walking into the weeds, they would shout to scare out the little animals. Next, we uprooted the weeds as tall as our knees.

(3) Count the stone carving components. Back then, after the ancient architecture was repaired, the stone carvings components were piled up in dozens of yards over time. We counted all of them and built an exhibition park to preserve them in Donghuamen (a subdistrict in Dongcheng District, Beijing). They are displayed to the public and the experts can study them, too.

(4) Clean up outdoor sundry things. Since long ago, various things have been stacked up under the eaves and in the passages. We removed all of them. A huge quantity of sundry things used to occupy the square on the east side of the garden of Palace of Compassion and Tranquility. Today, the vacated space is used for outdoor exhibitions such as the Peony Exhibition in spring and Chrysanthemum Exhibition in autumn, becoming a favorite spot for the visitors.

▣ Inspection of the environment of the Palace Museum (December 30, 2014).

(5) Remove the weeds on the roofs. Weeds grew wildly on the roofs of ancient buildings. To survive, they had to grow their roots deep in the tiles, thus loosening the tiles. As a result, rain could pour in and erode the roof trusses. We were determined to remove all the weeds. It took two years to make that happen. Today, the walls of the Forbidden City are open. Visitors standing on the walls will find absolutely no weeds growing on the 1,200 buildings in the Forbidden City.

(6) Replace exposed wires. Often, fires were caused by electricity leaking from wires and electrical appliances. In the past, the installation of wires and electrical appliances was not standardized and there were serious safety hazards. Accordingly, centralized efforts were made for improvement.

(7) Lay the municipal pipelines. In the Ming and Qing Dynasties, there were certainly no municipal pipelines in the Forbidden City. Today, as a modern museum, many pipelines for electricity, telecommunications, water supply, sewage, heating, firefighting, and security needed to be installed. Therefore, over a long time, hundreds of municipal pipelines have passed through red walls and ancient architecture, and spanned both banks of the Inner Golden Water River, and thick thermal pipelines occupied some ancient passages. It was a conundrum because we could neither dig open the foot of ancient walls to bury them underneath nor hang them in the air. In order to solve this predicament, we spent two and a half years on design and demonstration again and again, and eventually obtained approval. We adopted a shield approach, burying an assortment of pipelines 8 to 14 meters deep in the ground outside the palace walls, far from the ancient architecture. We avoided the thousand-kilometer municipal common trenches on the two cross sections of the cultural layer construction. There was no need to dig open the ground in the Forbidden City, or to go through the ancient architecture. For several years, the Palace Museum was open during the day, and the construction took place at night. Soil out and materials in. Thorough cleanup was conducted every morning so that it could welcome the visitors with a clean appearance.

(8) Improve the drainage for the squares. In the Ming and Qing Dynasties, a complete drainage system was installed in the Forbidden City. It took pride in the fact there was never a puddle of rain on the ground. However, since some squares were paved with cement bricks, drainage was not done well, and puddles formed after the rain. In some squares, after municipal pipes were buried, cement was smeared to cover them, as if there were patches on the ground, which also turned out bumpy. In response to these issues, we redid the drainage, and leveled the ground with traditional building materials such as bricks and stones. The Palace Museum can proudly promise to the public that no matter how heavy it rains in Beijing, there will never be a puddle in the Forbidden City.

(9) Improve protection measures. Some open areas are not particular about the protection facilities. For example, in the Imperial Garden, in order to protect bonsai

📷 Inspection of the environment of the Palace Museum (May 29, 2017).

and stone carvings, copper railings and iron railings are used to enclose the ground. The ground is bare land. When it is windy, dust fills in. Therefore, we removed these copper railings and iron railings, and then sealed the ground with green plants. This not only protected the bonsai and stone carvings, but also maintained the ground, and also improved the landscape environment of the entire Imperial Garden.

(10) Enhance the construction environment. The construction organization surrounded the construction site with iron plates when they worked, regardless of whether they were in harmony with the environment. Therefore, the Palace Museum designed a special construction fence. For example, when the ground was being repaired, transparent construction fence was placed, so that the status of the construction was visible, and simultaneously, illustrations were presented to the visitors, showing what kind of crafts and tools were being used for maintenance and preservation, thus popularizing the knowledge of cultural relics preservation.

(11) De-commercialization. For a long time, the visitors spent the most time on the central axis area of the Forbidden City. As a result, there were sales facilities operating at the Gate of Supreme Harmony, the Gate of Heavenly Purity, the Gate of the Thriving Imperial Clan, and the Gate of Good Fortune, which have seriously worsened the experience of visitors appreciating the magnificent ancient architecture. For example, when they reach the Gate of Heavenly Purity, the audio guide will tell them that this is the place where the Emperor of the Qing Dynasty held a daily morning court. But the shops surrounding them will surely distract them from an immersive experience. Therefore, we removed all of the shops and restored it as it was before. Another example is the Gate of the Thriving Imperial Clan. It used to be a restaurant for tourists. It was cold in winter and hot in summer, and unhygienic when there was smog. So, we simply opened the gate.

Next, the Imperial Garden, which is often the last stop for the tourists, used to have shops selling burgers, sausages, and popcorn. Weary tourists would eat and drink there. At noon, it smelt like a big food market. The air was filled with the smell of grilled sausage and popcorn. It was impossible for the tourists to feel the artistic conception of a classical garden. Therefore, we removed all catering business from the Imperial Garden and restored the old classic cultural atmosphere.

(12) Demolish temporary buildings. Over the past few decades, there have been 135 temporary buildings in the Palace Museum, of which 59 were the most dangerous color steel (temporary) rooms. It takes two weeks to build one but the material has poor flame retardance. It burns wildly if it catches fire. It is a dangerous threat for these 59 color steel rooms to remain in the ancient architecture complex, so we made the first move on them. The leaders of the Fire Department of the Ministry of Public Security and I agreed to first demolish the color steel rooms of the Ministry of Publicity and Education under the Sparrow Wing Towers of the Meridian Gate. The leaders of all departments of the Palace Museum came to witness the demolition because almost all departments had temporary buildings to be torn down. It delivered a message to them that they should speed up the demolition at their respective departments.

Demolished were the color steel office that the Information Department had used for eight years, the color steel dining hall for the 600 employees in the administrative department, the 13 rows of color steel offices, the color steel warehouse of the ancient architecture department, the color steel warehouse of the palace department, and the color steel rooms where the audit office, the infrastructure office, and the budget office used to be. On the day of the 2016 anniversary of the Palace Museum, concerted efforts were made to knock down the last color steel room in the Southern Residence.

There were more temporary buildings to be torn down. For example, back then, a garage was built with the red wall as one side and an ancient architecture wall as another. It had to be removed. There was also a staff shower room in the Palace Museum. After repairing and maintaining the ancient building, they would take a shower and return home clean. It was built on the side of an ancient building, which was quite dangerous. We called on all the staff to shower at home, and tore it down. The Southern Residence was the residence of the emperor's sons. The nine groups of courtyards in apple-pie order are covered with beautiful green glazed tiles. However, it was surrounded by seven greenhouses. For decades, the senior employees had never seen what the Southern Residence look like. Therefore, the Palace Museum opened the Forbidden City Classical Flower Center in Xibeiwang Town, in the Haidian District (a northwest district of Beijing), keeping the flowers together in the greenhouses there. In early spring, flowers are delivered to the courtyards of the Forbidden City, and in late autumn they are shipped back to the center. On this basis, the surrounding greenhouses were knocked down, and the Southern Residence was eventually visible.

The most difficult job was the thorough remediation of the environment of three most filthy and chaotic areas. They were the west riverside area, the south warehouse area and the Imperial Household Department area. How come there are such dirty spots in the Forbidden City? Between the end of the Qing Dynasty and the founding of the PRC, the ancient architecture of the Forbidden City lacked proper maintenance. Some parts of the ancient architecture were never repaired after they were damaged. Instead, they became vacant land to merely pile up an assortment of unwanted items. They were never properly utilized, and they posed a safety threat.

(1) The west riverside area. Wood has been piled up on the hundreds-meter-long strip on the west side of the Inner Golden Water River for decades. It was where wood processing and storage took place. We spent three years cleaning it up, restoring the sight of the ancient architecture on the ground, and built the modern Palace Museum Cultural Relic Hospital.

(2) The south warehouse area. In the past, as both the storage site and the processing site for building materials, it was in poor condition. Especially after the opening of the Sparrow Wing Towers of the Meridian Gate, it terribly stained the beautiful image of the Forbidden City. Therefore, the material warehouses in that area, as well as the Armed Police canteen and the warehouse of the Cultural Relic Exchange Center of National Cultural Heritage Administration were relocated, and the ancient construction was repaired, preserved, and completely restored to what it once was. Now it has been turned into the public's favorite furniture museum in the Palace Museum.

(3) The Imperial Household Department area. It was a vast area, below which was the underground warehouse built in the 1980s and 1990s. The ancient buildings on the ground have been long gone. For a long time, plenty of temporary buildings of construction units had been built there, construction vehicles parked there, and construction scaffolding wood and iron pipes stacked there. After the cleanup, the underground cultural relics warehouse was expanded, and the historical sight above the ground gradually restored.

In short, with the joint efforts of all the Palace Museum staff, after three years of arduous work on environmental improvement, the appearance of the Palace Museum, in and out, has been completely transformed.

We kept our solemn promise. Seven years ago, the Palace Museum promised to the society that it would "hand over a magnificent Forbidden City to the next 600 years intact." The goal was achieved. The Forbidden City was completed in 1420 during the reign of Emperor Yongle of the Ming Dynasty. 2020 was its 600th anniversary. We hope that when people walk into it again, they will see only magnificent ancient architecture and no modern buildings that pose a threat to its safety or its environment.

⊡ Natural light during the day and illumination at night.

However, a visitor, when touring the Palace Museum, will pay great attention to the surrounding environment. Therefore, it is necessary not only to clean up the environment, but to improve it.

The Palace Museum spent two and a half years to make overall environmental enhancements. Why this amount of time? Take the lids of the wells as an example. Many of them are of different heights on the square and passages. People have to pay attention to them and not trip when they tour the museum. They are especially dangerous for the wheelchairs of the disabled and baby strollers. It seems a piece of cake to level them but it turned out to be rather tricky. To make that happen, we must first run statistics and then make a declaration. Only with the approval of the relevant municipal departments could the 1,750 well lids be replaced with flat "Forbidden City well lids" before, the green areas on both sides of the pavement in the Forbidden City

▣ A leveled well lid of the Forbidden City.

used to be separated by iron railings or green fences. In fact, it was not an effective measure. Due to inconvenience of maintenance, the green areas were in poor condition. Now with the thousands of meters of iron railings gone, the green areas are receiving better maintenance. Also, in recent years, the 300 lamp poles in the Forbidden City have been replaced with 300 palace lanterns, so that they are a sight themselves during the day and illumination at night.

In order to improve the general environment, the Palace Museum has made painstaking efforts. We realize that no matter how simple it appears to level the well lid, to maintain the green space, or to improve the lighting, in the vast space of the Forbidden City, they become difficult tasks that require great effort and perseverance.

Good environment requires daily maintenance. There used to be rubbish on the ground in the open area: mineral water bottles, popsicle sticks, tissues, used

☙ With a sanitation worker of the Forbidden City.

tickets ... At first when we walked around the Forbidden City every day, we often had to bend over to pick up rubbish, repeating this action more than a dozen times in the distance between the Gate of Divine Prowess to the Meridian Gate. Therefore, the Palace Museum revised the invitation for bids, which clearly stipulated that within two minutes of a piece of rubbish touching the ground, the staff of the property company have to clean it. Under strict requirement, there were still companies bidding. The winner of the bid was ZHDB Property Management. In reality, the employees of ZHDB Property Management turned out to be lucky, because when they sweep the ground perfectly clean, nobody litters anymore. Without the first piece of litter, there is hardly a second. Their workload is greatly reduced, and the Palace Museum becomes generally clean. In fact, a clean environment has an effect on people. When visitor enter a clean environment, they are unconsciously willing to keep it clean, preserving the ancient architecture, the trees, and the lawns in the Forbidden City. Nobody will carve their names on the red wall or climb the rockery in the classical gardens.

In short, we hope that through unremitting efforts, when people visit the Palace Museum, they will see the beautiful scenery of green space, blue sky, red walls, and yellow tiles. Now, except that the blue sky is sometimes absent, everything else has been realized. In recent years, there have been more blue-sky days in Beijing. The Forbidden City with red walls and yellow tiles under the bright sun is particularly charming and fascinating.

However, the Palace Museum differs from other museums in one aspect, that is, visitors have to walk through the outdoor space from one exhibition hall to another, so both indoors and outdoors should be a continuous and wonderful visit experience. For this purpose, we continue to beautify the environment, growing peonies in spring, lotus in summer, ginkgoes in autumn, and winter plums in winter. Where can I appreciate the flowers? The Palace Museum has designed a "Flower Searching" app. On their phones, they can find out which flowers are blooming and where.

In terms of indoor lighting, we have also accumulated considerable experience. Visitors used to complain that the halls of the Forbidden City were dark. The brighter the weather, the darker the inside. Can't they be illuminated? For a long time, we had to patiently explain to them that these palaces are ancient wooden structures, so that no electrical circuits can be set up. The items displayed in the halls are antiquities. Especially, paper and embroidery items cannot be long exposed to illumination. Although these explanations make perfect sense, it is a fact that this does not make a satisfying tour experience. Visitors gather outside the railings of the main hall. It is often overwhelmingly crowded. It is no fun for the elders and the children. And it is happening every day. Is there a way to change the situation? To solve this conundrum, we conducted research and development and chose the cold light source of LEDs, which do not generate heat. The illumination does not come from individual light bulbs, but a group of scattered light sources. Moreover, the lamps are not hung on the ancient architectures, but fixed with a stone holder over 2.5 meters away from them.

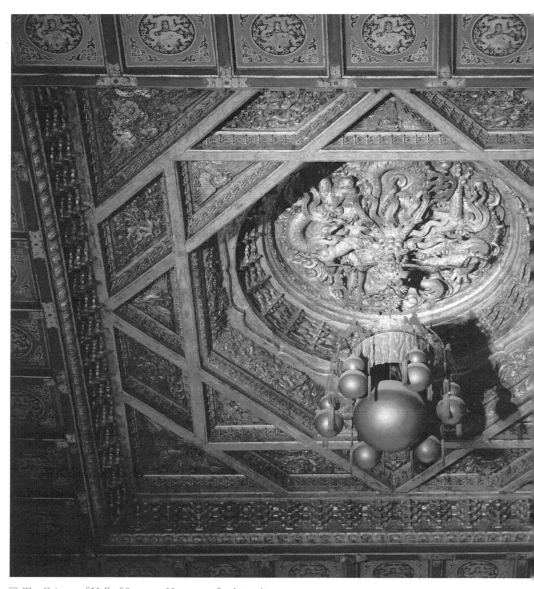

The Caisson of Hall of Supreme Harmony after being lit up.

When the lights are turned on, there is one employee on each side on duty. They use the light meter to repeatedly measure the light shining at the sensitive spots to ensure that it does not go over the limit. We have designed different indoor lighting for different halls for the best visual effects. After one and a half years of research and development, we have finally lit up the Forbidden City. The Hall of Supreme Harmony, which used to be dark, is now clearly visible. The Hall of Central Harmony, the Hall of Preserving Harmony, the Palace of Heavenly Purity, and the Hall of Union have all been lit up. These halls displayed in their original forms used to require systematical dusting every three months, but today dusting has to be performed every two weeks because the visitors can see them more clearly. Without better cleaning, every spot will be visible. This motivates us to do better in cleanliness. It is also a reminder that only when people have the right to understand and supervise the preservation of cultural relics can they be better preserved.

CHAPTER 2

The Abundance of
Precious Cultural Relics

In China, movable cultural relics are divided into precious cultural relics and general cultural relics, and precious cultural relics are further divided into grade-one, grade-two, and grade-three cultural relics. There are over 5,000 museums in China, with a total collection of 4.01 million pieces of nationally-graded precious cultural relics. The Palace Museum has collected 1.68 million pieces of them, accounting for 42% of all Chinese precious cultural relics. It is therefore the museum with the richest collection of precious cultural relics in China.

Almost all museums around the world share a pyramid-shaped collection structure. The spire is the best of the most precious cultural relics; the body is a vast number of wide-range general cultural relics; the bottom is the materials to be studied and graded. However, the Palace Museum is an exception. Its collection structure is an inverted pyramid because more than 90% of the cultural relics stored there are classified as precious.

The Exact Number of Collections
in the Forbidden City

———

It is a well-known fact that the Palace Museum is a museum. Therefore, it must store a collection of cultural relics. It not only holds the rare treasures collected by the Emperors of the Ming and Qing Dynasties, but also those scattered around the world since it was founded, especially after the founding of the PRC. Therefore, we have always been aware of the abundance of collections in the Forbidden City. Meanwhile, the newly collected cultural relics continue to increase every year, thus requiring proper enumeration and grading.

Enumerating the cultural relics is a basic assignment of a museum. The Qing relics in the Palace Museum are huge in number, diverse in variety, and scattered in storage. Therefore, it is the ultimate pursuit of generations of Palace Museum staff to thoroughly understand the exact number of the pieces in the cultural relics collection.

As early as 1934, Director Ma Heng explicitly stated in a report to the administration and the council of the Palace Museum that regarding the enumeration of cultural relics, "Without a solid determination, it is difficult to achieve the goal." In fact, as long as the work order is normal, the enumeration of cultural relics in the Palace Museum has never ceased. Historically, it performed four enumerations from 1924 to 1930, from 1954 to 1960, from 1978 to the end of 1980s, and after 1991.

After the first enumeration, 28 volumes of the six books of the *Enumeration Report of the Forbidden City Items* were compiled, registering a total of over 1.17 million items.

After the founding of the PRC, the enumeration the cultural relics collections was more arduous. In addition to the original cultural relics collections, there was the additional enumeration of considerable cultural relics transferred from other museums and cultural relics departments, a vast number of personal donations, and many old collections of the Forbidden City scattered around the world.

In 1990 and 1997, the first phase and the second phase of underground warehouses of the Palace Museum were completed. More than 900,000 pieces of cultural relics collections that used to be stored in the above-ground warehouses were moved there one after another, and those kept in the aboveground warehouses also received proper adjustment.

After Director Zheng Xinmiao took office in 2002, the Palace Museum carried out the fifth cultural relics enumeration from 2004 to 2010, which was a more comprehensive enumeration. It lasted for seven years and was the largest enumeration since the establishment of the Palace Museum. After the comprehensive and systematic enumeration, number of cultural relics in the Palace Museum has increased from nearly one million pieces to 1,807,558 pieces (sets), of which 1,684,490 are precious cultural relics, 115,491 general cultural relics, and 7,577 specimens. This is the first thorough and scientific number of the cultural relics collection of the Palace Museum since its establishment. So, when I took office on the first day, I was able to know that the exact number of cultural relics in the Palace Museum was 1,807,558.

For a long time, there was no full disclosure of the cultural relics in the Forbidden City to the public. As a result, in addition to the public, some professional researchers did not know much about the overall situation of the cultural relics in the Forbidden City. Since 2010, on the basis of the enumeration of the cultural relics collection, the Palace Museum has initiated the preparation and printing of the *General Catalogue of Cultural*

🖻 General Catalog of Cultural Relics Collections on the website of the Palace Museum.

Relics Collections in the Palace Museum, and published *Compendium of Collections in the Palace Museum* to serve the needs of people for research and appreciation, and to fulfill a museum's mission of public education and social service.

With the efforts of several generations of Palace Museum staff, the cultural relics collection of the Palace Museum has basically realized a sound management system, consistent accounts, accurate identification, complete archives, timely filing, proper storage, and convenient access. Every item can be found on the catalogue. Therefore, at the beginning of 2013, the *General Catalogue of Cultural Relics Collections in the Palace Museum* was released, disclosing the exact number and details about the collections to the public. It showed the abundance of collections in the Palace Museum, so that everyone knows what collections the Palace Museum holds and our work is open to social supervision and evaluation; to academics and professional researchers, we have disclosed the academic resources of the Palace Museum, making it easier to conduct studies in various aspects.

In rapid sequence, as the State Council initiated the first national survey of movable cultural relics, the Palace Museum performed a three-year collection enumeration from 2014 to 2016, and obtained new data on cultural relics collections.

As of December 31, 2016, the total number of cultural relics collection in the Palace Museum had increased from 1,807,558 pieces (sets) to 1,862,690 pieces (sets), of which 1,683,336 are precious cultural relics, 163,969 general and 15,385 specimens of animals, plants, etc.

In comparison with the data in 2010, there are 55,132 pieces more. By category, three types of cultural relics had the largest increase in number, including: 726 pieces of imperial manuscripts and letters by Emperor Qianlong, 16,511 pieces of inscriptions on bones or tortoise shells of the Shang Dynasty, 4,425 pieces of ceramics, and 7,808 pieces of specimens. Some were newly collected over the years, some donated by personages of all circles, and a considerable number newly discovered during the enumeration. These 1.86 million pieces of cultural relics have a complete system, span a wide range, possess high quality, and are rich in categories.

Among the visitors, there is a common misunderstanding that the cultural relics collections of the Forbidden City are all from the Qing Dynasty. The truth is that they are from different periods and regions. Often, the collections of the Qing emperors are historical relics of the former dynasties.

The more than 1.86 million pieces from collections are mainly cultural relics, ancient architecture, and ancient books and documents. Ancient architecture naturally requires no further introduction. In terms of ancient books and documents, there are about 600,000 of them in the Palace Museum, including the Hall of Martial Valor block-printed editions, fine block-printed editions from Yuan, Ming and Qing Dynasties, manuscripts from Ming and Qing Dynasties, local chronicles, special imperial collections, imperial archives, imperial opera scripts, and ancient books of ethnic characters. Among them, 240,000 books are of great importance, making the Palace Museum the museum with the largest collection of books of cultural relics in the world.

Ancient architecture and ancient books and documents, together with 23 categories of cultural relics, constitute the 25 categories of collections of the Palace Museum. This classification method takes into account both the texture and the usage of the collections. As a classification method that combines the two, in the Chinese museum collection classification system, it must have the most comprehensive number of categories. The classification method must also be the most characteristic because our collections are indeed vast in number and rich in variety.

Twenty-Three Categories of Cultural Relics

There are 23 categories of cultural relics collections: ceramics, paintings, model calligraphy, inscriptions and engravings, bronzeware, seals, embroidery, stationery, furniture, clocks and watches, enamels, lacquerware, sculptures, gold, silver, and tin ware, jade, glassware, bamboo, wood, ivory, and rhino horn carvings, imperial religious items, jewelry, flags and weapons carried by guards before an emperor, music and opera, living utensils, and foreign cultural relics.

(1) Ceramics. The Palace Museum holds the largest collection of ceramics in China, with more than 360,000 pieces of ceramics collected. In addition, it also houses thousands of physical materials on ceramics, and 30,000 pieces of ceramic specimens, which are collected from over 150 important kilns across China by the Palace Museum researchers since the founding of the PRC. The ancient Chinese ceramics in the Palace Museum create a system of their own, comprehensively reflecting the continuous history of Chinese ceramics production. In particular, the ceramic collections from the five famous Song kilns and the Ming and Qing official kilns, whether in quantity or quality, are second to none in the world.

(2) Paintings. In terms of paintings, there are a total of nearly 53,000 items in the collection, including masterpieces such as *Five Oxen*, *Along the River during the Qingming Festival* and *A Thousand Li of Rivers and Mountains*. The painting collection of the Palace Museum is mostly from the old collections of imperial courts of the Ming and Qing Dynasties. In the Qing Dynasty, especially during the reign of Emperor Qianlong, the imperial palace collected an abundance of famous paintings from past dynasties. But with the social turmoil in the late Qing Dynasty, some paintings were

scattered around China. Later, as the ancient relics were relocated southwards, some were transported to Taiwan. By 1949, the collection of paintings in the Palace Museum had been greatly reduced.

Since the founding of the PRC, with the attention and strong support of the country, National Cultural Heritage Administration handed over the collected paintings to the Palace Museum in several batches in the 1950s in all kinds of ways, such as inspection, enumeration, allocation, and reception. It also included treasures that China purchased back from abroad at huge costs. Plenty of patriotic collectors at home and abroad have selflessly donated their private collections, thus greatly enriching the Palace Museum's painting collection. Meanwhile, the Palace Museum, through persistent acquisitions and collections, discovered and added a multitude of fine paintings into the collection. Coupled with the gradual rise of art auctions since the 1990s, some painting treasures have at last returned to the Palace Museum after years of wandering. The level of painting collections in the Palace Museum is also believed to be second to none in China. It almost encompasses the famous works from all historical periods in the development of Chinese painting, and painting collections are regarded as priority among priorities in the art collections of the Palace Museum.

(3) Model Calligraphy. The Palace Museum accommodates about 75,000 pieces of model calligraphies. Some may wonder about the difference between this and common calligraphy. In fact, modeled calligraphy is a respectful name for the calligraphies of renowned ancient masters, and it means the role model for calligraphy works. In the Ming and Qing Dynasties, the imperial palace gathered the model calligraphies of the past dynasties. This is recorded in both the *Peiwenzhai Shu Hua Pu* compiled during the reign of Emperor Kangxi and *Shiqu Baoji* compiled during the reigns of Emperor Qianlong and Emperor Jiaqing. During the abdication of the Qing emperor at the beginning of the 20th century, parts of the model calligraphies were scattered. Before the founding of the PRC, some were transported to Taiwan by the Kuomintang authorities. They are now preserved in the National Palace Museum in Taipei. Since the 1950s, thanks to the support of the government and the contributions of collectors

such as Zhang Boju, Chen Shutong, Zhu Wenjun, and Luo Fuyi, many fine works of model calligraphy have returned to the Forbidden City, thus enabling the reconstruction of the calligraphy treasure house of the Forbidden City. Masterpieces such as *Preface to the Poems Composed at the Orchid Pavilion*[1], *Mid-Autumn Calligraphy*, and *Boyuan Calligraphy* have become paramount collections of cultural relics in the Palace Museum.

(4) Inscriptions and Engravings. Cultural relics with words are more precious than those without, so the 33,000 inscriptions and engravings in the Palace Museum are a very important type of cultural relics. They include the inscriptions on bones or tortoise shells of the Shang Dynasty, the bronze inscriptions of the Shang and Zhou Dynasties, and the seal, brick, tile, pottery, ceramic, clay, and stone carvings and rubbings since the Warring States, Qin, and Han Dynasties. The texts on them are inscriptions and engravings. Among them, there are 28,000 stone rubbings. It is common knowledge that the emperors of the past have been particularly fond of calligraphy. They extensively collected information on the wild stone rubbings in the famous mountains and rivers from all over China. Thousands of years later, the stone rubbings in the natural state have been weathered or destroyed, but those with clear historical information are preserved in the museums.

A small part of the stone rubbings in the Forbidden City are the old collections from the Qing Dynasty while most of them are newly collected after the founding of the PRC. The sum of the three types of model calligraphy, paintings, and stone rubbings is 156,000, a number that is unparalleled in the world of museums.

There are 10 stone drums among the inscribed cultural relics. They are the national treasures among national treasures. They carry the early Chinese characters. Their spread is extremely tortuous. It is miraculous that they have survived to this day. For these 10 stone drums, the Palace Museum built the special Hall of Stone Drums,

---

1. The original author was Wang Xizhi 王羲之 from the Eastern Jin Dynasty (317–420), and Feng Chengsu's copied edition dates from the Shenlong 神龙 period of the second reign of the Emperor Zhongzong (705–707).

which was previously located in the East Room of the Hall of Imperial Supremacy. Now, it is independently set up in the Palace of Tranquil Longevity.

In addition, the official webpage of the Palace Museum introduces that it has collected 4,700 pieces of bone inscriptions unearthed in the Yin Ruins of Anyang, Henan. In fact, there are a total of 23,000 pieces in the Palace Museum, but it will take six years to record all of them in the collection system after thorough research. These inscriptions of the Shang Dynasty are texts inscribed on tortoise shells and beast bones. About 5,000 characters have been discovered on inscriptions on bones or tortoise shells of the Shang Dynasty, and more characters are still being interpreted. Those inscriptions collected in the Palace Museum are recorded in books such as *Yin Xu Shu Xu Bian, Bu Chi Tong Zhuan, Yin Qi Yi Cun, Yin Qi Shi Duo, Yin Qi Shi Duo II*, and *A Collection of Inscriptions on Bones or Tortoise Shells of the Shang Dynasty*. They are priceless treasures from a long history.

(5) Bronzeware. Bronze culture is a product of the development of human civilization to a certain stage. In China, large bronzeware began to appear in the late Xia Dynasty, and in the early and late Shang Dynasty, there were a large number of bronzeware sets with magnificent and complicated patterns. In the Western Zhou Dynasty, Spring and Autumn Period, and Warring States Period, an abundance of bronzeware that later bore witness to historical events were made. The production and development of bronzeware were continuous in the past dynasties, but it was not until the pre-Qin years that it generated a greater impact on social life. There were thousands of pieces of bronzeware collected in the imperial palace during the reign of the Emperor Qianlong of the Qing Dynasty. Some were shipped to Taiwan, some were lost, and the rest are kept in the Forbidden City. With the addition of the bronzeware from governmental allocation, private donations, and purchases by the Palace Museum since the founding of the PRC, the total number of bronzes in the Palace Museum exceeds 15,000.

Bronzeware is common in collections of many Chinese museums. The Palace Museum is the one with the largest collection of bronzeware in China. It houses about 10,000 bronzeware from the pre-Qin period. The Palace Museum is also the museum

◨ Bronze tripod.   ◨ Inscriptions on a bone of the Shang Dynasty.

with the most bronzeware with pre-Qin inscriptions in the world. Its more than 1,600 pieces of bronzeware with pre-Qin inscriptions are of great research value.

(6) Seals. Seals are one of the proof tools. Nationally, publicly, and personally, the necessity to use seals as proof has resulted in various official and private seals. Seals appeared approximately in the Eastern Zhou Dynasty, and was passed down from generation to generation. The Forbidden City holds a total of 5,060 seals. A huge proportion of them belong to the emperors and empresses of the Ming and Qing Dynasties. They fully demonstrate the official seal system of the two dynasties and some personal preference of the emperors and empresses.

(7) Embroidery. The Forbidden City stores more than 80,000 pieces of ancient embroidery, including clothing, materials, embroidery for furnishings, and embroidered calligraphy and painting. Among them, clothing is divided into ready-to-wear, hats, crowns, boots, shoes, socks, accessories, Buddhist clothing, and handicrafts, etc.; materials include brocade, satin, silk, yarn, velvet, and cotton, etc.; embroidery for

furnishings covers bedding, cushions, hand cushions, chair covers, door curtains, tents, curtains, quilts, pillows, kang sheets, kang mats, table cloths, etc.; embroidered paintings and calligraphy are appreciative works of art that are modeled on paintings, calligraphy, and poetry, using embroidery techniques. Their binding forms include scrolls, books, striped screens, folding screens, fans, mirrors, etc.

Most of the embroidery collections in the Palace Museum come from the Qing Dynasty. Almost all of them were produced in Nanjing, Suzhou, and Hangzhou. In general, the Forbidden City collects an abundance of embroidery that are of various types, high specifications, high quality, and excellent preservation. Regarding embroidery collections, it is the best museum in China and in the world. It is of significant value for studying the Qing Dynasty clothing system, the technological level of silk weaving in the Qing Dynasty, the development of the silk weaving industry, and the history and culture, palace life, artistic aesthetics, and ideological concepts of the Qing Dynasty.

(8) Stationery. The Forbidden City holds more than 68,000 pieces of the Four Treasures of the Study—the writing brush, inkstick, paper, and inkstone. The Four Treasures of the Study are distinctive stationery in China. The name came from the Northern and Southern Dynasties. It refers specifically to the study stationery of the literati, namely, the writing brush, ink, paper, and inkstone. The most famous Four Treasures of the Study were a writing brush produced in Huzhou, an inkstick produced in Anhui, paper produced in Xuancheng, and an inkstone produced in Duanxi. They are not only of high practical value, but a work of art that integrates painting, calligraphy, sculpture, and decoration.

In fact, apart from these four treasures, stationery also includes the writing brush pot, writing brush holders, ink rests, ink cartridges, and arm resting pillows, writing brush washer, paperweights, water container for the inkstone, water spoon, small cup for adding water to inkstone, inkstone boxes, ink pads, seal box, cutters, stamps, rolls, etc. Most of the stationery items in the Palace Museum were made by famous craftsmen in the Qing Dynasty for the royal family to use exclusively, so fine materials were used and the craftsmanship was fantastic. Representing the development level of

📷 *Jasper Dragon Seal*—A Rare Emperor's Treasure.

ancient Chinese stationery and the creativity and artistic talents of skilled craftsmen, they are absolute treasures of the study rooms.

(9) Furniture. The Forbidden City houses over 6,200 pieces of Ming and Qing furniture. Among them, the number of Ming furniture exceeds 300 while Qing furniture covers beds, chairs, tables, cabinets, folding screen, pedestals, etc. There are also nearly 500 pieces of Eastern and Western furniture.

In terms of their materials, there is rosewood, rockwood, ebony, wenge, Mahogany, beech, nanmu, birch, elm, burl wood, boxwood, and more. In particular, those made of red sandalwood and rosewood are extremely precious. Except for some furniture that was made in the workshops of the Qing Dynasty, most of them came from all over China. Those made in Guangzhou, Beijing, Suzhou, and Shanxi are the most famous. The furniture in the Palace Museum basically presents the style and characteristics of Ming and Qing furniture. With useful guidance and reference value for the study of Ming and Qing furniture art and the ideology and culture of that period, it is a precious cultural heritage of China.

(10) Clocks and Watches. In China, there are few foreign cultural relics in museums, but the Palace Museum is an exception. The cultural exchanges in the past 500 years, especially the tribute paid by envoys and trade exchanges have accumulated the Forbidden City tens of thousands of foreign cultural relics. In terms of the collection of Western clocks and watches, the Forbidden City is the museum that holds the largest collection of 18th century western clocks and watches of the highest quality in the world. There are 2,200 (sets of) Western clocks and instruments, including 1,500 (sets of) clocks and 700 (sets of) instruments.

These clocks and watches make a rather special category among the many cultural relics of the Palace Museum. They are the products of the eastward spread of Western knowledge since the end of the Ming Dynasty, and also important relics that have witnessed the cultural exchanges between China and the West in the Chinese palaces during the Ming and Qing Dynasties. The missionaries who traveled to China at the end of the Ming Dynasty to spread their religious beliefs, after repeated exploration and consideration, adopted the missionary strategy that focused on displaying Western science. They either paid timepieces and instruments from Europe as tribute, or used their knowledge and skills to provide secular services to the Chinese society, especially the Qing palace. They manufactured or guided the craftsmen of the Qing Workshops to make many clocks and watches, thus influencing the style of study in the imperial palace at that time. Consequently, the court began to import, purchase, and manufacture clocks and watches. This historical situation determines the particularity of clock and watch collections in Chinese palaces. The representativeness, typicality, and extensiveness of the cultural exchanges and influences between China and foreign countries are unmatched by collections of the same kind in any other museums.

(11) Enamelware. The Forbidden City possesses the most ancient Chinese enamelware on the metal in the world. There are 6,600 pieces of enamelware, covering metal enamelware from the Yuan Dynasty to the Qing Dynasty and the Republic of

⊡ Cloisonné enamel incense burner with lotus patterns and hydra ears.

⊡ Cloisonné enamel vase with lotus patterns and dragon ears.

China. Among them, there are over 4,000 cloisonné enamelware, over 2,000 pink family enamelware, Basse-taille enamelware, Champlevé enamelware, and Plique-à-jour enamelware. Most of them were produced by institutions controlled by the imperial family during the Ming and Qing Dynasties, while a few were manufactured by private workshops. The enamelware in the Palace Museum has a wide range of uses, involving palace furnishings, religious ceremonies, architectural decorations in the palace, and daily life. They are valuable materials to study the ancient Chinese metal enamelware.

(12) Lacquerware. There are as many as 19,000 pieces of lacquerware in the Forbidden City, more than any other museum in the world. Lacquerware is an object made of wood or other materials with a lacquer coating. It has a practical function as well as ornamental value. China is the first country in the world to understand the characteristics of lacquer and tone it into all kinds of colors for beautification and decoration. The quantity of lacquerware collection in the Palace Museum ranks first in the world. Within the collection, the most are works handed down from the Yuan, Ming, and Qing Dynasties, and there is a small number of early works. Among the works of the Yuan, Ming and Qing Dynasties, most are royal works, and some are folk works. With diverse varieties, rich content, and a high level of craftsmanship and research value, these lacquerware are an important part of the world's arts and crafts.

(13) Sculptures. Sculpture is one of the main categories of the plastic arts. It is the general term for carving and modeling. Carving mostly happens to wood, stone, and metal, while modeling takes clay as the main material. The sculptures in the Palace Museum mainly include figurines of various colors, wood carvings, stone carvings, and porcelain carvings of Buddha from the Warring States Period to the Qing Dynasty, brick and stone portraits of the Han Dynasty, brick carvings of figures and animals from the Sui and Tang Dynasties, and brick carvings of twenty-four stories of filial piety in the Song Dynasty. Sculptures in the Palace Museum mainly come from the following sources: old collections in the Qing Palace, state allocations, acceptance of donations, and purchases. As one of the important collection institutions of Chinese sculpture cultural relics, the sculpture cultural relics collection in the Palace Museum is

famous at home and abroad for its complete variety, rich content, and high historical and artistic value.

(14) Gold, Silver, and Tinware. There are 11,000 pieces of gold, silver, and tinware in the Forbidden City, all of which are works of art handed down from ancient times. The gold and silverware in the palace have adopted various techniques such as casting, engraving, and threading. Uniquely shaped and exquisitely ornamented, they exhibit rich royal characteristics, and hold extremely high historical and artistic value. Among them, the goldware is mainly the remains of the Qing palace, most of which were made in the Qing Dynasty for the purposes of ordinances, rituals, traditional clothing, daily life, saddlery, furnishings, and Buddhist events. The vast majority of silverware was made in the Qing Dynasty, including silver pots, silver cups, and silver boxes. In different shapes, most of the tinware is engraved with poems, flowers, landscapes, and figures while some have customized patterns.

(15) Jade. The Palace Museum takes pride in its collection of 23,000 pieces of jade. The 5,000 years of Chinese civilization, even dating back 8,000 years, can be connected through the collections of the Palace Museum. For example, the Palace Museum collects an abundance of Hongshan Culture jade unearthed in the northeast, Liangzhu Culture jade unearthed in Zhejiang, and earlier Lingjiatan Culture jade unearthed in Anhui. These jade are mainly the remains of the Qing palace. Among them, jade ware accounts for the overwhelming majority. There are also a variety of exquisite ornaments made of crystals, agate, lapis lazuli, rose quartz, malachite, and coral.

(16) Glassware. The Palace Museum also collects glassware. It was called *liaoqi* in the Ming and Qing Dynasties. In fact, China's glass manufacturing process has a history of over 2,000 years, but it developed slowly before the Qing Dynasty. In the reign of the Emperor Kangxi of the Qing Dynasty, under the influence of Western science and technology, the Royal Glass Plant was established. Thereafter, the production of glassware exclusively for the royals continued until the end of the Qing Dynasty. During the reign of the Emperor Kangxi, the Emperor Yongzheng, and the Emperor Qianlong, it was the most thriving.

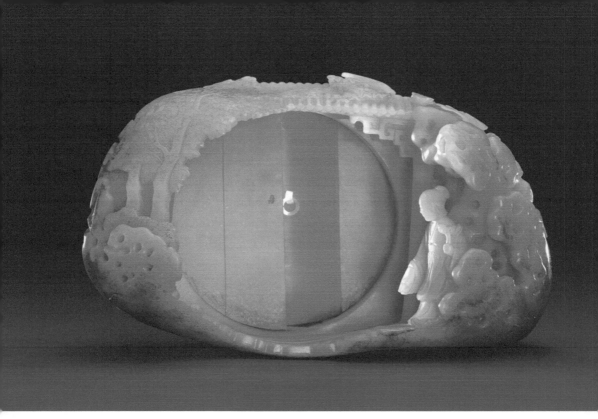

📷 *Gray Jade Moon Gate.*

(17) Bamboo, Wood, Ivory, and Rhino Horn Carvings. In addition, the Forbidden City stores 11,000 carvings, including carvings of bamboo, wood, ivory, and rhino horns. They are often labeled as "miscellaneous items." These types of crafts, with a long history, are closely related to daily life, but for a long time they had not formed a stable craft tradition. It was not until the Ming and Qing Dynasties, with the development and prosperity of the entire arts and crafts field, that bamboo, wood, ivory, and rhino horn carvings made unprecedented achievements. With unique craftsmanship techniques formed, they have left behind countless magnificent works, derived local products well-known across the country, and attracted the attention of the upper class. Based on the different texture of different materials, each of the bamboo, wood, ivory, and rhino horn carvings holds a complete and unique set of carving techniques with

🖼 *Silver-plated and gold-embedded jewel with five phoenix tails.*

their own orderly rules. There is a sea of works with different features that have been passed down to later generations.

(18) Imperial Religious Items. The Palace Museum has collected 42,000 religious relics, covering four major categories: Han Buddhism, Tibetan Buddhism, Taoism, and Shamanism. Items themed Han Buddhism are mainly various Buddhism classics handed down from the Qing palace and an assortment of Buddha statues collected since the establishment of the Palace Museum. There are more than 500 Taoist cultural relics stored in the Hall of Imperial Peace and the Hall of the Vault of Heaven (not open to the public); dozens of Shamanic cultural relics are kept in the Palace of Earthly Tranquility. None of them have been separated from the ancient buildings, thus their higher historical and cultural value than ordinary cultural relics. 80% of the religious

relics collected in the Palace Museum are Tibetan Buddhist relics, including 23,000 Buddha statues, 7,000 sacrificial artifacts, 1,970 thangkas from the 18th century. They used to be kept in many Tibetan Buddhist temples in the Qing palace. Most of them were gifts presented to the emperor by ethnic and religious leaders in the Qing Dynasty.

(19) Jewelry. The Palace Museum hoards an enormous collection of imperial jewelry from the Qing Dynasty. They were made by different offices of the Guang Chusi and the Imperial Workshops. According to custom, they are divided into headwear, neckwear, and accessories. Elegant in shape and exquisite in craftsmanship, they reflect a strict hierarchy.

(20) Flags and Weapons Carried by Guards before an Emperor. The Forbidden City still keeps many flags and weapons carried by guards before an emperor. Most of them were passed down from the Qing Dynasty, such as those used for inspecting troops, riding and shooting, and a huge quantity of ornaments. There are also the remains of the Eight Banners officers and soldiers, the sharp weapons that were given in tribute to the court from all over China, and a small number of foreign weapons. The weapons collected in the Forbidden City are divided two types: cold arms (those that do not use gunpowder) and hot arms (those using gunpowder or other explosive devices), including armor, bows, guns, swords, and artillery. They are made of steel, iron, copper, wood, leather, ivory, bone, and so on. They have witnessed the prosperity and decline of the military during the hundreds of years of the Qing Dynasty, and reflected the integration of traditional Chinese weapons and equipment with foreign weapons under the special historical background at the time.

(21) Music and Opera. Musical and opera cultural relics are a special type of cultural relics in the Forbidden City. They mainly consist of classical musical instruments of the Qing Dynasty, including the required instruments for *Zhonghe Shaoyue* and *Danbi Dayue* (Imperial music for formal occasions), as well as some national musical instruments and western musical instrument tributes from western countries. In addition, due to the prevalence of opera in the royal palaces of the Qing Dynasty, there are many accompanying musical instruments for opera, such as tanggu (a kind of drum used in Chinese operas) and yueqin (a four-stringed plucked instrument with

Self-Opening Music Fountain from the UK (after repair).

Gild Bronze Buddha Statue with Bead Inlay.

Prajnaparamita Hrdaya Sutra.

a full-moon-shaped sound box). Meanwhile, old costumes, hats, records, and scripts related to opera are able to paint a picture of the grand performance in the palaces during the Qing Dynasty. Apart from the music and opera cultural relics of the Qing Dynasty, the pre-Ming guqin (a kind of zither) in the Forbidden City is also extremely valuable treasure.

(22) Everyday Life Utensils. There are also 13,000 pieces of daily utensil cultural relics in the Forbidden City, including palace lanterns, bonsai, ruyi (an S-shaped ornamental object, usually made of jade), medical equipment, tea, tableware, and fire sickles. Basically, they are collected from the Qing palaces, and a small part come from the non-governmental sources or private donations. In other words, these cultural relics are mainly what the royal family used in their daily palace life. For example, there are children's toys, foods of the time, *pu'er* tea, and Chinese medicine, etc. Because of their wide variety and different uses, the materials vary greatly. There is wood, silk, wool, horn, gems, etc. At the same time, they have different craftsmanship, such as dyeing, gluing, embroidering, engraving, and inlaying. Among these utensils, the most difficult to keep are the bonsai because they are enormous, and unlike porcelain and jade, they cannot be packed and boxed. The branches and petals of these bonsai are generally made of jade, and some of the leaves are dyed. Therefore, there must be extra care when storing, transporting, or displaying them. These daily utensils in the Forbidden City contain rich cultural connotations, not only showing the mysterious palace life, but outstanding traditional Chinese craftsmanship.

(23) Foreign Cultural Relics. The Palace Museum also keeps some foreign cultural relics collected from the Qing palaces. The majority of them come from the UK, France, Germany, Switzerland, the U.S., and Japan. There are lacquerware, pottery, porcelain, glassware, paintings, books, and furniture made between the 16th and the 20th centuries. Most of them were produced in the 18th and 19th centuries. Among all foreign cultural relics, Japanese items ranked first in both quantity and type. These foreign cultural relics have distinctive regional characteristics, showing the culture of their motherlands and reflecting the exchanges between China and foreign countries and regions.

Collection Acquisition

Collection acquisition is a business to which all museums attach great importance. It is how collection continue to be enriched. The acquisition of museum collections is realized in the following ways: fieldwork, archaeological excavation, acceptance of donations, purchases, private acquisitions, and acceptance of allocations or transfers. Among them, acceptance of donations is an important way of acquisition.

To build the Palace Museum, the efforts of a handful of staff is certainly not enough. We have received public support for a long time, one of which was the donations from scholars and the common people, who donated their private collections. Since the establishment of the Palace Museum, over 700 people have donated precious collections to us. The Palace Museum therefore set up a donation board, the Board of Great Benevolence, to express the gratitude to these donors. In recent years, cultural relic donations have kept coming one after another, which means a great deal to the development of the Palace Museum and the protection of cultural relics.

I hope that these donations are seen and understood, so we increase the publicity every time we receive a donation. There are multiple ways to publicize the donations. On the one hand, a media conferences can be held. On the other, regular exhibitions of the donated cultural relics can be organized. We have specially set aside a donation hall in the Palace of Great Benevolence to exhibit part of the donated cultural relics to the public. Through publications, commemorative articles, and anniversary events, we strive to make kind deeds remembered. For the important collections, such as the cultural relics that were rescued and returned to the Forbidden City in the past, we always mark the donation details when publishing articles about them or exhibiting them. In short, in the future construction of the Palace Museum, I believe it is also "where many help to gather firewood, the flames shoot high."

The Palace Museum continues to collect and gather cultural relics, but there are rigorous collection principles. In particular, the Palace Museum expects to receive donations of the cultural relics that have been lost from the Qing palace for various reasons. For some extremely important pieces, it is ready to purchase them. For example, over a decade ago, the Palace Museum seized the opportunity to purchase valuable paintings and calligraphy by Zhang Xian, including *A Picture of Ten Poems*, *Chu Shi Song*, and *Yan Shan Ming*.

Throughout the history of the Palace Museum's acceptance of donations, it is noted that, in fact, the majority of the donated cultural relics are ancient artworks, especially those related to the culture of the Palace Museum. For example, *Silk Road Landscape Map* donated by Xu Rongmao, Chairman of the Board of Directors of Shimao Group in Hong Kong in 2018, has become a precious cultural relic of the Palace Museum. However, we hold a more cautious attitude towards contemporary artwork.

There are those who voice that the Palace Museum is the most demanding museum when it comes to accepting donations. It does implement three regulations for accepting contemporary art donations: first, the donated paintings and calligraphy or artworks must be from masters with domestic or international influence; second, the donations must not only be the original works of the masters, but also their iconic creations; third, no matter how famous the masters are, the Palace Museum accepts no more than 10 pieces of their contemporary artwork. This stipulation aims to provide collection opportunities for other cultural institutions while ensuring that in two hundred or two thousand years, the collections of cultural relics in the Palace Museum will still be the best in all historical periods. This practice also leaves more chances for other museums to collect cultural relics. If a sea of contemporary artworks go into in the Palace Museum's warehouse, due to limited exhibition space, they might never be exhibited, thus there is no effective social education and cultural communication.

Examples of Precious Collections
in the Forbidden City

———

As of December 31, 2016, the Palace Museum had accumulated 1,862,690 pieces (sets) of cultural relics. This is second to none in China. Around the globe, it is also among the best. Generally, museums around the world share the pyramid-shaped collection structure. The spire is the best of the most precious cultural relics; the body is the general cultural relics; the bottom is the materials to be studied and graded. But the Palace Museum is an exception. Its collection structure is an inverted pyramid: 90.4% of the cultural relics are precious cultural relics, 8.8% are general cultural relics, and materials account for 0.8. Almost all are precious cultural relics. For the Palace Museum, the more precious the cultural relics are, the greater their number is. In other words, being precious is the ticket for cultural relics to enter the Palace Museum. Therefore, the responsibility that the Palace Museum shoulders is enormous. This is also the most important reason why it continues to strengthen the preservation of cultural relics.

One of the main sources of the collections of the Palace Museum is the old collections of the Qing emperors. Therefore, it has an advantage in the cultural relics of the Ming and Qing Dynasties. Taking paintings and calligraphy as an example, the Ming and Qing paintings collected in the Palace Museum have great advantages in both the total quantity and the number of fine works. For example, it keeps a huge collection of paintings and calligraphy from the Wumen Painting School, including 167 paintings and 53 calligraphies by Shen Zhou, 134 paintings and 46 calligraphies by Wen Zhengming, and 85 paintings and 40 calligraphies by Tang Yin, and 105 paintings by Qiu Ying. Regarding Qing paintings, the Palace Museum has a unique advantage in court painting in that it hoards the works of foreign missionaries such as Giuseppe Castiglione, Jean Denis Attiret, and Ignatius Sickeltart (Jesuit painters), and the works of royal painters such as Leng Mei, Jin Tingbiao, and Ding Guanpeng.

The Palace Museum is not only advantageous on Ming and Qing collections, but also on the collection system. As mentioned before, the cultural relics of the Palace Museum span across an incredible 25 categories, including paintings, model calligraphy, bronzeware, gold, silver, tinware, lacquerware, enamel, and jade, etc. Historically, the important categories of the Palace Museum's collections are in a neat historical sequence. For example, there are sufficient ceramics collections to hold an exhibition of the development history of Chinese ceramics, and the jade collection covers all the periods from the stone age to the end of the Qing Dynasty. In this respect, no museum in the world outdoes it.

Here, I would like to list some precious collections of the Palace Museum.

In terms of ceramics, we possess many world-famous collections, such as *White-glazed Sunflower Bowls Made in the Xing Kiln* from the Tang Dynasty, *Three-legged Vase Made in the Ru Kiln* from the Song Dynasty, *Fish Ear Incense Burner Made in the Ge Kiln, String Pattern Vase Made in the Guan Kiln, White-glazed Vase with Embossment Made in the Jun Kiln, Celadon-glazed Phoenix Ear Vase Made in the Longquan Kiln, Porcelain Pillows in the Shape of a Baby Made in the Ding Kiln, Blue-glazed White Dragon-patterned Plate* from the Yuan Dynasty, *Blue-and-white Cup* from the Yongle period of the Ming Dynasty, *Blue-and-white Sanskrit Jar with Embossment* from the Xuande period, *Colored Chicken-patterned Cup* from the Chenghua period, *Yellow-glazed Golden Beast Ear Jar* from the Hongzhi period, *Multicolored Hollowed-out Cloud-and-phoenix-patterned Vase* from the Wanli period, *Violet Enamel Lotus-Patterned Vase* from the Kangxi period, *Enamel Pheasant-and-peony Patterned Bowl* from the Yongzheng period, and *Various Glazed Vases* from the Qianlong period, etc. These are the finest pieces of ceramics in past dynasties that represent the highest level of ceramic craftsmanship in various periods in Chinese history.

In terms of paintings, there are countless precious and famous collections in the Forbidden City, such as *Stroll About in Spring* by Zhan Ziqian of the Sui Dynasty,

□ *White-Glazed Vase with Embossment* made in Jun Kiln.

□ *Broken Stone Rubbings of the Marquis of Xixiang* in the Han Dynasty.

□ The twelve-character eaves tile of Qin Dynasty, "*wei, tian, jiang, ling, yan, yuan, wan, nian, tian, xia, kang, and ning.*"

Emperor Taizong Receiving the Tibetan Envoy by Yan Liben of the Tang Dynasty, *Five Oxen* by Han Fang, *Xiao and Xiang Rivers* by Dong Yuan of the Five Dynasties, *The Night Revels of Han Xizai* by Gu Hongzhong, *Dragon Stone* by Zhao Ji of the Northern Song Dynasty, *Along the River during the Qingming Festival* by Zhang Zeduan, and *Bamboo* by Ni Zan of the Yuan Dynasty. Among the 50,000 paintings, nearly 1,000 are grade-one national cultural relics, covering almost all the famous works of every historical period in the development of Chinese paintings. In particular, the number of the fine paintings of the pre-Yuan period exceeds 400, ranking the first in China. Moreover, many of the paintings of the Forbidden City are rare treasures, and some are even the only copies that have survived catastrophes, thus occupying a paramount position in the history of Chinese art.

Similarly, the model calligraphy in the Forbidden City is also an assembling of treasures. For example, there are two of the well-known "three rarities"—*Mid-Autumn Calligraphy* and *Boyuan Calligraphy*, the *Ping Fu Calligraphy* by Jin Luji of the Jin Dynasty, *Chu Shi Song* of the Sui Dynasty, *Poems about Zhang Haohao* by Du Mu of the Tang Dynasty, and *Dao Fu Zan* by Fan Zhongyan of the Song Dynasty. Like paintings, our modeled calligraphy collection is well-known both at home and abroad.

In terms of lacquerware, the Forbidden City houses *The Carved Gardenia-patterned Round Lacquer Plate* made by Zhang Cheng of the Yuan Dynasty, *The Carved Waterfall-view-patterned Octagonal Lacquer Plate* made by Yang Mao, and *The Carved Flower-view-patterned Round Box* made by Zhang Minde.

In terms of sculpture, the white stone statues of Quyang, Hebei collected in the Forbidden City span the late Northern Wei Dynasty and the Tianbao period of the Tang Dynasty; 50 wood carvings of Arhats of Nanhua Temple in Shaoguan, Guangdong were made between the 5th and the 8th years in the Qingli period of the Northern Song Dynasty. They are essential data for the study of secular beliefs; there are also the porcelain, bronze, and stone sculptures by He Chaozong, Shi Sou, Shang Jun, and Yang Yuxuan, brick portraits and stone portraits of the Han Dynasty, and twenty-four brick sculptures of the Song Dynasty. These sculpture relics, with high historical and artistic value, make up one of the important collections of the Forbidden City.

In terms of gold and silverware, the Forbidden City keeps Zhu Bishan's *Silver Raft Cup* of the Yuan Dynasty, a *Silver Square Wine Cup* of the Ming Dynasty, and *Qianlong Gold Everlasting Cup* of the Qing Dynasty, among a variety of fine pieces that either demonstrate the excellent craftsmanship of gold and silverware making or contain high historical value.

In terms of jade, the Forbidden City houses both ancient jade, such as the *Big Jade Dragon* and *Multi-Section Zong* (a long hollow piece of jade with rectangular sides), and the famous *Zigang Jade* of the Ming Dynasty. In addition, there is a rich collection of Qing Dynasty jade. In particular, huge jade with complex and exquisite carvings such as jade of *Sage King Yu Controlling the Flood*, jade of *Dantai Chunxiao*, and *Gray Jade Jar of Dragon Patterns* is extremely rare.

In terms of seals, the Forbidden City stores the official *Twenty-Five Seals* of the Qing Dynasty, as well as imperial seals and private seals. The seals of the Emperor Qianlong are the most outstanding among all.

In terms of embroidery, the Forbidden City keeps a complete collection of Qing Dynasty palace dresses, including hats, gowns, shoes, belts, and accessories. Together, they can outline the decrees and regulations of the Qing Dynasty, which is impossible in any other museum in the world.

Western instruments in the Forbidden City, including clocks, watches, and other technical instruments, suffice to narrate the history of cultural exchanges between the East and the West. Among them, the famous gilded bronze writing man clock, the gilded bronze elephant pulling chariot clock, and the gilded bronze tower clock with inlaid stone gems perfectly combine the Chinese elements with western elements, becoming both unique crafts and exquisite technical instruments.

Many of the collections of Tibetan Buddhism in the Forbidden City come from Buddhist temples in the Qing Dynasty. The Buddha statues, pagodas, thangkas and other religious musical instruments truly restore the development of Tibetan Buddhism in the Qing Dynasty and its prosperity in the Forbidden City. The *Gold Bell Jade Chimes* in the Forbidden City tells the importance of the ritual system in the Qing court.

☐ Western calculator.

☐ Silver enameled telescope.

As for ancient books, there is a variety of precious collections in the Forbidden City, such as various versions of Tripitaka, the blocked printed editions of the *Kangxi Dictionary*, and the *Compilation of Books of Ancient and Modern Times* kept in the Hall of Martial Valor. These ancient books are from multiple dynasties and of various forms, and many of them are extremely rare and even the only copies in the world.

In a nutshell, of the 1.86 million pieces of the collections in the Palace Museum, over 90% are precious cultural relics; of all 25 types of the collections, each is rich in variety and fine in quality. We have always wanted to exhibit them more to the public. Over the years, we have continued to improve the exhibition space, exhibition styles, and exhibition content of the Palace Museum, thus more precious cultural relics appearing in the exhibition hall one after another. I believe that as the Forbidden City continues to expand the open area and the exhibition quality continues to improve, visitors will definitely see more precious cultural relics in the exhibition halls of the Forbidden City.

The Palace Museum Exhibition Sensation

———

As the largest and richest treasure house of Chinese cultural relics, the Palace Museum hoards over 1.8 million pieces of cultural relics. However, in the past, the majority of them were "sleeping" in the warehouse, so that the tour of the Forbidden City used to be merely skimming the surface. In fact, the public's enthusiasm to go to cultural relics exhibitions and appreciate cultural relics collections is always there, and expanding day by day, but it is a pity that they could not see some of the rare cultural relics. Similarly, it is a regret for us Palace Museum staff, because we are dying to show more of its rich cultural relics collection to the general public. To this end, we must seek change and make cultural relics "alive."

Over the past few years, the Palace Museum has contrived to move an increasing number of cultural relics out of the warehouses for the public to appreciate by repairing and protecting ancient architectures, opening up new exhibition areas, expanding new exhibition galleries, planning new exhibition halls, holding new exhibitions, and transferring staff out of the Palace Museum.

In terms of exhibitions, we have enriched and improved permanent exhibitions, such as the newly upgraded exhibitions in the Treasure Gallery, the Gallery of Clocks, Gallery of Painting and Calligraphy, The Ceramics Gallery, and the Stone Drums Exhibition Hall; opened newly-themed exhibition halls, such as the Sculpture Gallery, the Furniture Gallery, the Gallery of Historical Architecture, and the Tools of War Gallery; and initiated the display of original forms for the Hall of Imperial Supremacy, the Belvedere of Literary Profundity, the Hall of All Peace, the Palace of Longevity and Health, and the Belvedere of Pleasant Sounds. In the meantime, there are more temporary exhibitions held each year, although most of them are thematic exhibitions of the Forbidden City cultural relics. Additionally, the number of cooperative exhibitions and introductory exhibitions continues to go up. Some are introduced from other museums and cultural institutions at home and abroad. More and more exhibitions with social influence continue to be presented to the general public.

Regarding the exhibitions on special subjects, the Palace Museum successively held the *Best of the Ancient Relics—Exhibition of Selected Donated Ceramics, Purity and Serenity—Ding Kiln Porcelain Exhibition, Fresh Breeze—an Exhibition of Fans in the Qing Palaces, an Exhibition of the Palace Museum Collection of Paintings and Calligraphy, the Special Exhibition of Paintings of the "Four Masters" of the Early Qing Dynasty, the Forbidden City and the Maritime Silk Road Exhibition, An Exhibition of the Paintings and Calligraphy of the Four Monks, the Special Exhibition of the Paintings and Calligraphy by Zhao Mengfu, A Thousand Li of Rivers and Mountains—a Special Exhibition of Landscape Paintings of Past Dynasties, Forever Remembered—the 120th Anniversary Exhibition of Zhang Boju, Refreshing Breeze—an Exhibition of Imperial Inkstones of the Qing Dynasty, Magical Carving—a Special Exhibition of Seal Cuttings by Wu Changshuo, Lunar New Year—Celebration in the Forbidden City*, and so on.

In cooperation with Chinese museums and cultural institutions, it successively held the *Joint Exhibition of Luoyang Peonies and Peony-themed Cultural Relics, the Joint Exhibition Kaifeng Chrysanthemum and Chrysanthemum-themed Cultural Relics, the Charm of Huizhou Craftsmanship—Special Exhibition of Traditional Crafts from Huizhou, Anhui Province, Secret Colors—the Archaeological Discovery of Secret Color Porcelains and Their Re-entering the Palace Museum, Everlasting Prosperity—a Special Exhibition of Ruilu Cultural Relics, Qing Ping Fu Lai—a Special Exhibition of Qi Baishi Art, Extreme Creation—the 2019 Olympic Expo Exhibition, Raging Beauty—Peony Appreciation in the Forbidden City, Liangzhu and Ancient China—Five Thousand Years of Civilization Through Jade, Globalizing Longquan—Longquan Celadon and Their Globalization, Viewing Fish For Fun—Joint Exhibition of Palace Goldfish Culture and goldfish-themed cultural relics in the Palace Museum, Longevity and Happiness—When the Tashi Lhunpo Monastery meets the Forbidden City*," etc.

The Forbidden City and the Maritime Silk Road Exhibition.

Special Exhibition of Paintings and Calligraphy by Zhang Boju.

🔲 *Born of Fire—an Exhibition of Treasures from the National Museum of Afghanistan.*

In cooperation with foreign museums and cultural institutions, it successively held the *Glory of the Indian Court: an Exhibition of the British National Victoria and Albert Museum Collections, Exquisiteness: the Royal Faberge Decorative Art Exhibition from the U.S., Brahma and East Earth: A Sino-Indian Sculpture Art Exhibition from 400 to 700 AD, Born of Fire—an Exhibition of Treasures from the National Museum of Afghanistan, Glamour—an Exhibition of Treasures from the Eighteenth Century, Princess Sissi and Hungary: The Life of Hungarian Nobles in the 17th and 19th Centuries, The Rarest—Al Thani Collection Exhibition of Qatar, Nobility—an Exhibition of the Grimaldi Dynasty of Monaco, Relics of the Aegean—an Exhibition of Underwater Archaeological Relics of Antikythera, Greece, Flowing Colors—an Exhibition of Ukrainian Museum Cultural Relics, Objects, and Decorative Arts, True Beauty—an Exhibition of Chinese Cultural Relics*

📷 *Nobility—an Exhibition of the Grimaldi Dynasty of Monaco.*

collected in the Vatican Museum, *Beyond the Boundary: Cartier—a Special Exhibition of Crafts and Restoration of the Palace Museum,* etc.

At present, as numerous modern museums have been built across China, the exhibitions of the Palace Museum can reach more cities. To especially thank various places for long-term support in the development of the Palace Museum, we held the *Homecoming Exhibition of the Cultural Relics* in the Palace Museum, including *Into the Imperial Study* held in Hefei—*a Special Exhibition of the Imperial Stationary of Qing Dynasty, Su Palace* held in Suzhou—*an Exhibition of Ming and Qing Su Works (Cultural Relics) Collected in the Palace Museum, Orchid Pavilion Homecoming Exhibition* held in Shaoxing, *an Unconventional February,* held in Yangzhou, *a Joint Exhibition of Paintings and Calligraphy of the Eight Eccentrics of Yangzhou, Looking at Fuchun,* held in Hangzhou, *a Special Homecoming Exhibition of Famous Paintings, a Hometown Exhibition of Shoushan Stone* held in Fuzhou, *an Exhibition of Mr. Zheng Zhenduo's Donation of Cultural Relics to the Palace Museum* held in Wenzhou, *Elegant Royal Taste* held in Yixing—*an Exhibition of Imperial Purple Sands, an Exhibition of the Fine Works of Women Artists of the Changzhou Painting School* held in Changzhou, *an Exhibition of the Paintings and Calligraphy of the Xin'an Eight Masters collected in the Palace Museum* held in Huangshan, *Oldtime Glory* held in Shenyang, *an Exhibition of the Cultural Relics in the Shenyang Palace Museum That Have Been Moved to the South, a Special Exhibition of Cultural Relics from Chengdu and on the Silk Road* held in Chengdu, *an Exhibition of Xinjiang Cultural Relics in the Qing Dynasty collected in the Palace Museum* held in Xinjiang, and Dialogue, held in Hainan—*an Exhibition of the Maritime Silk Road and the Forbidden City.* These cultural relics exhibitions that have a deep connection with local traditional culture have received the warmest welcome from the local citizens, enabled them to better understand their own urban culture, and strengthened their sense of pride in their hometown.

It is unforgettable that in 2015, the Palace Museum turned 90 years old, and we launched a series of exhibitions to celebrate this important moment, such as *Universal Jubilation—Exhibition of the Grand Ceremony of the Qing Dynasty Longevity* at the Meridian Gate, the *Special Exhibition of Shiqu Baoji* at the Hall of Martial Valor, *Porcelains of Imperial Kilns of the Ming Dynasty at Hall of Abstinence—Comparative Exhibition between Porcelain Unearthed from the Ruins of the Imperial Kilns and Porcelain during the Reigns of the Emperor Hongwu, the Emperor Yongle, and the Emperor Xuande, Fresh and Elegant* at Palace of Prolonging Happiness—*an Exhibition of Ru Kiln Porcelain, a Collection Exhibition of Old Photos of the Forbidden City* at the Gate of Divine Prowess, and *a Special Exhibition of Cultural Relics Conservation and Restoration in the Palace Museum* at Gate of Divine Prowess, and more.

In recent years, in addition to the increasing number of fixed exhibitions and original displays, the Palace Museum has held over 50 temporary exhibitions inside and outside itself each year, doubling the amount of cultural relics on display. It is especially gratifying that the continuous launch of a series of exhibitions has polished the exhibition level of the Palace Museum greatly, and built the concept of continuous active planning of exhibitions according to social needs. These exhibitions have not only caused a sensation in cultural circles, but generated a wide impact on the society. More and more visitors become more familiar with and fascinated by the culture of the Forbidden City through the exhibitions.

The *Special Exhibition of Shiqu Baoji* in 2015 and *A Thousand Li of Rivers and Mountains—a Special Exhibition of Landscape Paintings of Past Dynasties* in 2017 deserve more detailed description. They have caused an enormous public response, becoming exhibition sensations. Also, the proper term "Forbidden City Run" is derived, showing the status of the excellent traditional culture represented by the Palace Museum in the heart of the public and their respect and desire for of cultural classics. What is more delighting is that visitors under the age of 30 were 70% of those who came to the special exhibitions.

First, let's talk about the *Special Exhibition of Shiqu Baoji*. 2015 was the 90th anniversary of the Palace Museum. During the celebration, a large group of wonderful exhibitions were held for the public, and the *Special Exhibition of Shiqu Baoji* was one of them. Famous paintings and calligraphy works like *Along the River during the Qingming Festival* were exhibited. It attracted wide attention beyond our expectations.

In the past, people used to complain about their discontentment during the tour in the Palace Museum. It was common that 80% of visitors, once they entered it, would go straight to check where the emperor sat, slept, and got married, and pass through the imperial garden and end the visit. Too many visitors did not know or missed the opportunity to visit the exhibitions on both sides of the main road in the Palace Museum.

The *Special Exhibition of Shiqu Baoji* changed this situation. Once visitors walked into the Palace Museum, instead of marching straight, they ran to the west, because the Hall of Martial Valor, where this exhibition was held, is on the west road. More visitors joined the run, and they ran faster and faster. As a result, a network term

⬛ Visit order of the *Special Exhibition of Shiqu Baoji* (September 19, 2015).

was born—"Forbidden City Run," I saw it with my own eyes that there were indeed many visitors running to see it. An old gentleman, standing in front of the Gallery of Paintings and Calligraphy of the Hall of Martial Valor, asked me, "Why does the Palace Museum hold an exhibition like a sports meeting? Everyone has to run." He said that he had already turned 70, and he joined the line at the front early in the morning to get tickets. But people started to run after the exhibition was opened and he was left behind, thus unable to go in among the first group of visitors.

His words enlightened me. That moon, we convened a meeting to figure out how to better manage the event order. Overnight, we made 20 signs and 1,000 name badges. Before 7 o'clock the next morning, the signs were placed on the square to divide the visitors into groups A, B, C . . . People lined up accordingly, and the opening ceremony of the *Special Exhibition of Shiqu Baoji* was held. After that was the march-in ceremony. Before 8:00, the exhibition hall was opened 30 minutes early, receiving the first group, the second, the third, and more in turn. The elderly and the children simply had to follow the signs to enter the exhibition hall without the need to run. Allegedly, the Palace Museum is the only museum in the world that holds a march-in ceremony for the exhibitions.

Although this approach was adopted, there were still too many people, a total of 170,000, coming to the exhibition. Thousands of people lined up every day, with an average of six hours waiting. But no matter how long the waiting took, the audience insisted on seeing the exhibition, especially seeing the famous painting *Along the River during the Qingming Festival*. Therefore, we promised that the museum would not close until the last visitor saw it. I recall that one day, at 8 p.m., when we went to check on the visitors, there was still a long queue. I asked them if they were weary. They all replied: "We are hanging there, except there is no vending machine of bottled water in the Palace Museum at night. What if we get thirsty?" We immediately notified the kitchen to boil water and made 2,500 cups of tea for them.

At 12:00 p.m., I checked on them again and asked: "Have you got some water?"

They answered, "Our thirst is gone, but our hunger has come." We immediately took out another 800 cups of instant noodles. After a simple meal, they continued to wait in line. Later, I heard that the Palace Museum is the only museum in the world to offer free instant noodles during popular exhibitions.

At 4:00 a.m., the last group of visitors finished enjoying the exhibition. With their family photo taken, they left happily. The dawn broke when the last visitor left the Palace Museum. I particularly take fancy of the photo of the last visitor who just finished touring around the exhibition outside the Hall of Martial Valor—in the first glimmer of dawn, he wore a gorgeous smile of contentment.

Another fact that particularly touches me and makes me proud is that 70% of the visitors who queued up to see the exhibition were students from all over the world. To prevent them from wasting too much time waiting, we invited curatorial experts and volunteers to offer them a basic guide. In addition, the QR codes adopted at that time turned out enormously helpful. The visitors could check the details of each item displayed in the exhibition hall by scanning the codes with their mobile phones, thus lessening the boredom of their waiting. Meanwhile, books, magazines, and cultural and creative products published specifically for this exhibition have also attracted wide public attention.

We believe that the *Special Exhibition of Shiqu Baoji* has turned out to be a learning experience. Back then, at the old exhibitions held in the Palace Museum, a 10-to-20-meter queue was considered long. We did not expect to receive such a strong public repercussion this time. The queue that the visitors made extended as far as the Gate of Supreme Harmony Square. When there were the most visitors, thousands were waiting in line, as long as hundreds of meters. We did not expect such enthusiasm. It was romanticized as a beautiful sight itself. But for the visitors lining up, it was exhausting. We are grateful for their patience, and for their love for traditional culture and understanding of the meaning of cultural relics.

A Thousand Li of Rivers and Mountains—a Special Exhibition of Landscape Paintings of Past Dynasties held on September 15, 2017, at the Sparrow Wing Towers Exhibition Hall at the Meridian Gate centered on the famous painting *A Thousand Li of Rivers and Mountains* by Wang Ximeng from the Northern Song Dynasty. It aimed to go through and exhibit the development of Chinese landscape painting of past dynasties.

For the first time, the exhibition presented the best landscape paintings collected in the Palace Museum. It is common knowledge that Chinese landscape paintings not only simply depict the scenery of the mountains and rivers, but speak the painter's mind and create an ideal world. In order to fully present the spiritual connotation of landscape painting, the curators of this exhibition contrived to integrate the techniques, layout, and tension of landscape paintings and designed this entire exhibition into a blue-and-green landscape painting itself. This exhibition has great cultural significance, because blue-and-green is an essential category of Chinese landscape painting. But, as paintings by literati since the Yuan Dynasty developed rapidly and became the mainstream within art circles, our first impression of Chinese landscape painting is often ink wash landscape painting, and the status and value of blue and green landscape in the history of Chinese paintings are forgotten. The systematic display of the development of ancient Chinese blue-and-green landscape painting contributes to a more profound understanding of the concept of landscape painting and the spiritual world of Chinese arts. In addition, the Palace Museum, with the collections of precious works such as *Stroll about in Spring* by Zhan Ziqian, *A Thousand Li of Rivers and Mountains* by Wang Ximeng, *Autumn Landscape* by Zhao Boju, and *Ten Thousand Pines and Golden Towers* by Zhao Bosu, have an outstanding advantage in the possession of blue-and-green landscape paintings. Through this exhibition, the public can have a direct and specific understanding of the importance of the collections in the Palace Museum. In addition, after a thorough cultural relics numeration, the Palace Museum has published a catalog of all its collections to the public. The holding of special exhibitions themed with blue-and-green landscapes is a concrete embodiment of the achievements of the systematic numeration. It also reflects the practical significance of the numeration and research of the Palace Museum collections.

Certainly, the highlight and focus of this exhibition was *A Thousand Li of Rivers and Mountains* by Wang Ximeng of the Northern Song Dynasty. It was a blue-and-green landscape painting created for the Northern Song Emperor Huizong over 900 years ago by Wang Ximeng, a talented 18-year-old painter. It took him less than half a year to finish this 11.9-meter-long scroll that depicts both the splendid landscape and an ideal living environment full of vitality. This is one of the most famous landscape paintings in ancient China. It is usually believed that "paper lasts a thousand years, silk eight hundred." Despite its nearly-one-thousand-year-old age, it remains brightly colorful because it used mineral pigments, which prevent colors from fading. In addition to its artistic value, it can be used as a precious historical material for the study of ancient Chinese architecture. As early as 1979, Fu Xinian extracted the architectural complex in *A Thousand Li of Rivers and Mountains*, compared them with the records in literature, restored the layout and details of different types of buildings, and summarized the characteristics of urban and rural buildings and bridges in the Northern Song Dynasty. This scroll, which paints the fishing villages, open markets, and the long bridge over the riverside within the mountains and rivers, is an authentic portrayal of the ideal life in ancient China.

Exhibition of the Paintings and Calligraphy of the Four Monks Collected in the Palace Museum.

In fact, since the beginning of the 21st century, *A Thousand Li of Rivers and Mountains* has been exhibited three times in the Palace Museum, the first two times in the Gallery of Paintings and Calligraphy in the Hall of Martial Valor. My mentor, Professor Wu Liangyong, fancies this painting dearly, so I accompanied him to appreciate it every time it was exhibited. When it was exhibited for the first time, there were few visitors, and no long queue. But, when it was exhibited for the second time, an army of enthusiastic visitors flocked to see it, making a long line that took several hours to wait. To make it more comfortable for them to enjoy the exhibition and reduce the waiting time, the Palace Museum implemented the measures of issuing free different-slot-tickets to the main exhibition hall of the Meridian Gate where *A Thousand Li of Rivers and Mountains* was displayed. There were 16 time slots every day. Every half an hour was a slot, during which 150 visitors were allowed to enter the exhibition hall. The ticket was issued at the entrance of the special exhibition. Access was only granted when a ticket was shown.

This measure, together with the limiting and shunting that had been implemented at the beginning of the exhibition, operated an effective control of the exhibition in terms of time and space. At 8:30 a.m., the visitors could enter the Palace Museum from the Meridian Gate, and some of them marched straight to the entrance of the special exhibition. The Palace Museum staff would allow the first 150 visitors to enter the exhibition area, and issued free tickets to the rest of them for the remaining time slots. There was a sign indicating the current visit slot and ticket numbers for this period on the side of the entrance. If the visitors did not come to see *A Thousand Li of Rivers and Mountains* but still would like to check other exhibits in the Sparrow Towers of the Meridian Gate, they could enter the exhibition area without the special ticket.

With this series of measures taken, there was no longer a long queue of visitors at the entrance of the Meridian Gate exhibition area throughout the day. There was only a queue of about a dozen visitors at the main exhibition hall of the Meridian Gate. It took an average 30 minutes of waiting to see the *A Thousand Li of Rivers and Mountains*. There was no need to line up to see other exhibits. The implementation of different-slot visits by issuing tickets has several advantages: first, the waiting time was

🖼 *Exhibition of the Paintings and Calligraphy of the Four Monks in Hall of Martial Valor.*

greatly reduced, after receiving the tickets, visitors could freely visit other wonderful exhibitions in the Palace Museum or rest and dine; second, more visitors could enter the Sparrow Wing Towers and see many precious painting and calligraphy exhibits; third, the order was effectively improved, and the mood of the visitors, too. There is no longer the annoyance of a long waiting line, which is conducive to maintaining a delightful atmosphere in the exhibition hall. We have also called on the visitors not to line up blindly for such exhibitions, and not to focus only on a single exhibit and miss the other rare paintings and calligraphy treasures.

Like the *Special Exhibition of Shiqu Baoji* in 2015, about 70% of the visitors to *A Thousand Li of Rivers and Mountains—a Special Exhibition of Landscape Paintings of Past Dynasties* were under 30 years old. We were delighted to see that young people

⬛ The charm of Huizhou craftsmanship.

have taken an interest in the splendid Chinese culture, and that museum culture has become a part of their cultural lives. Perhaps in the past, *Shiqu Baoji* and *A Thousand Li of Rivers and Mountains* were known too little, but today they have become the hot topics, and their exhibitions are making larger and wider impacts.

In recent years, our wish that more visitors come to the exhibitions when they visit the Forbidden City is step by step being granted. Taking the National Day of 2017 as an example, in addition to waves of visitors attending the regular exhibitions at the Treasure Gallery, Gallery of Clocks, and the Ceramic Gallery, the thematic exhibitions at the newly opened the Sculpture Gallery at Palace of Compassion and Tranquility and the display of Palace of Longevity and Health in its original form received 183,000 and 126,000 visitors, respectively. Meanwhile, in the main hall of the Meridian Gate and the Sparrow Wing Towers on both its east side and west side, *A Thousand Li of Rivers and Mountains—a Special Exhibition of Landscape Paintings of Past Dynasties* received 126,000 visitors, of which 23,000 visited *A Thousand Li of Rivers and Mountains* in the main hall of the Meridian Gate in different time slots; a *Special Exhibition of the Paintings and Calligraphy by Zhao Mengfu* in Hall of Martial Valor received 35,000 visitors; *Princess Sissi and Hungary: The Life of Hungarian Nobles in the 17th and 19th Centuries* at Gate of Divine Prowess received the most visitors, reaching 213,000, because the city walls on both sides of Gate of Divine Prowess were opened for the first time; *Everlasting Prosperity—Special Exhibition of Ruilu Cultural Relics* held in Palace of Eternal Longevity and the garden of Palace of Compassion and Tranquility received 106,000 and 91,000 visitors respectively; *Porcelains of the Imperial Kilns of the Ming Dynasty—Comparative Exhibition between Porcelain Unearthed from the Jingde Town Ruins of the Imperial Kilns and Hongzhi and Zhengde Porcelain Collected in the Palace Museum* held at the Hall of Abstinence received 95,000 visitors. These exhibitions alone attracted about one million visitors during the National Day holiday.

It was imaginable in the past that this many visitors came to these exhibitions in the Palace Museum. Highlighting the culture and the characteristics of the Palace Museum, they have received positive social response. Also, because they were mainly distributed on the east and west roads, pressure was taken off of the central axis area, where most visitors gather, and the situation was changed where visitors went straight along the central axis when touring the Palace Museum.

Although the Palace Museum has made progress in expanding its opening area and improving exhibition services, its cultural resources are still far from full exhibition. At present, the exhibition halls of the Palace Museum are mainly the ancient architectures. Limited by exhibition space and conditions, merely around 30,000 pieces of cultural relics are exhibited, accounting for only 2% of the total collection of cultural relics of the Palace Museum. It fails to show the overall abundance of the Palace Museum's precious cultural relics to the public. Meanwhile, due to the limitation of the architectural characteristics of the cultural relics, the difficulty to maintain and restore cultural relics collections remains high. Therefore, it is the inevitable responsibility and mission of the Palace Museum to seek new developmental space and ensure the safety of its cultural heritage.

In the last couple of years, the Palace Museum has been expanding the first and second phases of the underground warehouses for the cultural relics. When the expansion is completed, about 1.1 million cultural relics of the Palace Museum, including nearly 200,000 cultural relics currently "sleeping" in the ancient architecture, will be classified into different categories and grades, and stored in their respective suitable warehouses with constant temperature and humidity.

At present, the Palace Museum has begun to plan the systematic opening of some ground-level warehouses so that they can act as warehouse-styled exhibition halls to display more cultural relics. For example, the big southern warehouse was first opened. This ground warehouse is enormous, with a length of 156 meters. We were determined to completely renovate it and turned it into the Furniture Hall of the Palace Museum. We are pleased to see the visitors having a blast touring the Furniture Hall, reluctant to leave. The Palace Museum then decided to open more warehouses to display the cultural relics in a warehouse style, such as the warehouse-style exhibition halls for ancient book editions, for ancient architectural components, for ceramics, for vehicles and horses, and for Zhonghe Shaoyue, etc. This has doubled the number of the cultural relics collections displayed each year, so that the visitors can appreciate more when they visit the Palace Museum. Warehouse-style exhibitions cannot only improve the storage conditions of the cultural relics collections, but exhibit them, so that more precious cultural relics can be seen. For example, the warehouse-style exhibition halls for ancient book editions under planning will be able to preserve and exhibit 240,000 precious book editions.

The upcoming completion of the north part of the Palace Museum, which is under preparation, will be able to solve the problem that a great many large and precious cultural relics, such as huge pieces of furniture, wide carpets, long scrolls of paintings, and enormous flags and weapons, cannot be protected and exhibited for a long time due to space limitations. In the meantime, it will show the traditional cultural relic restoration techniques, which are an intangible cultural heritage, to the public. I believe that everyone who comes to visit the Palace Museum will be deeply charmed by its culture.

On the 600th anniversary of the completion of the Forbidden City in 2020, over 100,000 cultural relics were exhibited. The proportion of the cultural relics collections of the Palace Museum on display in 2012 was only 1% of the total. We hoped that the number would increase to about 8% in 2020, and to around 30% in 2025. The Palace Museum possesses abundant cultural resources waiting to be discovered. It is the goal of the Palace Museum to systematically sort out these traditional cultural resources, bring the cultural relics stored in the Forbidden City, the heritage displayed on the vast land, and the words written in the ancient books back to life, and show the unique charm of Chinese culture in a variety of ways.

CHAPTER 3

The Palace Museum, an Educational Institution / Research Institution

The Palace Museum offers free educational programs for the adolescents, because we firmly believe that the generation of adolescents that grow up in the museums will fall in love with traditional Chinese culture as well as museum culture.

Mr. Geng Baochang, our ceramics expert, is nearly 100 years old. He comes to work when the weather is warm. The veteran experts of the Palace Museum have devoted their whole lives to academic research of the Palace Museum, becoming the most important pillar for its development. Now, we should make it comfortable for them to work in the Palace Museum so that they remain on their jobs and active in the research field. A couple of young apprentice scholars can work alongside with them, absorbing their experience and wisdom.

Volunteers—a Beautiful Sight in the Palace Museum

When touring around the Palace Museum, visitors must notice the presence of a group of people wearing badges and uniforms in every exhibition hall, such as the treasure hall, the clock hall, the painting and calligraphy hall, and the ceramics hall, who are patiently explaining the exhibits. Often, they are circled by visitors listening attentively. These are the lovely volunteers of the Palace Museum. They make a beautiful sight in the Palace Museum. And they contribute greatly to its publicity and education. From all walks of life, they are also of all ages. Their services range from lectures, consultations, educational programs, and promotional speakers. After over ten years of practical experience, the volunteer team of the Palace Museum has evolved into a high-quality service team.

On December 5, 2004, the Palace Museum put out a volunteer recruitment ad for the first time. More than 1,500 applications were received, 450 candidates were invited for an interview, and around 300 passed the training and assessment, and became the first group of volunteers of the Palace Museum. By the end of 2018, the cumulative number of registered volunteers was close to 3,000, reaching a total of 130,000, total hours of service rendered, serving an audience of nearly 600,000.

At first, the volunteers of the Palace Museum used to only undertake the exhibition explanations in the permanent halls of the Palace Museum. Now the explanation area has been expanded to ten exhibition halls of the Palace Museum, including the Gallery of Clocks, the Treasure Gallery, the Stone Drums Exhibition Hall, the Opera Hall, the Bronze Gallery, the Ceramics Gallery, and the Gallery of Painting and Calligraphy. They have also explained the exhibits of certain special exhibitions, such as the

Exhibition of Qing Emperor's Wedding Ceremonies, Special Exhibition of Ceramics of Palace of Prolonging Happiness, and *Special Exhibition of Orchid Pavilion*. In addition, they take care of the foreign exchange activities of the Palace Museum and the training of new volunteers, and participate in various cultural heritage promotion and protection activities organized by the Palace Museum, including visitor consultation, temporary exhibition explanations, visitor questionnaire surveys, and research and development and implementation of public education programs.

Volunteers of the Palace Museum take an active part in the themed publicity activities on the major theme days such as International Museum Day and China Cultural Heritage Day, as well as in the consultation service during the Golden Week (around the Chinese National Day in October) when there are the most visitors. For example, on the International Museum Day of May 18, volunteers hand out colorful bracelets with the Palace Museum logo and the tagline "Smoke-free Palace Museum" to the visitors, telling them not to bring fire sources such as lighters into the Palace Museum, and dissuading individual visitors from uncivilized conduct. At the Gate of Supreme Harmony Tourist Center, volunteers dressed in uniform patiently answer questions from the visitors, actively guide civilized tours, spread the concept of "safety in the Palace Museum," distribute the Palace Museum quiz cards, and give away souvenirs such as bookmarks.

They also actively spread and promote the culture of the Palace Museum outside the Palace Museum. On the International Museum Day in May 2012, the "Palace Museum Culture" promotion team was assembled. The team is entirely composed of volunteers of the Palace Museum. They took the lectures in the exhibition hall of the Palace Museum to the communities, thus breaking through the space limitations of the exhibition hall and expanding the scope of volunteer service. With the cooperation of Publicity and Education Department, volunteer teachers selected nearly 20 lecture themes based on the Palace Museum's history, ancient architecture, cultural relics collections, and exhibitions. Each lecture lasted about 20 minutes. Meanwhile, the Palace Museum volunteers are also involved in school education. For example, from September to December 2012, volunteers of the Palace Museum taught the last history lesson in every month to 11 classes of high school freshmen of Number 15 High School of Beijing. The content of the lessons was carefully selected stories of "Palace Museum Culture." And students learned about the profound cultural connotation of the Palace Museum through these easy-to-understand historical stories.

These volunteers are responsible for the recruitment, training and assessment of new volunteers, including foreign volunteers. Since foreign volunteers speak different languages, volunteers either participate in or take full charge of contacting, interviewing, and training foreign volunteers. For example, Ms. Chen Wenqing, a volunteer of the Palace Museum, with both experiences of studying abroad and volunteering in the Palace Museum, has played an important role in the recruitment and training of foreign volunteers.

Because of the special multiple cultural identities of the Palace Museum, not only a museum, a world cultural heritage, but a famous cultural tourism destination, its visitors, who are diverse and have different cultural needs, require volunteer service. Since its establishment, the Palace Museum volunteer team has made many good suggestions for the cultural heritage protection and opening services of the Palace Museum. Humbly, it listens to their voices. From the "The Favorite Cultural Relics of the Palace Museum Staff" event in 2012 to the several press conferences held by the Palace Museum in recent years, volunteers of the Palace Museum were invited to voice their opinions. Accordingly, measures have been taken for improvement and satisfying results achieved.

In December 2007, volunteers of the Palace Museum founded the first Palace Museum Volunteer Committee. It consists of seven members, including one chairman, one secretary, and five ordinary members. Their main responsibilities are to: fully implement the Palace Museum Volunteer Service Regulations; organize business training for volunteers under the guidance of the Publicity and Education Department; organize volunteer observation and exchange activities; write explanation drafts for special exhibits and related cultural relics in exhibitions that offer volunteer services; and assist the Publicity and Education Department in the daily management of volunteers of the Palace Museum. In order to continue to improve the level of explanation and strengthen their professionalism, the Palace Museum volunteers have created a training and assessment mechanism, under which regular training is organized every year, and "Palace Museum Volunteer Explanation Competition" is held, so that they can learn from each other.

The basic job requirement for the Palace Museum volunteers is a weekly service no less than two hours. Objectively, the Palace Museum volunteer team is one of the volunteer teams with the most standardized management, the most stable personnel, the lowest mobility and the most reasonable structure among all Chinese museum volunteer teams. The Palace Museum volunteers, with a hot passion for the cultural heritage of the Palace Museum, devote themselves to the volunteer service, and make selfless and important contributions to the public service cause of the Palace Museum.

In 2017, the Palace Museum volunteer team had 220 members. Although it was not a particularly large team among all museum volunteer teams, it put service quality over team size. In 2017, the vast majority of the 220 volunteers fulfilled their commitment to serve the visitors for at least 72 hours a year. In total, they have volunteered a total of 14,722.5 hours, giving explanations at the special halls and special exhibitions of the Palace Museum on theme days, preaching the Palace Museum culture at communities and schools, and assisting with educational activities, and served 88,142 visitors, setting a new record in recent years.

Over the past few years, I have personally witnessed the development and changes of volunteer services in the Palace Museum. The open environment of the Palace Museum is quite special. On the one hand, the exhibition halls are all ancient architecture, and on the other, the open-air open area is so enormous that volunteers often have to walk long distance during their service. For example, the Palace of Tranquil Longevity area, where the treasure hall is located, occupies a total area of 48,000 square meters. At the busiest hour, it opens nine exhibition rooms and displays over 400 cultural relics. As seasons rotate, it is faced with the burning heat in summer and freezing cold in winter. Therefore, I have noticed the volunteers in the exhibition hall are all plainly dressed. For the convenience of movement, they wear flat shoes. And to make it easier for the visitors to find them, they wear eye-catching yellow vests most of the time.

In fact, these volunteers are all "all-rounders" and "the real deal," which can be reflected in our annual volunteer summary meeting.

Volunteers of the Palace Museum come from all walks of life. For example, volunteer Wang Jiannan, who explains *A Thousand Li of Rivers and Mountains*, is a college professor, volunteer Wang Qianghui, who won the Full Attendance Award, is an executive of a foreign company, and volunteer Wang Shiling, who performs poetry recitation, is a professional radio announcer. The fact that they squeeze time out of their busy schedules to volunteer speaks to their love for the Palace Museum. Volunteer Zheng Liqing was employed at the Institute of High Energy Physics before retirement. He became one of the first volunteers of the Palace Museum after his retirement in 2004. Volunteer Ma Liang worked in the Beijing-Tibet Railway Team of the Beijing Railway Administration. After he became one of the first volunteers of the Palace Museum in 2004, he has overcome many difficulties to stay on volunteer duty. Many volunteer teachers of the Palace Museum have made positive contributions to the construction of the Palace Museum Volunteer Team while performing their volunteer service well. Volunteer Su Li, as one of the first volunteers of the Palace Museum, has devoted himself to serving the Palace Museum Volunteer Team. Volunteer Wang Hui, as one of the second group of volunteers, once participated in the Palace Museum Volunteer Storytelling. He told the visitors fascinating stories on the International Museum Day of May 18. Next, he was engaged in storytelling in dozens of communities and schools. As one of the first group of volunteers, Wang Xinhua often used his medical experience and cooking skills for the service.

At every volunteer meeting, some will take the stage and perform their special skills, spreading joy. Divided into different groups by the special halls they are responsible for, they compete on the same stage, showing their explanatory skills and personal talents. The cultural relics that they explain are all well-known classic exhibits in the themed halls, and their rhapsodizing makes them more fascinating. There is popular singing, recitations, elegant Kun Opera, orchestral music, refreshing sand art, and light paintings at this talent show. Also, at every volunteer meeting, the Palace Museum commends and rewards the volunteers who had gave outstanding service and great contributions. There are three awards, 1,000 Hours of Voluntary Service,

Excellent Volunteer Service, and Full Attendance, and 36 winners. Among them, Full Attendance is the most difficult to get as it requires volunteers to be at a fixed post at a fixed time every week throughout the year and render explanation and consultation services to the visitors. One of the winners of this award, Yan Baosheng, is a senior volunteer with 13 years of volunteering experience in the Palace Museum and 1,240 hours of interpretive service. The 52-year-old "most beautiful volunteer" Huo Manyi has been a volunteer explainer in the Palace Museum for 10 years. Her total service record is 656 times and 1,932 hours.

In the past few years, I have attended the year-end summary meeting of the volunteer team multiple times. Personally, I am friends with many volunteers. Every year, I recognize the familiar faces in the volunteer team. Also, I notice the new faces. At the summary meeting in 2017, I was introduced as a "special guest," which I found inaccurate. I identify myself as the gatekeeper of the Palace Museum. In fact, I am also an explainer of the Palace Museum. I have experienced the hardships and pleasures of publicizing and explaining the exhibits.

In 2015, the 90th anniversary of the Palace Museum, a photo album called *Staff of the Palace Museum* was published. It contains the photos and materials of all the staff of the Palace Museum at the time, with one chapter written about the volunteers.

The episode, aired at the end of 2017, of the first season of *National Treasure*, sent an invitation to the Palace Museum, asking us to recommend "Palace Museum treasures" and "treasure guards." I believed there was no better candidate than the volunteers to take on the role of "treasure guards." Therefore, the Palace Museum decided to invite its volunteers to represent the Palace Museum staff on CCTV and introduce the cultural treasures of the Palace Museum to audiences at home and abroad. And their appearance on national television was well received by the audience.

The achievement that the Palace Museum volunteers have made is the fruit of their joint efforts, including not only the enthusiastic devotion and self-management of all volunteers, but the diligence of the Palace Museum staff, especially those of the Publicity and Education Department. It is also inseparable from the strong support from the volunteers' families, the encouragement and tolerance of the public, and the great attention of media. As a hub and bridge between the visitors and the Palace Museum, the Palace Museum volunteers are a lovely, dedicated and competent team. They have become a business card and a mirror of the Palace Museum.

In 2018, the volunteer services expanded again. At the time, after three years of preparation and more than one year of trial operation, the Palace Museum Cultural Relics Hospital was basically ready. It had received many professionals of the cultural relics museum circle and important foreign guests. We were exploring how to attract tourists to go inside the Palace Museum Cultural Relics Hospital and learn about the repair of its cultural relics. To avoid interrupting the daily work of the cultural relic doctors during the open visits but enable the visitors to watch the repair up close and have a high-quality visit experience, we have decided, after thorough discussion, to control the opening hours and number of visitors of the Palace Museum Cultural Relics Hospital, and to recruit volunteers from the public. This volunteer recruitment ultimately aims to enable the museum culture to reach the public in a deeper and more diverse manner.

On March 15, 2018, the official website, the official Weibo, and the official WeChat of the Palace Museum released the volunteer recruitment notice to the public. And a total of 871 valid resumes were received. The applicants varied in age, gender, occupation, and educational background, and most of them were young and middle-aged employed women with bachelor and master diplomas. The resume screening team of the Palace Museum Cultural Relics Hospital set up the multi-faceted evaluation criteria. After a rigorous preliminary screening, a total of 75 résumés passed and those applicants were invited for an interview.

On the afternoon of April 16 and the morning of April 17, 2018, the interview for the first batch of volunteers for the Palace Museum Cultural Relics Hospital took place. 75 candidates were expected to be interviewed, and 73 showed up. The Palace Museum Cultural Relics Hospital set up five groups of interviews with three interviewers per group. In the first round of the interview, each interviewee was asked to select a favorite cultural relic within six minutes, and complete introducing it within three, so as to investigate their expressive power, logic and appeal. There was also Q&A. The questions

📷 Activities at the Palace Museum on May 18, International Museum Day (May 18, 2012).

were set as three parts according to the age of the applicants: 20 to 30 years old, 30 to 50, and 50 and above, to specifically examine their appearance, personality, physical condition, expressive power, logical thinking, time arrangement, and knowledge and interest in cultural relics museum operation, etc. It was a comprehensive evaluation according to their performance. The top seven of each group, thus 35 in total, moved on to the second round of interviews. Those who made it to the second round were notified on the afternoon of April 17.

The second round of interviews also took place in five groups. The interviewees were asked to explain *Along the River during the Qingming Festival* within five minutes. Then, they were given a short story to read. And they had to tell it again in their own way to the interviewers. The evaluation was carried out from four aspects: how much knowledge was delivered, how fun it was, how much information was condensed, and how good the organizational competence was. Next, interviewers could ask relevant

📷 Palace Museum Volunteer Recruitment Interview (April 28, 2017).

questions based on the specific performance of the interviewees. At last, their ranking was based on the score of each test, and the top 25 were admitted to the pre-job training. During the training, according to their interests and educational background, they were divided into three groups, A, B, and C. They received targeted training corresponding to the three architectural functional divisions of the Palace Museum Cultural Relics Hospital. Senior volunteers explained them the fixed points. After on-site simulation practice, they were officially put on duty. These new volunteers have undergone rigorous tests. Almost all of them were well-educated. They were teachers, college graduates with a master's degree or PhD, and TV and radio hosts. All of them were talented, different, and passionate. After one month of training, 18 of them were selected as prospective volunteers of the Palace Museum Cultural Relics Hospital based on the comprehensive evaluation of the two-part test scores. To some degree, it was more difficult to pass the volunteer test of the Palace Museum Cultural Relics Hospital than the entrance exam to key universities. I attended the second round of interview and was deeply impressed. The interview was so difficult that the Beijing TV Station reported it to be "equally as difficult as an art exam."

June 9, 2018, happened to be the Cultural and Natural Heritage Day, which was a big day for the Palace Museum volunteers. The Palace Museum Cultural Relics Hospital welcomed the first 40 visitors who had made a reservation, and its volunteers officially took up their posts to provide explanation services to visitors from all over the world. On the same day, the Palace Museum set up information desks at Gate of Supreme Harmony Square and the entrances of various halls. The volunteers were dispatched at the desks to answer visitors' questions, plan their tour routes, and promote the explanation service. Visitors could also interact with the volunteers on site, participate in the quiz, and win exquisite Palace Museum prizes. In the themed halls, volunteer explanations for the visitors were conducted as scheduled. In front of the dazzling collection of cultural relics in the exhibition halls, visitors listened to the stories narrated by the experienced volunteers of the Palace Museum, thus embarking on a wonderful cultural journey.

For the Children

———

Children are our future. They have always been the center of education. The Palace Museum, a world cultural heritage and the most famous museum in China, should be known to more children. Getting to know it is not only a chance to see the rich Chinese history, a great variety of exquisite cultural relics, and the finest craftsmanship and superb techniques, but understand how it has become a public museum from a feudal palace, how it has cultivated a persistent artisan spirit, and how it carries on the mission of cultural relics protection in different times. In these senses, it is of great necessity for the Palace Museum to invest more in educating children.

Social education, especially adolescent education, is the key emphasis in the work of the Palace Museum. In terms of adolescent education, it has been exploring the methods suitable for the characteristics of adolescents, so that it becomes the second classroom outside the school. Since March 1, 2004, the Palace Museum has offered ticket-free visits and explanations to primary, middle, and high school students: every Tuesday is set as a ticket-free day for student groups, including organized groups of primary, middle, and high school students and of college students, too. Since 2006, the "Palace Museum Classroom" has opened during the holidays of primary, middle, and high school students, with rich content, diverse forms, and an active atmosphere, and it has been rather popular amongst students and parents. On the International Museum Day and China Cultural and Natural Heritage Day, a tour in the Palace Museum is organized for the students, so that they can participate in various activities and spend a day as a volunteer. In cooperation with the Beijing Palace Museum Cultural Relics Conservation Foundation, projects like Make Children's Palace Museum Dream

Come True have been launched to take the cultural activities to primary schools in remote villages and open children's courses that combine knowledge and practice. The "Digital Palace Museum" project suitable for adolescents was initiated, where video clips, interactive designs, adolescent version of the Palace Museum website, and apps are used to allow different social groups to understand the cultural connotation of the Palace Museum, and a series of cartoon cultural products for adolescents have been developed.

The Palace Museum strives to build a bridge of communication so that more young people understand and pass down the excellent traditional culture in the form of off-campus classrooms with rich content and fun activities. Among them, the public education project "Palace Museum Classroom" officially launched in 2006 has gained popularity for the ease to promote itself in various cultural activities as well as for fun, liveliness, universality and easy participation. For more than a decade, tens of thousands of students have walked into the Palace Museum and into the "Palace Museum Classroom" to feel traditional Chinese culture. For example, based on the ancient architecture of the Forbidden City and the collections of the Palace Museum, the following activities were organized: Looking up at the Bucket Arch of Hall of Supreme Harmony, The Colorful Paintings Under the Eaves, The Intricate Mortise and Tenon Joints, Finest Embroidery and Best Porcelain, Court Beads DIY, Blue and White, the Magical Brushes, the Emperor's New Clothes, and Ruyi in the Court; based on the exhibitions, projects, including Colorful Dresses, Searching for Stone Drums, Finding the Porcelain Pieces, Attending the Royal Wedding, and Sino-India Buddhist Sculpture Exhibition—Teachers' Workshop were created; based on the history and culture of the Ming and Qing courts, themed events, such as Skillful Hands, Dragon Boat Festival in the Palace, Summer Zongzi, Books Welcome the Spring, Fun with Qianlong Seals, and Armor of the Eight Banners were launched. These combine knowledge lectures, on-site interaction, and hands-on production, thus popular amongst teenagers and parents. For example, we once organized a puppet DIY called The Adorable Eight Banners Dolls and invited the 8-to-12-year-olds. It aimed to teach them the content, origin, development, and rules of the Eight Banners system

■ "One Hour in the Palace Museum," a themed children's event, on International Museum Day.

and their respective garrison position and deployment as the main military force to maintain the stability of the Qing Dynasty. We have prepared materials bags for them so that everyone could make their own Eight Banners dolls, expressing their unlimited creativity and unique personality.

To further enhance its social education function and promote its publicity and education projects, the Palace Museum opened the Palace Museum Education Center at the end of 2016. Located in the north and south rooms of the Gate of Glorious Harmony in the west side of the Gate of Supreme Harmony Square, it covers an area of about 800 square meters and consists of four classrooms with different themed functions, including education project displays, theme activities, daily operations, volunteer workstations, and auxiliary space. As an important base

for public education, it fully integrates the existing educational resources of the Palace Museum, and organizes education or training activities for visitors of different ages. In particular, it offers to primary, middle, and high school students and families all year round a variety of thematic educational programs with the characteristics of the Palace Museum, rich content, and different forms. It is a flexible and convenient venue. At the same time, the Palace Museum has utilized more space for social education, adding a number of spacious classrooms, so that more students can attend a class in the Palace Museum. There is one more unique advantage of the Palace Museum, that is, dozens of courtyards are absolutely safe. When the weather is charming in spring, summer, and autumn, many courtyards are used to organize fun activities for the students, and they become their open classrooms.

 ⊡ "Palace Museum Classroom" at Yixing Museum (January 12, 2017).

 ⊡ Hosting students from Gansu and Qinghai (February 28, 2017).

In recent years, the social education activities of the Palace Museum have left foot-steps in more cities, such as Chengdu, Changchun, Bijie, Dongguan, and Qinhuangdao. In addition to that, they have gone abroad to Malta, Singapore, Thailand, Australia, and more. The vivid knowledge explanation and handicraft courses have won the love of adolescents from all over the world. For example, in 2017, the Palace Museum was invited by the Overseas Chinese Cultural Center to hold 12 educational activities in Bangkok and Sydney with the themes such as Court Beads DIY, Ruyi in the Court, Lessons about the West for Emperor Kangxi, Painted Robe, and Origami Dragon Robe. About 350 adolescents participated in the activities with great enthusiasm.

The Palace Museum grasps the new trends in the fields of culture and museology and designs more and better educational courses. For instance, as intangible cultural heritage has been receiving greater attention in recent years, in 2018, the Palace Museum selected two traditional techniques, namely, making rubbings and woodblock printing, as the themes for the intangible cultural heritage technique trial class offered to dozens of primary and secondary school students who had made an appointment. Making rubbings is a traditional technique of printing the characters or patterns cast on bronze and stone tablets with paper, ink, and special tools. As an ancient traditional Chinese technique, it originated in the Southern and Northern Dynasties and survives today. Thanks to it, a great deal of literature of precious documents has been intactly preserved and passed down to the present day. Thirty middle school students took the making rubbings trial class to learn about rubbings and the long history of making rubbings, experience and learn the wonderful craftsmanship, and make a rubbing of their own. Woodblock printing, invented on the basis of making rubbings, is a special technique that uses knives to engrave texts or patterns on a wooden board, prints them with ink and paper, and binds the printed pages into books. It was officially included in UNESCO Intangible Cultural Heritage Lists in 2009. In the woodblock printing trial class, 15 primary school students' families learned about the history of woodblock printing in the form of parent-child activities. Together, they made woodblock print pictures, feeling its unique charm and fun. Through these classes, the students not only mastered a practical skill, but gained a deeper understanding of an intangible Chinese traditional culture.

I always believe that what truly matters in life is not what happens, but what is remembered and how. When I was little, my parents took me to the Palace Museum. I remember every second of that trip. It has become a precious memory that will remain forever in my life. In the past few years, whenever I joined the parent-child education activities organized on the International Museum Day of May 18, whenever I saw adolescents making court beads, painting imperial robes, and wrapping zongzi in the full "Palace Museum Class," I believe that these participatory educational activities would surely enchant them with traditional Chinese culture and that this fascination from childhood would have a subtle influence on their future paths. Whether it is learning to paint, practicing calligraphy, or making crafts, they will have a special memory of the Palace Museum. When they enter adulthood, they must be active communicators of the Palace Museum culture, staunch supporters of its development, and its enthusiastic volunteers. They are the future of the Palace Museum.

Since its initiation in 2012, Make Children's Palace Museum Dream Come True, a collaborative project between the Palace Museum and the Beijing Palace Museum Cultural Relics Protection Foundation, has left footprints in Weining County, Bijie City, Guizhou Province, Zhenfeng County, Qianxinan Prefecture, and Wanshan District, Tongren City. It has visited ten local primary schools, offered dozens of public educational programs, donated over 6,500 books, received 2,500 student participants, and at last achieved satisfying social effects. After several years of development, this project has been upgraded since 2017 to Make Dreams Come True. It offers an opportunity for rural primary school students in Guizhou to understand the Palace Museum, visit it, learn history, and experience culture, so that traditional culture is inherited and promoted, via various forms of dissemination, in this information age, and truly, the children's palace museum dream is realized.

It is common knowledge that the Palace Museum is one of the earliest museums in China that adopted digitalization, and also one of the earliest to develop new media

The Palace Museum Education Center in operation.

Establish Children's Cultural and Creative Experience Store.

business. And we never forget to open more customized "adolescent" sections on the Palace Museum website, apps and new media.

We have created a special version of the Palace Museum website for teenagers that is more lively and better fits the characteristics of teenagers in both form and content design. It is no longer awkward with situational interactive maps. They can feel the architecture, exhibitions, and cultural relics collections of the Palace Museum through visual exploration. The whole experience is accompanied with various types of games, as well as illustrations and easy-to-understand cultural themes. Children of today are active online. We hope that with the help of this website, they will show more interest in the Palace Museum and pass on the amazing traditional Chinese culture to the next generation.

The Palace Museum has been creating a series of apps since 2013, and so far there have been ten in wide use, each of which is an award winner, which encourages us deeply. For example, through the app *Emperor's Day*, children can find out what books the emperors read in the past, what scientific instruments they used, what food they had, and with whom he had contact, etc. It is so interesting that it has accumulated some young fans.

The dissemination of the Palace Museum culture requires more help. Therefore, the Palace Museum actively seeks diversified cooperation with important cultural institutions, and well-known foundations and enterprises. In 2015, The Forbidden City Publishing House joined hands with the studio of Chiu Kwong Chiu from Hong Kong to set up a cultural research and development team for the Palace Museum culture. It launched the "Little Forbidden City" educational workshop project, which has performed compulsory education promotion in primary and secondary schools at home and abroad, narrating the stories on different topics, such as the imperial palace, architecture, royal figures, gardens, objects, and ornamental patterns. The promotion event was held almost 5,000 times, attracting over 53,000 participants. Also, several multimedia exhibitions for schools and the public were organized, with an audience of over 110,000 attending.

Pear Blossoms at Palace of Celestial Favor.

The Palace Museum and the China National Theater for Children entered a strategic cooperation agreement. The first move of the cooperation between the two parties is two consecutive charity shows in the Palace Museum and the China National Theater for Children respectively. In the morning, the former received more than 260 students from the Hope Primary School. In the afternoon, the latter launched the show free to disadvantaged groups, including the children of migrant workers in Beijing, families with subsistence allowances, orphans, and disabled children, so that over 700 kids who hardly have the opportunity to enter the theater could also enjoy elegant art.

The Palace Museum is striving to plant the seeds of Chinese civilization in the hearts of children in a unique way. The Palace Museum offers free educational programs for the adolescents, because we firmly believe that the generation of adolescents that grow up in the museums will fall in love with traditional Chinese culture as well as museum culture. The Palace Museum is the museum with the most visitors in the world. It has the power to carry out more social education activities. It is going to work harder to turn itself into a cultural oasis in social life through a variety of cultural activities. In the future, we will continue to launch various educational programs with the characteristics of the Palace Museum, rich content, and various forms, so that the cultural experience is more educational, and it performs better social education function in a more comprehensive manner.

It is hoped that after participating in the educational activities of the Palace Museum, children will have a profound understanding of the unique value of the Palace Museum culture and become the inheritors of the fantastic traditional Chinese culture. They shoulder the responsibility and carry the hope of future cultural heritage protection and research.

From "Gugong Studies"
to "Palace Museum Academy"

———

The museums in modern China took off in 1905. Twenty years later, in 1925, the Palace Museum was established on the basis of the Ming and Qing imperial palaces, thus completing the historic transformation from a palace of the feudal dynasties to a public museum. It gathers thousands of years of Chinese culture. Its establishment has made the royal treasures accessible for public academic research.

Research is one of the essential functions of a museum. When the Palace Museum was first founded, it was clarified that academic research there should "recruit more scholars and experts, and documents must be made available for it." It attracted a group of top-notch experts and scholars, exhibiting the characteristics of sociality and openness. After the 1950s, a group of renowned experts and scholars at home and abroad, such as Tang Lan, Luo Fuyi, Chen Wanli, Feng Xianming, Shan Shiyuan, Yu Zhuoyun, Liu Jiu'an, Zhu Jiajin, and Xu Bangda, were active there. Thereafter, the Palace Museum became a vital center for academic research in China. It has played an important role in the formation and development of Chinese museology. And it holds an important and unique position in the fields of Ming and Qing history and palace culture, Chinese art history, and Chinese ancient architecture and cultural relics protection and identification.

Since 2000, the Palace Museum has picked up the pace of foreign exchanges and cooperation. In academic research, it has made achievement after achievement, and cultivated talent after talent. In October 2003, Zheng Xinmiao proposed to establish "Gugong Studies" based on the understanding and positioning of the Forbidden City and the Palace Museum. It is a science that studies the Forbidden City and its abundant collections. Its research fields cover the Forbidden City palace complex, cultural relics collection, palace history and culture, Ming and Qing archives, Qing classics, and the Palace Museum history. Therefore, it has rich and profound disciplinary connotations.

The academic sector of the Forbidden City is so broad that it involves plenty of disciplines, and its complexity is almost parallel to that of a comprehensive university. The Gugong Studies sees the Forbidden City as a cultural entity that consists of ancient architecture, cultural relics collections, historical remains, and the people and things that used to be there. In the past centuries of the continuation of the Forbidden City, although there have been changes, it is relatively stable, fully reflects the mainstream traditional Chinese culture, and possesses the characteristics of multi-ethnic cultural integration. The Forbidden City culture that the Gugong Studies study is a richer and broader cultural sector that includes royal culture. It involves history, politics, architecture, ancient artifacts, archives, books, art, religion, folklore, science and technology, museums, etc.

In 2005, the Palace Museum founded Ancient Ceramics Research Center and Ancient Calligraphy and Painting Research Center. The former was officially approved as the "Key Scientific Research Base for the Protection and Research of Ancient Ceramics of the State Administration of Cultural Heritage (The Palace Museum)" in February 2008. It mainly studies the 367,000 pieces of ancient ceramics cultural relics collected in the Palace Museum, the 60,000 or 70,000 pieces of ancient ceramic specimens collected at ancient sites, the over 10,000 pieces of ceramic specimens left in the Qing palaces, and ancient Chinese ceramics collected around

故宮研究院

⊡ Founding assembly of the Palace Museum Academy (October 23, 2013).

the world. Specifically, it studies their raw materials, craftsmanship, structure, and related properties of these ancient ceramics of different periods, different origins, and different types; their age, kilns, and authenticity; their scientific preservation, restoration and replication, etc. There is a sufficient talent team, rich ancient ceramic sample resources, and advanced instruments and equipment at the base. It is the perfect place and institution to conduct comprehensive research on the key areas and difficulties of ancient ceramics.

In October 2013, the Palace Museum Academy was founded. Zhang Zhongpei served as its honorary director, and Zheng Xinmiao as its director. It is a non-organizational comprehensive academic institution established by the Palace Museum to conduct cooperative research and exchanges with prestigious experts and scholars

at home and abroad with the purpose of making an "academic Palace Museum." This establishment not only inherits the fine academic traditions of the Palace Museum, but embodies new thinking on its development concept. It strives to plan a new layout of the academic Palace Museum, and make a high-end research platform with systematic innovation, flexible mechanisms, and academic democracy. And it aims to promote the Palace Museum culture and its highly valuable research, and achieve high-quality comprehensive research results. The Palace Museum Academy, mainly composed of in-service and retired experts and scholars of the Palace Museum, is actively attracting well-known experts and scholars at home and abroad, and building an open high-end academic platform. Multiple scientific research projects have been carried out as planned, and some have achieved fruitful results, such as the Wu Bamboo and Wooden

Slips Sorting Out Project and the Sorting Out and Research of Oracle Bone Script collected in the Palace Museum.

Under the Palace Museum, after integration, enrichment and supplementation, there are one office, one program, and 26 institutes: Research Office, Postdoctoral Program, Institute of Gugong Studies, Institute of Archaeology, Institute of Ancient Literature, Institute of Ming and Qing Archival Research, Institute of Heritage Architecture, Institute of Court Opera, Institute of Ming and Qing Imperial Handicrafts, Institute of Museum Legal Affairs, Institute of Ceramics, Institute of Painting and Calligraphy, Institute of Tibetan Buddhist Cultural Relics, Institute of Palace Gardens, Institute of Chinese Paintings, Institute of Sino-Foreign Cultural Exchange, Institute of Chinese Calligraphy, Institute of Clocks and Watches, Institute of Palace Original Conditions, Institute of Forbidden City Cultural Relics Relocated Southwards, Institute of Ancient Civilization, Institute of Film and Television, Institute of Traditional Chinese Medicine Culture, Institute of Jade Culture, Institute of Ancient Paintings and Calligraphy Appraisal, Institute of Cultural Relics Protection Technology, Institute of Intellectual Property, and Institute of Architecture and Planning. Basically, the overall academic layout and institutional construction of the Palace Museum are complete. Among them, only the Research Office, Institute of Gugong Studies, and Institute of Archaeology are organizational institutions. The Research Office is an organizational office and liaison agency that guarantees the normal operation of over 20 non-organizational units. It is a new exploration under the new situation.

How to organize and develop massive academic research institutions in museums is a brand new challenge. In the history of museum development, there is no precedent of the establishment of massive academic research institutions in museums featuring cultural accumulation and inheritance.

The Palace Museum Academy is non-administrative and sticks to being non-organizational. Instead of wearing a false reputation, it gets down-to-earth on projects and results, formulates plans, focuses on practicality, stays distinctive, and builds a brand. The "scientific research project system" is the basic principle of the Palace Museum Academy to promote academic research. All academic organizations and implementations are based on the "scientific research project system"; all academic research and activities revolve around real projects; and all equipment allocating, staffing, work promotion, and method exploration are matched with specific national scientific research projects, so that the progress of the projects is clear and the results predictable.

Through the integration of the academic management mechanism, the academic research activities of the Palace Museum are upgraded from the individual level to the overall level of the whole organization, so that there is collaboration to expand the space for development of the academic research in the Palace Museum. In particular, the Palace Museum Academy builds an academic research platform that concentrates intelligence, materials and funds. For example, in March 2016, The Institute of Ming and Qing Imperial Handicrafts, the Institute of East Asian Culture of the French Academy of Sciences, the Limoges Enamel Art Museum, Guimet Museum, and the Louvre Laboratory jointly established the Chinese Enamel Art Research Group. Since the research started, Sino-French cooperation has been sailing smoothly, and there have been more and stronger bilateral exchanges.

In recent years, the Institute of Archaeology of the Palace Museum has collaborated with the Historical and Cultural Research Committees of the Indian states, the Department of Archaeology of Durham University, the United Arab Emirates and Uzbekistan to study the cultural relics unearthed in China and perform archaeological excavation in India, Ras Al Khaimah, and Uzbekistan. After years of hard work, the archaeological research of the Palace Museum has basically evolved into a multi-angle research on the Maritime Silk Road and the Land Silk Road. It has become one of the main tasks of the Palace Museum to improve the discipline construction while expanding the scope of its academic research.

As research horizons are widened, the Institute of Tibetan Buddhist Cultural Relics of the Palace Museum Academy has successively conducted a continuous and planned cultural relics investigation in Sichuan, Gansu, Qinghai, and Tibet, especially in Western Sichuan and Tibetan regions. The ten-year-long investigation turned out to be fruitful. Since 2013, we have started to digitalize the protection of Tibetan Buddhist

Press Conference on the Establishment of the Institute of Clocks and Watches of the Palace Museum (June 2, 2017).

Exchange of Academic Achievements of the Palace Museum Academy (May 5, 2016).

cultural relics and completed the digitization of the collections and murals of seven Tibetan Buddhist temples, including those of the famous Jokhang Temple. We also helped it build a database, which is one of the most advanced databases in Tibet and even in China. Therefore, the protection of the cultural relics of the Jokhang Temple soon joins the advanced ranks. Our work will definitely have a positive impact on the protection and research of Tibetan Buddhist cultural relics in the future.

Another example is the Institute of Traditional Chinese Medicine Culture. The Palace Museum has collected more than 3,000 medical cultural relics. They are an important and distinctive category in the museum's abundant collections. Specifically, they are the physical remains and written records of the medical activities in the Qing court and possess a unique value. For academic research, these are the first-hand materials to study the medical history, court history, and even the cultural exchange history between China and the West. To some extent, they make up for the lack of certain medical literature and records. However, due to the complexity and professionalism of the research on medical cultural relics in the Qing courts, some research remains on the surface, and there are still some topics that have been never discussed. The establishment of the Institute of Traditional Chinese Medicine Culture of the Palace Museum aims to integrate the advantageous resources of the Palace Museum and all walks of life, and help to excavate, sort out, and study the medical relics of the Qing Dynasty, so that they can serve the health care of the general public, that the traditional Chinese medicine culture spreads wider to the world, that traditional Chinese medicine culture is innovated, and stronger cultural confidence is built.

It must have been noticed that among our many research institutes, there are two special ones, the Institute of Forbidden City Cultural Relics Relocated Southwards and the Institute of Film and Television. In June 2010, the Palace Museum and the National Palace Museum in Taipei jointly organized an investigation named *Retracing the Southward Road of the Cultural Relics*. In October that year, *Exhibition of the Forbidden City Cultural Relics That Were Moved Southwards* was held in the exhibition hall of Gate of Divine Prowess. It was a sensation. This was an important way to

🔲 Meeting with Director Feng Ming-chu of the National Palace Museum in Taipei at the Palace Museum Academy (November 9, 2013).

carry on the spirit of diligence of the Palace Museum and review the history and culture of the same root. In March 2017, at the Fifth Session of the 12th CPPCC National Committee, I submitted *Proposal on the Protection of the Historical Traces of the Forbidden City Cultural Relics That Were Relocated to the South*, urging to promote the "Historical Traces of the Forbidden City Cultural Relics That Were Relocated to the South" as a national key cultural relic protection unit. In June that year, the Palace Museum Academy established both the Institute of Forbidden City Cultural Relics Relocated Southwards and the Institute of Film and Television at the same time. It was hoped that in the wave of the development of academic media in the new times, these two institutes would, based on the needs of the Palace Museum's development, put the cultural relics and their history back in the spotlight, and make the studies of the ancient Forbidden City popular. In December 2017, the Palace Museum Academy produced the Wisdom Tree Online Course into the Forbidden City, introducing its architectures and collections of cultural relics, telling stories of their southward relocation, raising the awareness of cultural relics protection, and spreading the spirit of craftsmanship. In 2017, 677 colleges and universities included this course as an elective credit course for the students, and nearly 200,000 students enrolled in and obtained the credits, with a satisfaction rate of 96.3%. In August 2018, the themed comic *Echo of the Forbidden City* was launched on the official platform of Tencent Comics. Based on the historical facts of the cultural relics of the Forbidden City that were moved to the South, it is targeted at game developers and young colleges students. The platform attracted 4.7 million viewers, and the rating for the comics is as high as 9.5/10.

Also, the Palace Museum Academy has opened the groundbreaking Institute of Museum Legal Affairs. It is the first research institution in China that specializes in the legal issues of museums. It started with the legal problems encountered when the excellent traditional Chinese culture tried to go abroad. In particular, it aims to thoroughly implement the strategy of law-based governance of the country and spread the spirit of law-based governance of the country, and further enrich the theories of the rule of law for museums. It was founded specially for the legal issues regarding the protection of the Forbidden City. And it will conduct thematic research on legal issues related to the cultural relics and museums, and provide intellectual support for the realization of law-based governance.

The unique Institute of Palace Gardens is expected to explore and study the history and culture of imperial gardens and the cultivation history and skills of traditional imperial flowers and plants, and improve the protection level and scientific protection methods of famous ancient trees in the Forbidden City, so as to drive and guide the garden management of the Palace Museum. The establishment of this institute has opened a new chapter in the research on imperial gardening in the Forbidden City, provided stronger theoretical and technical guarantee for the maintenance of those Imperial Gardens, made it more possible to perform cross-studies in related fields such as Ming and Qing palace history, architectural design, and archaeology, and cultivated more talent for the maintenance of the Forbidden City gardens. Consequently, it is conducive to enriching the research content of the Palace Museum Academy, expanding

🖻 Postdoctoral Programme of the Palace Museum (June 25, 2016).

its research scope, strengthening the multi-disciplinary and interdisciplinary research force, and building researchers with a broader and more free research platform.

In addition to the establishment of many research institutes, the Palace Museum has also launched its own Postdoctoral Programme. In August 2013, the application for this Postdoctoral Programme went through. Usually, it takes three years for a new Postdoctoral Programme to hold independent recruitment. However, the outstanding achievements and orderly management of the Postdoctoral Programme of the Palace Museum received high commendations from the management department. In June 2015, the National Post-Doctor Regulatory Commission approved it to hold independent recruitment of postdoctoral researchers one and a half years earlier. The Postdoctoral Programme of the Palace Museum is, on the one hand, a platform for the talent training and introduction to the Palace Museum, especially the short-term introduction of high-end academic talents to cope with the short-term understaffing; and on the other, encourages the researchers to perform innovative research at the forefront of the discipline. At present, the research directions of this Postdoctoral Programme include archaeology, ancient architecture, Ming and Qing archives, Ming and Qing court history, the history of ancient Chinese paintings and calligraphy, tomb records unearthed since the founding of the PRC, the sorting of inscriptions on bones or tortoise shells of the Shang Dynasty, scientific and technological protection, ancient kiln sites, the history of court crafts in Ming Dynasty, the history of arts and crafts in Ming Dynasty, imperial opera, history of Palace Museum, ancient books of Qing Dynasty, Chinese calligraphy, and more.

The Palace Museum Academy and its affiliated institutes are research institutions. Certainly, an indispensable element of them is the researchers. The Palace Museum, as an academic research institution, needs to work harder on academic research. There are currently over 400 senior researchers in it, but many older experts and scholars have either retired or are about to. As the most valuable talent resources of the Palace Museum, they have given all their wisdom to it. Despite retirement, they still care about the development of the Palace Museum and hope to continue their research. After the Palace Museum Academy was founded, retired experts were hired back by its non-organizational affiliated institutes. The bottleneck of organizational recruitment requirement that museums used to make has been broken through. According to the "scientific research project system" model, the Palace Museum Academy based on the different needs of various research projects, make flexible recruitment. Retired business directors or veteran experts will be the honorary heads of the institutes, giving full play to their academic influence. In this way, the 70-to-90-year-old experts and scholars are still active at work, attracting a group of young scholars. They can impart academic knowledge to these young talents, cultivate in them research literacy, and pass on to them the spirit of the Palace Museum, so that they can grow quickly. For example, Zheng Xinmiao was employed as Director of the Academy, and Zhu Chengru, Li Ji, Jin Hongkui, Cheng Lihua, and Wang Su, as the respective Directors of the Institute of Ming and Qing Imperial Historical Archives, the Institute of Archaeology, the Institute of Ancient Architecture, the Institute of Ming and Qing Imperial Handicrafts, and the Institute of Ancient Literature. The Director of the Palace Museum is responsible for the general coordination between itself and the Palace Museum Academy, and provides strong support in terms of policy guarantee, administration, and resource allocation. He is the "general logistics man" of the Palace Museum Academy.

It is no secret that there are a flock of experts in the Palace Museum. In particular, the older experts have set great examples and made enormous contributions. For example, Tang Lan, a famous ancient philologist, bronzeware expert and historian, broke through the old theory of ancient characters and built the theory of "Three Books" for Chinese characters. He proposed to divide ancient Chinese characters into four series, and created the theory that bronzeware dating in the Western Zhou Dynasty had no successors and the practical system engineering, which are new inspiration and new contributions to academic circles. Du Jiasong wrote in *The Scholar Style of Tang Lan*: "Mr. Tang had been researching until his last breath, whether at home, in a hotel or on the road . . ."

Shan Shiyuan, a well-known expert of Qing history, archivist, and scholar of ancient architecture, is the first to propose the studies of archive bibliography in the circle of Chinese archives, and the first to include ancient architectural technology research into the research scope of Chinese architectural history. With the support of Director Wu Zhongchao, he set up the Ancient Architecture Research Office, the Ancient Architecture Management Department, opened the glazed tile plant, and assembled a capable ancient architecture repair team. By applying his years of the achievements in architectural theories and techniques to the repair, management, and protection of ancient architecture, he has greatly improved the research and practical technical level of ancient architecture in China.

Zhu Jiajin, a famous cultural relic expert and historian, who has worked in the Palace Museum for 60 years, knows it like the back of his hand. In 1992, National Administration of Cultural Heritage assembled an expert group to identify the grade-one cultural relics collections that provinces and cities reported in local museums and archaeological institutes across China. Within this expert group, there were experts of ceramics, of bronze experts, and of jade while Zhu Jiajin dealt with the other cultural relics.

Xu Bangda, a Palace Museum expert in the appraisal of ancient paintings and calligraphy, and is also a scholar and artist, appraises the paintings and calligraphy as they are, without bias from the collector's character, status, and influence. The accuracy and authoritativeness of his appraisals are universally recognized. His writings are the most systematic, comprehensive, and credible textbooks for the younger generation engaged in studying ancient paintings and calligraphy and their appraisal.

In recent years, experts and scholars of the Palace Museum have made remarkable achievements, claiming award after award. For instance, four senior experts, Yu Jian, Zheng Minzhong, Geng Baochang, and Xu Bangda, won the honorary title of Outstanding Figure in Chinese Cultural Relics and Museums. These experts and scholars of the Palace Museum have not only worked diligently and rigorously throughout their lives, but taught others tirelessly. They encourage their apprentices, cultivating generations of scholars. Together, they embody the characteristics of "the Palace Museum staff," that is, love the Palace Museum, take pride in it, make selfless contributions to it, be rigorous and conscientious, do their jobs well, and serve the public.

The oldest re-employment of the Palace Museum at present is naturally the 100-year-old ceramic specialist Geng Baochang. Mr. Geng was born in Beijing in 1922 and became an apprentice at Dunhua Zhai in Beijing since childhood. He came to work in the Palace Museum in 1956 and that has lasted until today. For over 60 years, he has never stopped loving his career and the Forbidden City. Despite his over-90-year-old age, he keeps leading the compilation of the *History of Chinese Ceramics*. At the ceramic exhibition on the 90th anniversary of the Palace Museum in 2015, he actively organized the *Exhibition of Ceramics of Ru Kiln,* the *Exhibition of Celadon of Yue Kiln*, and the *Comparison Exhibition of Porcelain Unearthed from Imperial Kiln Sites and Chenghua Porcelain*. He deserves to be called a representative master of the Palace Museum, and a real treasure of the talent team.

The Palace Museum inherits and promotes a good tradition of openness, attaches importance to the release, dissemination, and exchange of research achievements, and keeps introducing them to the public in an easy-to-understand form. Via publications, seminars, and symposiums, the research findings of the Palace Museum have a positive impact not only in the area of expertise, but in the public. *The Palace Museum Journal* has been rated one of the Top 50 Chinese Journals with Overseas Academic Influence among thousands of journals for its characteristics of traditional culture studies. *Academic Palace Museum* is the academic journal of the Palace Museum Academy. Known for the profound articles, it expresses the scholars' academic rigor to the utmost, thus is widely praised in academic circles. The *Beijing Central Axis—Ancient Architecture Measured Atlas,* co-compiled and co-published by Institute of Ancient Architecture, supports the research on the city's central axis. The special exhibition and seminar of *Shiqu Baoji* co-organized by the Institute of Painting and Calligraphy has attracted great attention. With the technical support of the data and information department, scholars' new findings on cultural relics collections have been presented on the smart phone apps.

Academic openness is the trend of the times. In the face of the rapidly growing demands of the public to mold a more sophisticated character and cultivate a better cultural taste, the Palace Museum has clarified new objectives in the following aspects, including collection and preservation, exhibition, publicity and education, and cultural creativity: standardize the collection storage and bid goodbye to untidiness; design the exhibitions in a more sophisticated manner and stay away from "piling up the exhibits randomly"; make publicity and education more fun and no more "dull lectures"; make cultural creativity more tasteful and eliminate poor imitations to reflect the development concept of the Academic Palace Museum; and require the researchers of the Palace Museum to stay both academically rigorous and personally approachable.

Certainly, this research institution, the Palace Museum, pays attention to not only the academic impact of the research findings, but their inspiration for the development of cultural and creative products. We require every cultural and creative product to have a clear origin based on the seven-year numeration of the cultural relics collections of the Palace Museum. For example, the books published by The Forbidden City Publishing House, whether the best-sellers *The Palace Museum Calendar* and *The Forbidden City 100,* or the book project *The Palace Museum Collection Compendium,* are all owed to a numeration of the cultural relics, which presents the Palace Museum culture alive on paper. As mentioned earlier, all the rich information available in the app *Emperor's Day*, which is designed especially for children, has been validated through meticulous and in-depth research. Such requirements for academic research ensure the correctness and forward-looking of the culture carried and disseminated by the cultural creativity of the Palace Museum, and truly reflect the culture of the Palace Museum and the mellow charm of traditional Chinese culture.

Today, as the scope of academic research in the Palace Museum expands, a research feature that emphasizes textual research has been formed. Significant research findings keep coming, the research team is expanding, and talent is emerging in large numbers. After long training and practical experience, professional talents have matured, continuously making remarkable academic achievements with a social impact. The balanced research team structure ensures a supply of qualified successors for the academic development of the Palace Museum. The Palace Museum is both an educational institution and an academic institution, meaning great efforts are invested to guarantee effective popular education and academic research. The Palace Museum is special, as is its equal emphasis on education and academics. It holds 5,000 years of Chinese civilization and 600 years of history of the Forbidden City. It is at a critical moment of development. Looking back on the past, there were ups and downs, but more inspiration; looking towards the future, there will be difficulties, but more confidence and hope. In the future, we will strive to continue the system with the characteristics of the Palace Museum, which places equal emphasis on popular education and academic research, and to keep enhancing and expanding the influence of the Palace Museum in these two aspects, so as to present more to the society.

CHAPTER 4

The Inspirational
Artisan Spirit

I wonder how many have watched the documentary *Masters in the Forbidden City*. It was a huge sensation. It's rating on Douban .com is 9.4/10, even surpassing that of (the very popular food documentary series) *A Bite of China*. What impressed me the most is that it received the most likes from the students. I did not expect that they would be fascinated with this slow-paced cultural documentary. However, they are deeply fascinated because in the following year after it was aired, there were tens of thousands of students who applied to repair cultural relics in the Palace Museum.

I hope that before signing up, students should understand that the repair and protection of cultural relics is a profession that requires full commitment. This job is never as easy as shown in the documentary, where there is picking fruit, teasing wild cats, and playing the guitar. Those are merely the documentary director's artistic expression of the romantic souls of the masters of cultural relics repair. In fact, they stick to their posts, 100% concentrated on the cultural relic repair, day after day, year after year. This is their lifelong commitment. Students must be mentally prepared before signing up for the job.

Masters in the Forbidden City

Visitors who have recently been to the Palace Museum must have noticed that some of the ancient architecture is covered with thick green enclosures with dense scaffolding around them. Many construction workers in safety helmets are working hard inside and outside the architecture. Some people may see it as a pity that they are temporarily closed to the public; others may be curious because it is lucky to witness the repair of ancient architecture in the Forbidden City. I suggest that we should look forward to the renovation of these ancient architecture, because it is the largest maintenance and preservation of ancient architecture in the Forbidden City in the past 100 years. We call it the "century renovation."

In history, every major renovation of the Forbidden City has been accompanied by the inheritance of the craftsmen's skills.

In the first major renovation of the ancient architecture of the Forbidden City, the repair of the northwest Corner Towers attracted the most attention. These Corner Towers are a symbol of the Forbidden City. Tourists often can't help but stop to admire their beauty. *The Qing-style Construction Regulations* divides large wooden roofs into hip roof, flush gable roof, overhanging gable roof, and gable and hip roof. The Corner Towers has no roof like these. It is usually described to have nine beams, 18 columns and 72 ridges, but the truth is that it is far more complicated. The three-layer eaves have a total of 28 upturned roof-ridges, 16 roof corners, 28 roof corner grooves, 10 pediments, and 72 ridges and 10 hidden ridges behind them. There are 230 ornamental beasts on the roof, more than double the number of those in Hall of Supreme Harmony.

After the founding of the PRC in 1949, in response to the problems in the Forbidden City, the first five-year renovation plan in the history of the renovation of ancient architecture in the Forbidden City was proposed. As a result, in the Forbidden City, mountains of garbage which accumulated for years were cleared, the river channels were dredged, the river walls of the Inner Golden Water River were repaired, the subdrains were harnessed, a large number of unattended ancient buildings were mended, and the outer eaves of the Hall of Supreme Harmony, the Hall of Central Harmony, and the Hall of Preserving Harmony were repainted. In 1956, the major repair of the northwest Corner Towers was initiated.

Considering the complex structure of the Corner Towers, the Palace Museum sincerely hired the master carpenters Ma Jinkao and Du Botang from the old Xinglong Wood Factory, known for "the best woodwork," to instruct the repair of the wooden structure, so as to ensure that everything returned to what it was. In terms of color painting, He Wenkui, Zhang Lianqing, and other famous craftsmen in the Beijing were hired. These craftsmen are all extremely skilled. Together, they were nicknamed the "Ten Elders" of the Forbidden City. It is these ten craftsmen that made up the first generation of craftsmen of the Palace Museum. And the second generation of craftsmen were also able to grow and stand out in this major renovation project. Dai Jiqiu, Zhao Chongmao and Weng Keliang continued to learn model making for 10 years after their apprenticeship under Ma Jinkao, Du Botang and other masters during the repair of the Northwest Corner Tower. Today, the Department of Ancient Architecture of the Palace Museum still retains the quarter model of one corner of the northwest Corner Tower

and the model of the four-column and octagonal pavilion in the Imperial Garden. Pu Xuelin, Deng Jiu'an, and Wang Youlan learned to lay the foundation of the roof and tile the roof from Zhou Fengshan and Zhang Guo'an; Zhang Deheng, Zhang Decai, and Wang Zhongjie followed Zhang Lianqing and He Wenkui to repaint the Hall of Supreme Harmony, the Hall of Central Harmony, and the Hall of Preserving Harmony. They facsimiled most of the Forbidden City's paintings in proportion, such as those in the Qianlong Garden, the Hall of Supreme Harmony, the Hall of Central Harmony, and the Hall of Preserving Harmony, the Areas of Six Eastern Palaces and the Areas of Six Western Palaces, totaling 300 pieces, which were later compiled in the *Forbidden City Architectural Color Painting Catalog.*

The second major renovation of the Forbidden City began in 1973. The Palace Museum Engineering Team (the predecessor of the Ministry of Craftsmanship) recruited 300 young craftsmen. Under the leadership of Zhao Chongmao and Dai Jiqiu, they participated in the renovation projects of the main building of the Meridian

🖻 Apprenticeship Meeting at the Ancient Architecture Renovation Center (February 4, 2013).

Gate, the East and West Sparrow Wing Towers, the East and West waiting rooms of the Gate of Supreme Harmony, the Palace of Accumulated Purity, the Palace of Great Benevolence, the Hall of Mental Cultivation, the Garden of the Palace of Compassion and Tranquility, the southeast Corner Towers, etc. The bricklayer apprentices followed their mentors to the small stone bridge dormitory construction site and participated in the construction of the new dormitory; the oil painting apprentices joined their mentors at the Gate of Divine Prowess, practicing oil painting and color painting; the carpenter apprentices made and installed the general wooden structures under the instructions of their mentors. When winter came and it was too cold to work outdoors, the second generation of craftsmen taught the work to the new apprentices. And out stood the third generation of craftsmen represented by Li Yongge, Huang Youfang, and Weng Guoqiang of woodworking, Wu Shengmao, Li Zenglin, and Bai Fuchun of tile work, Liu Zengyu and Zhang Shirong of oil painting, and Zhang Zhiquan of color painting.

■ Evaluation of the Inheritors of the Construction Techniques of Official Ancient Architecture of the Forbidden City (June 25, 2014).

■ Visiting the Palace Museum's North Research Center of Horticulture (April 4, 2014).

In December 2005, the traditional apprenticeship that had stopped for nearly half a century re-appeared in the Palace Museum. Bai Fuchun of the tile works was formally apprenticed to Piao Xuelin, an expert on ancient architecture of the Forbidden City, and Huang Youfang and Jiao Baojian of the woodworks to Weng Keliang, an expert on ancient architecture of the Forbidden City, and Zhang Zhiquan of color painting to Wang Zhongjie, also an expert on ancient architecture of the Forbidden City. These apprentices stand out among the third-generation craftsmen of the Forbidden City in terms of skills. Through apprenticeships, they are given the opportunity to learn more refined skills from the masters, and better continue and inherit the ancient architectural skills, so as to smoothly renovate the Hall of Supreme Harmony and other buildings.

The third major renovation is the "century renovation." Since 2002, the Palace Museum has launched the Overall Maintenance and Preservation Project of the Ancient Architecture of the Palace Museum, which is the largest, most extensive and longest maintenance and preservation of the ancient architecture therein for over 100 years, since 1911. This unprecedentedly large-scale protection operation is also known as the "century renovation." The Forbidden City was built during the reign of Emperor Yongle of the Ming Dynasty in 1420. It turned 600 years old in 2020. We expect that after 18 years of hard work, the ancient architecture of the Forbidden City will be maintained in a stable condition, so that we can hand over a magnificent Forbidden City intact to the next 600 years. This overall maintenance project adheres to the principle of "on the ground before above ground, outdoors before indoors." It preserves and repairs the infrastructure, outdoor environment, individual ancient architecture and interior decoration, and opens some repaired areas one after another. I still recall that when the project just started, as director of the State Administration of Cultural Heritage, I visited the Ministry of Housing and Urban-Rural Development in order to ensure the quality of the maintenance and protection for a series of world cultural heritage sites such as the Forbidden City, Temple of Heaven, Summer Palace, and Ming Tombs. I explained to it the differences between the maintenance and protection of ancient buildings and other types of civil projects, with a special emphasis on the historical responsibility of cultural inheritance. And I made a suggestion that a special management mechanism be established, which the Ministry of Housing and Urban-Rural Development took well and offered strong support. As a result, the Ministry of Culture and National Administration of Cultural Heritage co-formulated rules and regulations, and set up a qualification system for the survey, design, construction, and supervision of ancient architecture maintenance and protection industry, which still remain effective.

In 2012, to train the inheritors of its own official-style ancient architectural skills, the Palace Museum recruited 14 candidates through social recruitment. After one year of learning, they held the apprenticeship meeting together in 2013. Ten masters of the renovation of ancient architecture, Zhang Shirong, Ding Yongli, Wu Shengmao, Bai Fuchun, Bai Qiang, Weng Guoqiang, Huang Youfang, Zhang Jinian, Liu Zengyu, Zhang Zhiquan took the young apprentices, Zhang Fengbing, Liang Lijun and Xue Yongdong under their wings. The future for the cause of renovation of ancient architecture is therefore of great promise. And the artisan spirit is expected to be passed on from generation to generation.

Those who have been to the renovation site of the ancient architecture of the Forbidden City must have noticed the obvious differences between the work scene there and elsewhere: there are no cranes, and construction materials are shipped to the construction site by handcarts. When there are overweight wood materials, the tool that has been in use for a hundred years comes to play—the pulley block. The renovation of the ancient architecture of the Forbidden City follows the "four originals," namely original materials, original craftsmanship, original structure, and original shape. As long as the presentation of the characteristics of traditional craftsmanship and techniques is unaffected, craftsmen may use electric tools, such as a middle filling machine and docking saw, but traditional tools are used most of the time: carpenters use ink markers, painting notes, brush pens, square chi, rods, and rope to draw lines. Rods; tools used for processing and making wooden components are adzes, chisels, axes, saws, planers, etc.

What best reflects the difficulty of renovation the ancient architecture of the Forbidden City is laying the foundation of the roof, which is part of the tile work.

Laying the foundation of the roof means adding a waterproof layer to a wooden building. There is a pithy formula "three layers and three compressions," that is, lime mortar is applied three times and compressed three times. But this may not be enough. On a sunny day when drying happens fast, "three layers and three compressions" can meet the requirements. When it is cloudy, it may take "six layers and six compressions." An error at any link may lead to rain leakage, which results in fatal damage to the ancient architecture.

Shan Shiyuan, a senior craftsman of the Forbidden City, once stressed that the ancient architecture and their various practical and artistic components must be strictly kept to their original forms during the maintenance and renovation. He pointed out: "Where the damage is so serious that major repair is needed, repair must happen immediately. This architecture must be treated as a cultural relic during the repair, meaning to keep their original form and various practical and artistic components. Since the Forbidden City is the most complete ancient palace complex in China, its architectural structures and engineering practices are the best materials for later architects to conduct research. During their ongoing maintenance and repair, in addition to original forms that are required to be kept, some buildings' renovation will use the original construction materials as much as possible."

When he instructed the painting project of the important palaces on the central axis of the Meridian Gate to the Gate of Divine Prowess on the National Day in 1959, he continued to consult documents and experienced craftsmen and technicians. At the Hall of Supreme Harmony and the Gate of Supreme Harmony, the crude colored painting on the outer eaves that was painted when Yuan Shikai was proclaimed emperor was removed. Instead, the original colored painting painted during the 16 years of Emperor Kangxi's reign was restored after meticulous literature consultation. In the arduous work of repainting the eaves of the Hall of Supreme Harmony, he climbed the tall scaffoldings many times to instruct the key points of each process. Under his leadership, this maintenance and renovation project of the ancient architecture of the Forbidden City was finished on schedule and won public praise and respect.

Opening Ceremony of the Official-Style Ancient Architectural Skills Training Program (November 9, 2013).

During the maintenance and renovation, the professional repair team has gradually established a set of palace architecture construction techniques with strict requirements, which not only helps to maintain the original appearance of the ancient architecture of the Forbidden City, but directly promotes the development of ancient Chinese architectural technology. Traditionally, the construction techniques of official-style ancient architecture include tile, wood, clay, stone, scaffolding, painting, color painting, and pasting, and hundreds of traditional crafts subdivided under them. Ancient architecture under the strict feudal hierarchy must strictly follow construction rules from materials to construction. Representing the highest level of official-style ancient architecture, the ancient architecture of the Forbidden City is undoubtedly the pinnacle of this set of construction techniques.

The Chinese character 工 (gōng, meaning craft) appeared as early as in the bone inscriptions of the Yin Ruins (one of China's oldest and largest archeological sites and

🖼 The major renovation of the Forbidden City.

a World Heritage site, in Henan Province). Both the *Rites of Zhou* (also known as *Zhou Guan*) and the *Chronicles of Zuo* recorded that the Zhou Dynasty (the Western Zhou and Eastern Zhou Dynasties in northern China, 1046–256 BC) and the vassal states thereof had set up institutions in charge of construction. Countless skilled craftsmen have left a great number of magnificent architecture for future generations, except rarely were listed in historical records to be known to the later generations. They were called master craftsmen not only because they possessed some certain skills, which after all can be developed over time, but because their respect and love for ancient architecture, which could only be found over a long history.

It relies deeply on these anonymous craftsmen to hand over the magnificent Forbidden City intact to the future. The maintenance and renovation of the ancient architecture of the Forbidden City is an endless relay, where they are the best relayers.

Greenlight the "Century Renovation"

As the imperial palace complex of the Ming and Qing Dynasties, the Forbidden City is the highest achievement of traditional Chinese official-style ancient architecture as well as the model of their final stage. The various types of Ming and Qing official-style ancient buildings preserved in the Forbidden City demonstrate the appearance of the imperial palaces in the Ming and Qing Dynasties in an encyclopedic manner. Every ancient architecture in the Forbidden City is unique, so every renovation of them should be a research protection project, should bear an unavoidable historical responsibility, should strive to set an example for ancient building maintenance and preservation, and should not be treated as general civil engineering or general construction engineering.

This "century renovation" of the Forbidden City has attracted global attention. Every employee of the Palace Museum could not have been more cautious. In a sense, during the protection and inheritance of the ancient buildings of the Forbidden City, there were not only problems of craftsmanship and techniques, but of understanding and attitude, that is, what kind of concept should be held towards traditional Chinese culture and human cultural heritage. Therefore, while we repaired them, we also kept thinking and trying to deepen and change the concept of protection.

Since 2010, due to the adjustment of the system and mechanism, the "Forbidden City Ancient Architecture Maintenance and Preservation" project was faced with a series of new problems about the professional team, material supplies, construction cycles, and technology inheritance, which put off the implementation. The first problem was the professional team. This project required such professionalism that ordinary enterprises often fail to guarantee the required renovation quality. The Palace Museum's old ancient architecture maintenance and preservation team is highly professional and the best in the industry. However, the new policy forbade it from bidding on the museum's own projects. It was forced to disband in 2010. The second problem was material supplies. In the past, to ensure the best quality, the materials used in the ancient architecture of the Forbidden City were mostly hand-made, thus costly. The new rule stipulates that the materials used for the maintenance and preservation of the ancient architecture must be obtained through government procurement, which negotiates a more reasonable price but compromises the quality of maintenance and preservation. The third problem was the work cycle and funding. The annual maintenance and preservation fund for ancient architecture is often in place in November, but at the end of August and October of the following year, there will be the "spending rate" check. If there are residual funds, it will be returned, and the next year less funds are granted. Therefore, it is necessary to speed up the construction progress. Because it was difficult to guarantee a reasonable cycle of maintenance and preservation, some problems that required thorough consideration and meticulous decision-making were often laid aside, and some became permanent regrets. The fourth was technical inheritance. The age structure of the Palace Museum's experts in ancient architecture repairs is old. Most of them were about to retire or should have, and restricted by the personnel system, they could not be rehired. Also, the talent they trained via the "apprenticeship program" was subject to the limitations of the household registration system, thus it was difficult to obtain permanent employment, and some walked away. If this went on, the construction skills of the official-style ancient architecture in the Forbidden City would be lost.

Fortunately, in this predicament, an opportunity for change presented itself. In November 2015, the National Committee of the Chinese People's Political Consultative Conference (NCCPPCC) held a fortnight forum on the Inheritance and Preservation of Intangible Cultural Heritage. I was given the opportunity to give an eight-minute speech, in which I reported the difficulties and problems in the maintenance and preservation of the ancient architecture of the Forbidden City. Comrade Yu Zhengsheng, the then-Chairman of NCCPPCC, took my speech seriously. During my report, he asked, "Has the construction team of the Palace Museum been dismissed? Is it necessary to bid for the renovation project of ancient architecture? Why not make it possible to rehire the senior craftsmen with traditional skills?" After the questioning, he instructed me to write a special report to the State Council to explain the problems in the preservation and inheritance of the ancient architecture of the Forbidden City. I asked if it was ok to write to him, a member of the Standing Committee. He replied yes. Next, the report of the Palace Museum was approved and forwarded to the State Council. The leaders of the State Council paid great attention to it. The Ministries of Culture, Finance, Human Resources and Social Security conducted research and proposed solutions based on the principle of "special greenlights."

The "special greenlights" are the important opportunity for the Palace Museum to improve the maintenance and preservation mechanism of ancient architecture. In my opinion, not only should the preservation and maintenance of the ancient architecture of the Forbidden City receive "special greenlights," but those of ancient buildings across China, so that the cultural characteristics of Chinese ancient architecture are respected, the renovation regulations of ancient Chinese architecture followed, and the technical content required for the maintenance and preservation of ancient Chinese architecture ensured.

In 2015, based on the summary of the past experience in the maintenance and preservation of ancient architecture, the Palace Museum selected four ancient architecture complexes, namely Hall of Mental Cultivation, Qianlong Garden, Hall of

High Heaven and the Forbidden City walls, which were in urgent need of maintenance and preservation, as pilot architecture for the "research protection project" to explore new implementation mechanisms and inheritance methods for the maintenance and preservation of ancient architecture.

We attached extraordinary importance to the Hall of Mental Cultivation. Built in the 16th year (1537) of Emperor Jiajing's reign in the Ming Dynasty, it is one of the royal palaces with the best preserved construction data. The Hall of Mental Cultivation got the name from a verse from Mencius (the ancient philosopher), "*mental cultivation comes from few desires.*" Its main building is the remains of an official-style building in the Ming Dynasty. It used to be a side hall of the emperor's resting chamber. Since the Emperor Yongzheng, it has been used as the emperor's resting chamber and the center of daily administration. The emperors since the middle Qing Dynasty all used it as their actual resting chamber, so that it has almost witnessed the occurrence of all major historical events since Emperor Yongzheng of the Qing Dynasty. It was the center of the highly centralized political system of the emperors.

The Hall of Mental Cultivation area is located in Gate of Mental Cultivation, west of the Palace of Heavenly Purity and south of the Area of Six Western Palaces. It is a group of independent courtyards surrounded by red walls. It is about 94.8 meters long from north to south and 81.3 meters wide from east to west, covering an area of about 7,707 square meters. It contains 18 buildings including the Hall of Mental Cultivation, the I-shaped Corridor, the Back Hall, Wintersweet Dock, and so on, which covers around 3,887 square meters. The Hall of Mental Cultivation is a model of the administrative space in the heyday of the Qing Dynasty. It is the most representative artistic expression in the Forbidden City that Emperor Qianlong's lifelong pursuit, dream of peace and literary accomplishment, as well as the harmonious coexistence of multiculturalism and the artistic crystallization of the cultural exchanges between China and the West. The Hall of Mental Cultivation is in the shape of capitalized letter I. The front and rear halls are connected by corridors, forming the pattern of administrative space at the front and resting chamber at the back. The interior of the Hall of Mental Cultivation is well utilized and designed. The main hall, study, resting chamber, and small rooms are used for reviewing memorials, secret conversations, sleep, and worshipping Buddha respectively. There are side halls on the east and west of the front hall, and side rooms on both sides of the rear hall, named the Room of Health and Room of Joy.

Though the layout and furnishings of the Hall of Mental Cultivation varied in different periods, it retains the original display in different periods since Emperor Yongzheng of the Qing Dynasty. It is valuable historical data to study the development of Qing arts and crafts and the administrative and resting spaces of the Qing emperors. There are 1,890 pieces of indoor and outdoor exhibits in the Hall of Mental Cultivation, including bronzeware, jade ware, porcelain, woodcrafts, paintings and calligraphy, and ancient books, all of which hold extremely high cultural relic value.

At the end of 2015, the Conservation Project of the Hall of Mental Cultivation was officially launched. It was treated as scientific research and cultural engineering, and operated as a team event. We expected to take the lead in realizing the scientific renovation centered on "research and prevention," and set an example for the preservation of cultural relics in China. Before the maintenance and preservation started, we mobilized professionals from relevant departments to conduct academic research first, from its historical evolution to cultural events, from its cultural relics architecture to cultural relics collections, from outdoor landscaped to indoor environments. Experts and scholars reported 36 related scientific research topics, of which 33 were approved by the Academic Committee after thorough discussions. A total of hundreds of researchers participated in the preliminary research on the maintenance and preservation of the Hall of Mental Cultivation. They performed more detailed survey and mapping, so that the project was based sufficient scientific research, and could become a model for the maintenance and preservation of ancient architecture.

In April 2016, these 33 special topics of the Hall of Mental Cultivation Research Protection were set up as a project to provide supporting academic findings and talent. The Palace Museum hoped to open up a new way of cultural heritage protection, establish a mechanism for craftsman recruitment, assessment, and training, open a supply base for official-style ancient architecture renovation materials, formulate material performance standards, so as to save the construction, decoration, and renovation technologies of ancient architecture from extinction.

Before the repair began, we first removed all the exhibits from the Hall of Mental Cultivation. On May 30, 2016, the removal of the movable cultural relics in Hall of Mental Cultivation started. We made a detailed schedule, as well as related systems and measures. The removal took place in the halls. According to their types, the department in charge of display in the original forms counted and handed over the cultural relics to the relevant business departments, and then the professional divisions in each business department were responsible for the warehousing of the corresponding cultural relics. The specific removal order was:

First, the flat displays, such as jade, lacquer, enamel, glass, bonsai, and clocks (the utensils department, the court department, and the library received them);

Second, the furniture and curtains, and cushions (the court department received them);

Third, lanterns (the court department and the utensils department received them);

Fourth, super-large furniture (the court department received them);

Fifth, books, paintings, and calligraphy (the painting department received them).

Packaging for these cultural relics was adopted public bidding, and professional companies with qualifications and rich experience in cultural relic packaging and transportation won the bid. At the same time, the dusting and photographing of the cultural relics were conducted as the removal was unfolding.

On September 3, 2018, the Hall of Mental Cultivation Research Protection Project officially kicked off. This was the first comprehensive research renovation project of movable and immovable cultural relics in China, so it was of great importance. While repairing the Hall of Mental Cultivation, we filmed the documentary *New Diary of the Forbidden City*, through which, the audience can learn about the whole process of the renovation of the Hall of Mental Cultivation. In addition, I would like to disclose that before the renovation, only 17% of the Hall of Mental Cultivation was open, and after the renovation, more than 80% of the area will be, and visitors can see the inside at last.

⬛ Visiting the Bower of Friendship in Qianlong Garden (March 14, 2013).

The Qianlong Garden, also known as the Garden of the Palace of Tranquil Longevity, is one of the four gardens of the Forbidden City (the Imperial Garden, the Garden of Palace of Established Happiness, the Garden of the Palace of Compassion and Tranquility and the Garden of Palace of Tranquil Longevity). Qianlong built it for fitness keeping for the years after his abdication. It stands in the northwest corner of the Palace of Tranquil Longevity area of the Forbidden City. It took six years to finish its construction. In the later reign of Qianlong, remodeling of the Palace of Tranquil Longevity was forbidden, which is an important reason why the Qianlong Garden has been fully preserved to this day. It is 160 meters long from north to south, and 37 meters wide from east to west, covering an area of 5,920 square meters. Divided into four courtyards, it accommodates more than 20 buildings, of which the main ones are the Bower of Ancient Catalpa, the Hall of Tracing Origin, the Tower of Appreciation, the Tower of Prolonging Delight, the Bower of Friendship, the Pavilion of Hope, the Bower of Jade, the Studio of Exhaustion from Diligent Service, etc.

The renovation of the Qianlong Garden was scheduled to be completed in 2020. During the repair, every step must be recorded in detail, and the repair report must be published; every traditional craft must be repaired with the original materials and original techniques; the plaques, couplets, and calligraphy removed from the walls must be returned accurately to their old position.

Take the Studio of Exhaustion from Diligent Service as an example. As early as March 2003, the Palace Museum began the cooperation with the World Monument Funds of the United States to carry out the interior protection and renovation project of Studio of Exhaustion from Diligent Service. With the joint efforts of both parties, in November 2008, the project declared a success even though the process was extremely challenging.

The Studio of Exhaustion from Diligent Service was designed by Emperor Qianlong himself. The floor is tiled with golden tiles made in Suzhou; the embroidery is double-sided silk embroidery made in Suzhou; the 176 windows and beams are inlaid with 2,640 pieces of Hetian jade. In addition, bamboo products are used extensively in the interior design of the Studio of Exhaustion from Diligent Service. Among them, the upper and lower sill walls of the East Five Immortal Towers are all decorated with *zhuhuang* (handicraft articles made from bamboo with its green covering removed), which is exclusively used there in all decoration of the Forbidden City, thus extremely valuable. He Fuli, a Chinese master of bamboo craftsmanship, devoted his life to studying this lost craft. *Zhuhuang* has to be softened to be as thin as a sheet of paper, and can be pasted on uneven wood carving patterns like cloth. Therefore, bamboo, either too old or too tender, does not work. Moreover, the softer the bamboo, the less fiber there is, meaning too brittle. This shows how amazing the craftsmanship mastered by our ancestors.

There is also a landscape painting inside, which depicts a wisteria trellis full of blossoms. When repairing it, it was found that the paper on which it was painted was a kind of handmade mulberry bark paper. In order to find paper with the same level

📷 The renovation site of the Hall of High Heaven in the Forbidden City (November 8, 2016).

of craftsmanship, experts traveled around cities, and at last found the inheritor of the craftsmanship of handmade mulberry bark paper in Anhui. It was not until hundreds of trial and error that the paper was recreated and used in the repair.

The repair of the landscape painting of the Studio of Exhaustion from Diligent Service has promoted the restoration of mulberry papermaking technique, which was listed as a national intangible cultural heritage in 2008. Although visitors cannot see the efforts behind this painting, the technique and craftsmanship to repair it have been well preserved, so that they can be learned and inherited by future generations. This is the very point of the renovation projects, "to guard the present for the future."

The Hall of High Heaven is located outside the Gate of Divine Prowess and adjacent to the northwest corner of the Forbidden City. Built in the 21st year (1542) of the Emperor Jiajing in the Ming Dynasty, it was an imperial Taoist temple of the Ming and Qing Dynasties. Historically, it has endured a series of tribulations and suffered serious damage. It was not until 2014 that it was returned to the Palace Museum, which initiated the comprehensive examination and repair. First, 6,000 square meters of illegal buildings and temporary buildings were demolished. At the same time, as it was a "research protection project," we adopted the maintenance and preservation methods that integrated multiple disciplines so that more academic institutions and research units could participate. It is particularly worth mentioning the introduction of archaeological research not only on the ground of the ancient architecture, but on the roofs and beams. Drawing on the concepts of stratigraphy and typology in archaeology, the relevant personnel recorded and carefully studied the entire life course of the Hall of High Heaven from the Ming Dynasty to the present day without missing one cultural trace nor one historical clue. Every inscription on the tiles and every note on the wood has been scrutinized. They studied information on craftsmen throughout history and the place of origin of the materials, applied modern technology to make scientific records, and determined the information to be retained and the measures to be taken during the repair. The first phase of the maintenance and preservation project of the cultural relics architecture commenced on April 2, 2015, and finished at the end of 2016. Most of the hall base in the Hall of High Heaven complex still retain the wooden structure and shape of the Ming Dynasty, which holds significant historical, artistic and social value. It is another important example of the official-style architecture of the Ming Dynasty in the Forbidden City. This renovation shouldered the important mission of pioneering and accumulating experience for the research protection project of the Palace Museum.

Since 2016, we have also included the Forbidden City walls in the Research Protection Project. The total length of its city wall is 3,437.6 meters. Excluding the total length of the city platform, the number is 2,914.3 meters. The top width of the city wall is 6.63 meters and the bottom width 8.55, and it is 9.3 meters tall. The main structure takes rammed earth as the core and wears a brick setting outside. There are four city gates in four directions. On each city gate, there is a city platform and

The groundbreaking ceremony for the renovation of Hall of High Heaven (April 2, 2015).

a city tower. The hidden safety hazards of the city wall were mainly the disrupted, weathered, and bloated surface bricks, and there was bulging in the bloated areas, whose maximum size was up to 20 cm; there were many vertical cracks on the side wall, and many loosened and missing brick settings due to the loss of mortar; there were also cracks on the floor of the city wall along the central line; the ground of the city wall has subsided, the rammed earth has been lost, and there grew plants or vines on the ground and sides of the city wall. All of these problems were serious safety hazards. Should the rain pour, there would be a possibility of partial collapse. The repair was urgent. We commissioned a survey unit to conduct a detailed survey of the entire city walls of the Forbidden City. It made a danger analysis, formulated a feasible repair plan for the most dangerous parts, and started the first phase of the city wall repair project.

🖼 The maintenance and preservation project of Big South Warehouse (April 16, 2016).

Among them, the "sickness" of a section of the city wall was most concerning. It was located north of the First Historical Archives on the north side of West Prosperity Gate, with a total length of 233 meters. Records show that it was repaired twice between the 1950s and 1970s, and the repairs carried out in the 1990s were mainly on the outer side of the city wall. Once we discovered the serious hazard of this section of the city wall in 2013, temporary propping reinforcement measures were taken for the serious fracture of the surface bricks and the hollow parts in 2014. This major repair was mainly focused on the inner side of the city wall. It was accompanied by the general repair of the ground and the inner surface of the city wall, and of the parapet and its inner surface.

In addition, during the repair, we made a scientific record with experiments on traditional crafts and materials, and figured out the suitable materials and crafts for this

📷 Renovation of Sparrow Wing Tower of Meridian (June 12, 2015).

repair by exploring the traditional crafts and materials, visiting senior craftsmen, and conducting experiments. Consequently, we paved the way for subsequent renovation of the city wall. The first phase (pilot) of the infrastructure maintenance and renovation project, which was carried out simultaneously with the repair of the city wall, aimed to eliminate the hidden threats such as aging of supporting equipment and insufficient supply capacity in the drainage, power supply, and heating systems of the Palace Museum, to cultural relics buildings. This phase of renovation covered a total area of about 169,485 square meters.

At the beginning of the overall maintenance and preservation project of the ancient architecture of the Forbidden City in 2002, merely 30% of the Forbidden City was open; by 2015, the number had gone up to 65%; in September 2018, the opening of the Hall of Furniture of Big South Warehouse increased the percentage to 80%; we strive to open 85% of the Forbidden City by 2025. For the public, such an opening is indeed gratifying news that called for a celebration. We look forward to more and more comprehensive displays of the complete appearance and diversity of the ancient architectural complex of the Forbidden City, to providing more effective display space for the abundant collection of the Palace Museum, and to alleviating the congestion during the busiest hours by expanding the area to accommodate more visitors. Whether from the perspective of meeting the public's visiting needs to the fullest, or from the perspective of displaying the charm of historical and cultural heritage and improving the service level, the practice of the Palace Museum to gradually expand the open area is worthy of commendation. This is also a rational response to the increasing public visit expectation index.

The overall maintenance and preservation project of the ancient architecture of the Forbidden City presents visitors a more real Forbidden City while retrieving and preserving the many lost traditional cultures and skills. The three major renovations in the history of the Forbidden City have respectively nurtured three generations of craftsmen, and also forged the artisan spirit of the Forbidden City. The reverence and love for the ancient architecture, which is condensed in the craftsmanship, should be forever remembered.

Masters in the Forbidden City

In the early morning, amid the melodious bird chirps, the vermilion gate of the Palace Museum slowly opened, and Min Junrong of the Ministry of Cultural Protection and Science and Technology, began to repair the royal folding screen of the Emperor Kangxi. Like a magician, through meticulous polishing, he restored these dusty and damaged historical treasures to their past glory . . .

The documentary, *Masters in the Forbidden City*, about the restoration of cultural relics of the Forbidden City was broadcast. Every ordinary shot in this documentary presents the meticulous repair over the years of the cultural relics by masters in the Forbidden City.

This documentary made the little-known restoration of cultural relics in the Forbidden City popular. It was the first time in recent years that the Palace Museum attracted numerous fans. If there is a trending chart for the keywords of the Forbidden City, the "Forbidden City Cultural Relics Hospital," where the masters of restorations are, will definitely top it.

In 2016, the Palace Museum and Central China Television (CCTV) jointly launched the cultural relic restoration documentary *Masters in the Forbidden City*. CCTV decided to shoot it because, pleased with the continuous new achievements in the restoration of cultural relics of the Forbidden City, it believed that this scientism, especially the artisan spirit, deserves to be seen. *Masters in the Forbidden City* records the restoration process of rare treasures of paintings and calligraphy, bronzeware, clocks and watches, woodwork, ceramics, and lacquerware of the Forbidden City. It presents how best "cultural relics doctors" of the Palace Museum brought them back to life. After it was broadcast, it immediately won the public over with its profound ideological connotation, distinctive artistic style, exquisite craftsmanship, and elegant cultural taste.

Although there are only three episodes, it quickly became viral on the Internet, receiving more than one million views, and attracted continuous media attention and reports across the country. It was rated 9.4/10 on Douban.com, where 70% of the audience gave it five stars, surpassing the sensational documentary *A Bite of China* and the hit TV series *Nirvana in Fire*. It became the most influential documentary of the year. On Bilibili, *Masters in the Forbidden City* was such a hit, with nearly two million reviews and more than 60,000 live comments. Netizens sent live comments to express their love for the production, such as "please make more episodes," "best job advertisement for the Palace Museum," etc. There is no doubt that cultural relics preservation is getting unprecedented attention.

More importantly, 70% of the audience who liked this documentary are the young people between the ages of 18 and 22, which moved me deeply. At first, we intended to popularize the techniques of restoration of cultural relics in the Forbidden City through this documentary, and expected the positive response from the middle-aged and elders. Unexpectedly, the younger generation admire the spirit of lifelong devotion to a cause, which has encouraged us deeply. We thought that students would prefer the more exciting films, but it turned out that this documentary of quiet and endless repairing cultural relics moved them. Therefore, I apologize for making incorrect assumptions about them.

Masters in the Forbidden City is particularly influential among young students. In 2017, there were 15,000 applications to work for the Palace Museum, and many of the applicants hoped to work as a cultural relic restoration technician. Unfortunately, the Palace Museum only recruits 20 talents a year. Therefore, it is common to notice young people's love of culture in the Palace Museum. For example, during the special exhibition of Zhao Mengfu, when I entered the exhibition hall, I found that more than 70% the visitors were young people. After simple conversations with them, I realized that many have come three times, and some even six times. I never expected them to be so deeply fascinated with paintings and calligraphy. We should present more of their favorite works, including film and television productions, into their lives.

Masters in the Forbidden City profoundly reveals the preservation and restoration of the cultural relics collection in the Palace Museum, which are also called "behind the scenes," and sings the praises of the group of experts, who are persistent, yet unknown, meticulous, and keep endeavoring for perfection in the post of preserving and repairing cultural relics. For example, the documentary introduces a refined watch repairer, Wang Jin, who has become a well-known "star." Many young audience members nicknamed him "the Fantastic," which he deserves. These 18th century Western clocks and watches, after his careful restoration, run accurately again. It is no piece of cake to make the water flow, the birds chirp, the figurine to pop out, the alarm to chime, the music to play and the several sets of watch movements to be linked smoothly. What's more amazing is that one day I met him in the cafeteria and he told me that he was going to go to the United States to accept an award. It turned out that he won the Platinum Award for Outstanding Contributions at the Houston Film Festival. I asked what role he played. He said he played none but worked as usual, which was filmed and won the award. In addition to him, the popularity of *Masters in the Forbidden City* shows the work value, work attitude, and work skills of all cultural relic restoration experts and scholars in the Palace Museum, such as Professor Shan Jiajiu, an expert in the restoration of the mounting of ancient paintings and calligraphy, and Wang Youliang, the inheritor of the intangible cultural heritage of bronzeware restoration. All the experts of the restoration of porcelain, woodwork, lacquerware, musical instruments, inlay, hanging screens, ivory, mother-of-pearl inlays, kesi (a type of weaving done by the tapestry method in fine silks and gold thread), thangkas, and embroidery are widely recognized in society for their work.

After the documentary was broadcast, we were wondering: How to handle the unprecedented enthusiasm of the public for the preservation of cultural relics? How to preserve historical information to the greatest extent during the cultural relics preservation and restoration? How to combine modern science and technology with traditional restoration techniques in the process of cultural relics preservation and restoration? How to popularize the correct concepts and scientific knowledge of cultural relics preservation and restoration to the public? How to ensure the public's right to know, to participate, to supervise and to benefit from the preservation of cultural relics? How to keep the artisan spirit passed down from generation to generation and expand it

🖻 Preservation and restoration of cultural relics collections (August 13, 2014).

in social life? In other words, now that these "Forbidden City Cultural Relics Doctors" are there and known, the "Forbidden City Cultural Relics Hospital" must keep up.

In fact, every piece of cultural relic collections stored in the cultural relics warehouse and every piece of cultural relic exhibits displayed in the cultural relics exhibition hall have their own life course. They carry extensive precious historical information, and have witnessed some little-known historical events. Therefore, it is necessary to retain more of these historical information during cultural relic preservation and restoration, and to reveal these historical events in depth. To this end, the restoration of cultural relics should not only be the exclusive task of a department, an industry, and a profession, but be a comprehensive task across departments, industries, and professions; it should not be a closed field, but an open system that integrates multiple disciplines.

Back then, medicine around the world was traditional medicine, and doctors treated patients with their own experience. It was not until the middle of the 19th century that scientists introduced scientific instruments in the laboratory into medical

◨ Preservation and restoration of cultural relics collections (August 13, 2014).

practices, thus laying the foundation of modern medicine. Dr. Song Jirong, Founder and Director of the establishment of the "Forbidden City Cultural Relics Hospital," believes: "If we see traditional cultural relics restoration techniques as traditional Chinese medicine, modern science and technology is Western medicine. To build a cultural relics restoration hospital with modern scientific concepts, there must be the integration of traditional Chinese medicine and Western medicine to both treat the symptoms and effect a permanent cure. And the unique traditional cultural relics restoration skills, coupled with modern science and technology, enable the Palace Museum to build a general hospital of cultural relics restoration with modern scientific concepts."

Now if an ill person seeks medical help at the hospital, doctors will not directly prescribe medicine to or perform surgery on the patient, but check his/her previous medical records to better understand his/her past medical history; then there are a series of essential physical examinations, including measuring body temperature, blood pressure, heartbeat, or performing urine and blood tests if necessary, or running more detailed tests through stethoscope, electrocardiogram, X-ray, ultrasound, CT, and MRI, so as to accurately locate the cause of the illness, and scientifically determine the treatment plan; it is not until after that treatment can take place, and the right medicine can be prescribed to cure it. During the course of treatment, doctors must constantly observe the patient's condition and take corresponding measures to obtain the expected curative effect. All these processes are recorded in detail, and after the patient recovers, they will be incorporated into the medical record file for future reference.

Cultural relics have a life course, too. For one piece of the cultural relics collection, a detailed diagnosis is an absolutely necessary step of the restoration work. For example, when a bronzeware enters the "cultural relics hospital," its life course should be investigated first, including the age of production, the place where it was unearthed, and the characteristics of the manufacturing process; then, there is the comprehensive test analysis on it, including the components and information accumulated on it; next, its health status is evaluated, and detailed research on its illness conducted, and its disease mechanism and the cause clarified; finally, on the basis of a comprehensive and detailed examination, in-depth research is performed to make an accurate judgment, and through expert consultation, a scientific restoration plan is formulated, so that restoration takes place in an orderly manner. At the same time, during the restoration, each restoration step is recorded in detail, such as what technology, what materials, and what processes are used, and photos are taken in time. After the restoration is completed, a work report should be prepared in a timely manner and published. This "medical record," that is, the restoration file, will always be there throughout the life course of the cultural relics, so as to help future experts to understand their "medical history" and re-perform the restoration as before. For example, the full-colored parts, the parts that have been through mold treatment, and the parts that have been repaired can be clearly reviewed, thus there will be a reference for the preservation and restoration of cultural relics in the future.

In fact, the preservation and restoration skills of many types of cultural relics applied in the Palace Museum have been passed down from generation to generation.

For example, the restoration of the mounting of ancient paintings and calligraphy has a history that exceeds 1,700 years. During the Tang and Song Dynasties, the imperial mounting had formed a quite strict style. During the Ming and Qing Dynasties, there were formed the "Jing mounting" centered on Beijing, the capital of China, and the "Su mounting" centered on Suzhou, while the Imperial Workshop integrated both their advantages and created a unique mounting restoration technique. There is another example, in that bronzeware casting had reached the peak as early as the Spring and Autumn Period, and its restoration and reproduction techniques emerged. During the Ming and Qing Dynasties, there were different schools in the field of bronzeware restoration. The bronzeware restoration techniques of the Palace Museum originated from the "Bronze Zhang School" of the "Beijing School." Today, the restoration techniques of the mounting of ancient paintings and calligraphy, and of bronzeware have been included in the national intangible cultural heritage.

In the 1950s, the Palace Museum established a cultural relics restoration factory. In the 1980s, it was expanded into the Ministry of Cultural Protection, and Science and Technology, a department specializing in cultural relics protection, restoration, and research. In the past, the cultural relics repaired in the Ministry of Cultural Protection, and Science and Technology only had a repair list, which recorded simple information such as their code, damage condition, name, people who send for repair, and parts to be repaired. In recent years, the Palace Museum's Ministry of Cultural Protection, and Science and Technology has begun to archive cultural relics restoration in detail. Any cultural relics to be repaired at the Ministry of Cultural Protection, and Science and Technology shall go through a detail documentation of their conditions first. The conditions before, during, and after the restoration are archived in the form of high-definition photos. Today, accumulating research data is regarded a pivotal link in the preservation and restoration of cultural relics.

Meanwhile, during the preservation and restoration of cultural relics, more modern science and technology should be applied for analysis and testing. For example, when repairing cultural relics of paintings and calligraphy, it is necessary to use modern instruments to test and analyze them, so as to determine the proper treatment plan

🔳 Bronzeware Restoration 1—Sort the fragments.

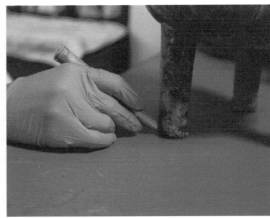

🔳 Bronzeware Restoration 2—De-rust via physical methods.

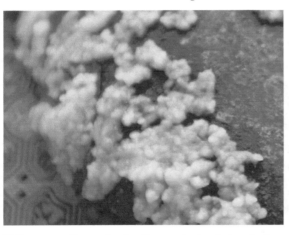

🔳 Bronzeware Restoration 3—De-rust via chemical methods.

🔳 Bronzeware Restoration 4—Reshape.

🔳 Bronze Restoration 5—Weld.

🔳 Bronzeware Restoration 6—Splice.

⬚ Bronze Restoration 7—Refill.

⬚ Bronze Restoration 8—Color.

for different damages such as missing corners, broken pieces, moldiness, discoloring, hollowing, and adhesion. Another example is the restoration of embroidery cultural relics, which also requires the help of modern instruments to magnify the mold invisible to the naked eye by dozens or hundreds of times, so that the state of mycelium growth is seen.

The "Forbidden City Cultural Relics Hospital" is a two-row building 361 meters long. The exterior is traditional while the interior is a modern workshop, with a construction area of 13,000 square meters, which is connected with the underground cultural relics warehouse through an underground passage to ensure their safety during transportation. The number of personnel in the "Forbidden City Cultural Relics Hospital" has been expanded to 200, thus realizing multidisciplinary integration. At present, some world-class museums have 30 or 40 personnel on cultural relics preservation and restoration. Why does the Forbidden City Cultural Relics Hospital gather 200 "cultural heritage doctors?" The truth is that over half of them are professionals in natural science research. They can analyze, test, and detect damages of the cultural relics collections, prepare analysis and research reports, and draw restoration plans.

In the meantime, we have also equipped the Forbidden City Cultural Relics Hospital with a complete set of around 100 advanced precision instruments and equipment suitable for the restoration of cultural relics, including elemental analysis equipment, such as an energy dispersive X-ray fluorescence spectrometer, a wavelength dispersive X-ray fluorescence spectrometer, and a laser-induced breakdown spectrometer; molecular structure analysis equipment such as an X-ray diffraction phase analysis equipment, a micro-infrared spectrometer, a micro-laser Raman spectrometer, a near-infrared spectrometer, an ultraviolet-visible spectrophotometer, a pyrolysis gas chromatography-mass spectrometer, an ultra-high performance liquid chromatography-mass spectrometer, a supercritical chromatograph; environment, pests and aging analysis equipment, such as an environmental real-time monitoring system, a xenon lamp aging test chamber, a constant temperature and humidity aging test chamber, an automatic kinematic viscosity measurement system, a fiber optic spectrometer; thermal performance and physical performance equipment, such as a synchronous thermal analyzer, a thermal dilatometer, high temperature physical properties testers and impact testing systems; nondestructive imaging and measurement equipment, such as microfocus X-ray damage detectors, general-purpose cultural relics CT systems, optical coherence tomography systems, hyperspectral imaging systems, multispectral imaging systems; microscopic observation equipment, such as scanning electron microscopes, ultra-depth-of-field 3D video microscopy systems, confocal lasers microscopes, polarizing microscopes, metallographic microscopes, biological microscopes, and solid microscopes, as well as 3D printers and thermoluminescence measurement systems.

There are more examples. The Palace Museum has always been best in the industry in terms of the restoration of the mounting of ancient paintings and calligraphy, and when it encounters new difficulties, there are more restoration methods to choose. For example, Qianlong Garden was under preservation and repair in recent years. The tallest building in the garden is the Belvedere of Viewing Achievements. There used to be a huge painting on one wall of the Belvedere of Viewing Achievements. During the war of liberation 70 years ago, this painting fell and the old staff at the time wrapped it up. Seventy years later, when it needed to be repaired and protected, it was found broken into thousands of pieces when unwrapped. However, with the assistance of a computer system, the cultural relic restoration experts actually pieced it back together in three months, and it took over a year to complete the entire restoration. What hangs there today is a beautiful painting by Dong Gao, a famous scholar in the Qing Dynasty. It has been brought back to life.

A piece of bronzeware had already been broken into 200 pieces when it was unearthed in Shangcai, a county in Henan Province, and there was no way to study it. However, with the support of non-destructive testing equipment, under the patina of the largest piece, an inscription of more than Chinese 20 characters was discovered. Therefore, experts were able to determine that it is a bronze tripod with pre-Qin inscriptions made in the Spring and Autumn Period. It is extremely precious and has now been preserved and repaired.

⬛ *The Spring and Autumn Tripod* unearthed in Shangcai, Henan, before restoration.

⬛ *The Spring and Autumn Tripod* unearthed in Shangcai, Henan, after restoration.

Let me give one more example. Although there are thangkas makers in Tibet, Sichuan, and Qinghai, no one knows how to repair ancient thangkas, because without understanding the materials, pigments, and embroidery used before, ancient thangkas will only be repaired into modern thangkas. The Palace Museum has collected over 2,000 thangkas, which had been left unattended for a long time. Today, the Forbidden City Cultural Relics Hospital has mastered the preservation and restoration techniques of thangkas. For example, in Hall of Mental Cultivation, there is a small Buddhist shrine on the north side of the room where Emperor Yongzheng reviewed memorials to the throne day and night. There are 48 thangkas hanging on the second floor of the small Buddhist shrine, which have been there for over 200 years. They required urgent restoration. I often introduce the Number 34 thangka, Shang Le King Buddha among them—the contrast before and after the restoration. Through the preservation and restoration, we understand that there are 25 layers of embroidery, 50 small Buddha heads, and 632 millet beads on this thangka, and 32 different materials were used. After being magnified 20 times, their noses, eyebrows, eyes, and mouths are clearly shown. How these millet beads are connected in series and in parallel can be easily observed. Zooming in 100 times, it is super clear how each gold and silver thread is woven and how each detail is made. Therefore, in the process of restoration and protection, the original state of the thangka will not be changed. Therefore, we can proudly say that the Palace Museum has mastered the preservation and restoration techniques of ancient thangkas.

In fact, in recent years, whether it is through *Masters in the Forbidden City*, which records the restoration of cultural relics, or *New Diary of the Forbidden City*, which shows the progress of the research protection project of the Hall of Mental Cultivation, the audience can understand that the experts of the Forbidden City have been making the greatest efforts in the protection of cultural heritage. Also, they learn a term— artisan spirit. The success of *Masters in the Forbidden City* owes greatly to the artisan spirit deeply hidden in the Palace Museum that has attracted public attention.

A documentary has made the cultural relics preservation and restoration in the Palace Museum known to the public. I reckon the reason why it has attracted great

attention is not only the fantastic skills of the cultural relic restorers, but the artisan spirit of generations of experts condensed onto the artifacts themselves. For the cultural relic restoration experts of museums, on top of the technical craftsmanship, is their respect for the cultural relics and the cultural treasures of the Chinese nation. Each piece of cultural relic carries the hard work and wisdom of the artists or craftsmen from thousands of years ago. They are material carriers of the spiritual life of the ancients; it is almost a miracle that they have been passed down through thousands of years, so the restoration cannot afford the slightest mistake. As a cultural relics restorer, one must be meticulous, patient, and responsible at work, and involuntarily have higher pursuits, that is, respect for cultural relics collections and traditional skills.

In fact, in the Palace Museum, like these cultural relic restorers, there are many employees who silently devote themselves to the protection of the ancient architecture and cultural relics of the Palace Museum year after year. The artisan spirit is actually the spiritual wealth accumulated and passed down by generations of Palace Museum employees.

When I first started to work in the Palace Museum, I saw an expert repairing one lacquerware in the Ministry of Cultural Protection, Science and Technology. After a few months, I came back to the cultural relic restoration room. He was still repairing it, so I asked how long it would take. His answer left a deep impression on me that it would take months, because in Beijing, only in the hot summer and humid seasons can he paint two coats a day, and in normal days, only one per day, and to repair it entirely requires more than 100 coats of paint. I believe that this is the artisan spirit that we sing praise of.

Since the construction of the Forbidden City, an "artisan spirit" has run through it, such as the Lei family (a family of imperial architects and craftsmen). The majestic and splendid ancient architecture of the Forbidden City was usually designed by the best architects and craftsmen employed in the royal architectural designing studio affiliated to the engineering department, which was set up by the princes and cabinet officers the emperor selected. The craftsmen made the architectural plans, designs, sketches, modules, guided the construction, and co-edited the *Engineering Practices*. From the Emperor Kangxi to the end of the Qing Dynasty and the beginning of the Republic of China, the Lei family dominated the royal architectural designing studio. With their superb skills, they made remarkable achievements, thus were well respected from the imperial court to general public. They earned themselves the title "the Lei style." Whether it was the construction, reconstruction or repair of the Forbidden City architecture, they were all designed after careful procedures and thorough discussions, and carried out in accordance with the design drawings, models, and construction design instructions under a strict management system. The artistic structure of most of the ancient architecture in the Forbidden City carries the painstaking efforts of the "Lei family." It is an unparalleled miracle in the history of Chinese architecture, and even of world architecture, that this outstanding family of architects with a continuous heritage has designed so many everlasting masterpieces of such a large scale and such a great variety.

The documentary *Masters in the Forbidden City* brings cultural relic restorers closer to the people, but there is a serious shortage of talent in this profession. According to the results of the first national census of movable cultural relics, there are a total of 108.15 million pieces (sets) of movable cultural relics in China, and 37.12% of these treasures need mending. Taking the Palace Museum as an example, it will take at least a century for the current restorers to repair the existing cultural relics. Craftsman Wang Jin became well-known because of *Masters in the Forbidden City*, but it is little known that compared with the large number of cultural relics collections of clocks and watches in China, our skills to repair them are quite weak, and there isn't enough talent. The Palace Museum alone holds more than 2,200 ancient clocks and watches, but there are merely four craftsmen skilled in their restoration. For the protection of intangible cultural heritage, the most important measure is to give full play to the shared value of these amazing cultural heritages, to cultivate strong inheritors, and to attract more people to participate in their protection.

In my understanding of craftsmen, when the artisan spirit is born out of their crafts, values, ideology, and culture are involved. The artisan spirit should be passed on, but how? Germany and Japan set good examples. I started my study in Japan in 1980, and returned to China four years later. The content of my study included vocational education. Therefore, I believe that only by attaching importance to vocational education while being able to sort out and inherit traditional culture from generation to generation can there be a society that respects the artisan spirit. As a result, the artisan spirit achieves more, which will continue to be reflected in people's daily life and continue to benefit them.

Many senior craftsmen in the Palace Museum have to retire when they reach retirement age because they are not cadres. Also, they cannot be rehired. Inheritors of the traditional craftsmanship have left one after another. Most of the young apprentices they have trained come from the surrounding areas. Without a Beijing household registration, they cannot be hired by the Palace Museum, either. Few of the local young people in Beijing have the interest to learn bricklaying and carpentry. In 2015, the Palace Museum and Beijing International Vocational Education School jointly set up the major of cultural relic preservation and restoration for the first time. The Palace Museum restoration experts were the main teaching faculty, but due to the limitations of an academic diploma, it remained difficult for graduates of this major to work at the Palace Museum to restore cultural relics. In order to change this situation, in May 2017, Beijing Union University, Beijing International Vocational Education School and the Palace Museum jointly launched the pilot project of high-end technical and skilled personnel in cultural relics preservation and restoration, which was quickly approved. Thirty middle school graduates from Beijing will learn the craftsmanship from Palace Museum experts. Once they complete the learning, they will obtain a bachelor's degree.

In the 2016 government work report, Premier Li Keqiang proposed to cultivate the artisan spirit. It was a clear signal and positive orientation. The artisan spirit represents the spirit of an era that strives for perfection, pays attention to details, and pursues ultimate achievement. The forging of the artisan spirit in a great country requires strong support from all walks of life. The artisan spirit is the national spirit that China has possessed since ancient times. The research and development of cultural and creative products also need the artisan spirit of traditional Chinese culture. Today, the Palace Museum will infiltrate the artisan spirit into all fields, remove impetuousness and the simple profit-seeking psychology, and sow the seeds of humanistic feelings, artistic attainments, and the spirit of the times behind the cultural relics in the hearts of the general public.

Because of the artisan spirit, the 600-year-old Forbidden City can stay young and beautiful forever. In the next 600 years, and another 600 years, it will be forever ancient but full of vigor. And it is precisely because the craftsmen of the Palace Museum choose to devote their lives to their work that the Palace Museum can stand forever.

◨ *Desk Clock Inlaid with Fi Flowers in a Wooden Frame*, after restoration.

🏛 *The Ivory Tower of Gods Celebrating Longevity,* after restoration.

CHAPTER 5

Management Reform

We witnessed the unopened area on the map of the Forbidden City shrink, the closed doors open one after another, and the quiet courtyards liven up. In 2014, the open area of the Forbidden City increased to 52%, and by 2018, the number was almost 80%.

We also held exhibitions in the off-season. January to March is the off-season for the Palace Museum, which used to receive 20,000 to 30,000 visitors per day. From January to March 2019, we held the *Lunar New Year—Celebration in the Forbidden City* exhibition, which attracted up to 80,000 visitors.

Many people who had been to the Palace Museum were not expecting new changes, so they do not come again. Now that open area is constantly expanding and interesting exhibitions are held, they have returned to the Palace Museum.

Better Service

When visiting the Forbidden City, tourists share a common experience in that it is overcrowded. The large influx of visitors is a stern test for the reception capacity and reception quality of the Palace Museum. Recently, it has been the fastest growing museum in the world in terms of numbers of tourists. In 2002, the number of tourists exceeded seven million for the first time. And in 2012, the year I started working at the Palace Museum, it surpassed 15 million, more than twice the number 10 years ago. The Palace Museum has become the only museum in the world that receives more than 10 million visitors every year.

In addition, the number of visitors of the Palace Museum shows a distinctive feature, that is, the obvious gap between the off-peak seasons. During off-season (November 1 to March 31, excluding the Spring Festival holiday), there are around 20,000 visitors every day, and in the peak season (April 1 to October 31), especially the Labor Day (May 1) holiday, the National Day (October 1) holiday, and the summer vacation, the daily reception of visitors often exceeds 80,000, and sometimes reaches 100,000. The busiest day in the Palace Museum's history was on October 2, 2012, when 182,000 visitors filled it up.

The rapid increase in the number of visitors has put huge security pressure on the 600-year-old ancient architecture of the Forbidden City and the Palace Museum's cultural relics collections. Meanwhile, it is likely that visitors would get a less good tour experience, and there are hidden dangers like a stampede. These are the unprecedented challenges to the service and reception of the Palace Museum. It shoulders the heavy responsibility of a safety guarantee.

To this end, we have taken a number of measures. For example, "close" and "open"—setting closing days and increasing open space; "dividing" and "limiting"—launching time-slot online reservation, and limiting the daily number of tourists to 80,000. These measures are effective to some extent. Of course, because of the increasing influence of the Palace Museum and the greater attention from the entire society in recent years, the number of visitors grew again after a brief minor drop. In 2017, it reached 16.7 million, ranking first in the world. In the same year, the Louvre received 8.3 million visitors, the second largest in the world and nearly half of that of the Palace Museum.

Many people who had been to the Palace Museum were not expecting new changes, so they do not come again. Now that open area is constantly expanding and interesting exhibitions are held, they have returned to the Palace Museum.

I believe, with the development of museums from "object-oriented" to "people-oriented," that visitors have a satisfying experience has become more of the key factor in measuring the success of a museum. Focused on the service object, we have done a lot in recent years. It is no exaggeration to say that to better serve the visitors, we have carried out a management reform.

"Closed" and "Open"—Set the Closing Days and Open More Space

Every museum at home and abroad has certain day offs. It is perhaps once a week, or twice a month. This is conducive to daily maintenance of the museums and staff rest. But for a long time, Palace Museum operated 365 days a year without a break. In the past, it was open all year except on the afternoon of Lunar New Year's Eve and the morning of Lunar New Year's Day. Because of this, the exhibition halls or showcases could not be repaired in time, the service facilities failed to be maintained in time, and there was no time to train the service personnel. As a result, many problems have accumulated and required urgent solutions. All the Palace Museum employees used to work without sufficient rest, making great efforts to serve the visitors and the society.

Since January 1, 2013, the Palace Museum began a trial of closing every Monday afternoon (excluding national holidays) for half a day. It opened at 8:30 a.m. every Monday, and closed at 12:00 a.m., and stopped selling tickets at 11:00 a.m. This contributed to promoting the orderly development of various tasks of the Palace Museum. When we first made the decision, we were worried that the public would not understand. Therefore, we held a press conference to explain the purpose of this change, invited the media to see what and how the work were carried out in the Palace Museum when it was closed, and won the support of public media.

After a one-year trial of closing itself on Monday afternoons, on January 1, 2014, the Palace Museum implemented the new policy of closing all day on Mondays, except for statutory holidays and summer vacations This decision has been widely understood and appreciated by all sectors of the society.

The closing has bought more time for the comprehensive promotion of the Safe

Palace Museum project, where the safety and health of ancient architecture and cultural relics in the Palace Museum received proper maintenance. The short rest essentially prolongs the longevity of the cultural relics of the Palace Museum.

One-day closing allows the ancient architecture and cultural relics exhibits in the open area to take a break. Normally, the rest for the staff should come first but for the Palace Museum, that for the precious ancient architecture and cultural relics exhibits is equally important. Closing the museum for one day aimed to enable cultural relic experts to maintain the protected objects without interference; to enable the staff of the open department and the security department to check and repair the facilities and equipment in the open area in time; and to enable the visitors to get a safer, more comfortable, and satisfying visiting environment. Therefore, various departments of the Palace Museum deeply cherish the closed day, on which they organize staff training, cleaning of the open environment, indoor maintenance of the exhibition hall, technical protection of cultural relics exhibits, and demolition of the "color steel rooms" in the open area. Systematic training also takes place during the day-off, so that the employees who have been tense all the time can catch their breath. The expectations of Palace Museum staff for many years have finally come true.

I recall that on the first full-day of closing, we conducted the Safe Palace Museum engineering safety training. The day-off is so precious that it must not be wasted. About what we are going to do on this day and what we can do, we must think carefully, plan thoroughly, and organize and implement it safely. Why did we conduct the Safe Palace Museum engineering safety training on the first closed day of the Palace

◉ The Palace Museum ran fire drills on Monday, January 6, 2014 (the museum was closed).

◉ Cultural relics preservation and cleanup on Monday, January 20, 2014 (the museum was closed).

Museum? Because safety is the lifeblood of the Palace Museum. Ensuring the safety of the visitors, of the ancient architecture, and of the cultural relics is always our top priority, and it is extremely challenging and arduous. Great ideas are the first step to safety. To build a wall of safety requires everyone's wisdom, a common understanding, and unified and conscious actions. It is happening that we have worked relentlessly to make sure the precious treasures are well rested and maintained.

There are both attempts to "close" and measures to "open." We have opened up quite some more new areas compared with before.

Before 2002, only about 30% of the Forbidden City was open. By 2012, that percentage had climbed to 48%. Some parts were not open because some buildings were warehouses, some were the offices of the Palace Museum, and some were long occupied by external units. And we realized that more areas should be opened to the visitors. First, this would be an effective measure for people to know and understand the Forbidden City, especially when these buildings were turned into special exhibition halls to display cultural relics, more visitors can understand the cultural relics collections in the Forbidden City and become more familiar with the museum attribute of the Forbidden City. Secondly, it would be an effective way to divert the visits. In the past, most of the visitors of the Forbidden City gathered on the central axis, and paid little heed to the buildings and exhibitions on both sides. We have run statistics that in the past 80% of them only had a quick browse of the Forbidden City without checking the exhibitions of the Palace Museum. This led to overcrowded visits on the central axis, which was a threat to the safety of ancient architecture, cultural relics and tourists. Opening more areas is also a way to rationally divert and guide crowds with different needs to different areas. Certainly, it would be more effective with more active and vigorous publicity.

Recently, the Palace Museum has made great efforts to expand the open area. We evicted some external units from the Forbidden City, moved some of our own offices out of the ancient buildings, and transferred some cultural relics stored in the ground warehouse. Since the beginning of Zheng Xinmiao's directorship, we started the overall maintenance and preservation of the ancient architecture of the Forbidden City, which was the premise of the expansion of open area. At last, with the joint efforts of every employee, the open area of the Forbidden City has witnessed significant improvement in recent years.

Since 2014, the Palace Museum has opened many doors that were closed for years, and more and more areas have been open to the public, including Palace of Compassion and Tranquility, Palace of Longevity and Health, Meridian Gate Sparrow Wing Towers, Forbidden City Wall, Big South Warehouse, Palace of Prolonging Happiness, etc.

The opening of the Gate of Thriving Imperial Clan symbolizes that the west part of the Forbidden City is opened for the first time. That area is mysterious because it was never opened to the public. The emperors' mothers used to live there, and they built some shrines and gardens. The largest palace there is Palace of Compassion and Tranquility. Built by Emperor Jiajing of the Ming Dynasty for his mother, it was enormous. Today, it houses five exhibition halls of sculptures, also known as Hall of Sculptures of the Palace Museum.

Palace of Longevity and Health on the west side of Palace of Compassion and Tranquility was opened at the same time. On the first day of the opening, it received waves of young visitors, who believed that this was where Zhen Huan (a popular fictional TV character) lived. In fact, it was Empress Dowager Chongqing, mother of Emperor Qianlong, that lived there the longest, a total of 42 years. After detailed research by Palace Museum experts on the royal history, the furniture, utensils, and display used by the Empress Dowager Chongqing during her residence have been restored to their original state. Emperor Qianlong was a dutiful son. He would greet his mother every morning at East Belvedere of Warmth in Palace of Longevity and Health. The interior of that palace that visitors can see today is basically the same as what Emperor Qianlong saw back then.

Meridian Gate Sparrow Wing Tower used to be a warehouse of cultural relics. Later, the cultural relics were moved out to make way for the repair of the Sparrow Wing Towers. Its appearance remains what it was the same, but the inside has been turned into the world's largest temporary exhibition hall, which can undertake the

◢ Palace of Longevity and Health on display (September 11, 2015).

◢ The Palace Museum implemented the preservation procedures of the cultural relics in Hall of Supreme Harmony during the full-day off on Monday (January 6, 2014).

◉ Interior of the Palace Museum's Hall of Furniture.

exhibition of any precious cultural relics in the world. Since the opening of the Sparrow Wing Towers, many large exhibitions have been held there.

We have also opened the city walls of the Forbidden City. The visitors will have different experience when ambling on the city walls, overlooking the sceneries inside and outside the Forbidden City. There are surprises along the city walls. Visitors can now enter the Corner Towers that could only be seen and photographed from a distance in the past. Inside, a 25-minute virtual reality clip is played to show the visitors how to combine tens of thousands of pieces of wood, through mortise and tenon structures, into a beautiful Corner Towers with triple eaves and 72 ridges.

Big South Warehouse on the south side of Hall of Martial Valor is now accessible, too. The Palace Museum holds over 6,200 pieces of furniture from Ming and Qing Dynasties, the largest quantity in the world. Dating from Emperor Yongle of Ming Dynasty to Emperor Xuantong of Qing Dynasty, most of them were for the imperial use of Qing Dynasty. And among the furniture of Qing Dynasty, the majority was from the years of Emperor Qianlong. Previously, these precious furniture and cultural relics had been kept deep in the warehouses and unknown to the public. In fact, most of the furniture had been stacked in over 90 warehouses for a long time. Since they were checked into the warehouses, they have never come out again. It was impossible to ventilate them, repair them, study them, or display them. Some warehouses stacked up 11 layers of furniture. It was absolutely not good storage condition. When I noticed this, I wondered why these cultural relics had to be stored in the warehouses all year round. The truth is that only when they are displayed will they receive meticulous maintenance; only when they are appreciated by the visitors can they gain the respect they deserve. Therefore, it was decided to turn Big South Warehouse into a special exhibition site for imperial furniture. After three years of preparation, it has become a modern professional exhibition hall for cultural relics. First, there is modular furniture exhibition that displays imperial furniture related to the imperial ritual system and the daily life of the emperor for the visitors to appreciate at close range; then, there is a situational furniture exhibition that presents different cultural spaces designed according to the different scenes of study room, musical instrument room, and courtyard; the third exhibition focuses on the warehouse-style furniture. In fact, the warehouse-style display effectively relieves inventory pressure, expands the exhibition area, and increases the number of cultural relics displayed, so that the cultural relics have a bigger chance to be seen. Through this warehouse-style exhibition, the ancient architecture can be better maintained, preserved and utilized, while the furniture receive proper sorting, protection, and exhibition. Moreover, the visitors can better appreciate the exquisite materials, delicate design and rich connotation of the imperial furniture. Therefore, there is a "new must-see" in the Forbidden City trip.

The open area of the Palace Museum continues to grow, such as the Palace of Prolonging Happiness area, which has been accessible only in recent years. Palace of Prolonging Happiness was burned down multiple times in history, and the last tragedy happened during the reign of Emperor Daoguang. Superstitiously, the last emperor Puyi decided to build a fish-watching Western Building Crystal Palace there to avoid

◳ Interior of Hall of Furniture.

◳ Interior of Hall of Furniture.

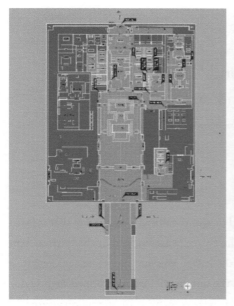
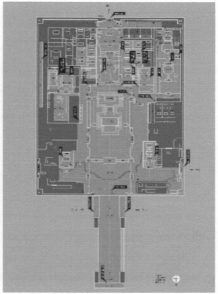

⬛ 52% of the Palace Museum was open (2014).   ⬛ 76% of the Palace Museum was open (2016).

fire. The main body of the building adopts a metal structure while the walls and floors are made of glass materials. And ponds have been dug around it to store water. But soon after the construction started, Puyi was forced to abdicate, and the project was halted. It became the earliest "unfinished building" in Beijing, but left an architecture that rarely combines both Chinese and Western styles in the Forbidden City. Taking advantage of it, the Palace Museum decided to build a hall of foreign cultural relics. The Palace Museum hoards a great many precious cultural relics from all over the world. When hall of foreign cultural relics is complete, it will be a feast for the eyes of visitors.

I believe it is widely noticed that over the years, there have been fewer and fewer "no entry" areas in the Forbidden City. We witnessed the unopened area on the map of the Forbidden City shrink, the closed doors open one after another, and the quiet courtyards liven up. In 2014, the open area of the Forbidden City increased to 52%, and in 2018, the number was almost 80%. By 2025, when the Palace Museum celebrates its centennial, we hope this number will have gone past 85%.

"Divert" and "Limit"
—Balance between Peak Off-Seasons

There is probably no museum in the world or world cultural heritage site that is faced with as many management challenges as the Palace Museum, and or that attracts tens of millions of visitors every year. Recently, the Palace Museum has witnessed the fastest growth in the number of visitors. In 2013, the number of visitors dropped slightly due to the half-day closing on Mondays, but there were as many as 14.56 million visitors. In 2014, the number was on the rise again. For the Palace Museum, the biggest difficulties in receiving visitors are the continuous growth of their number, and the obvious gap between the off-season and the peak season. On all the annual visitor quantity graphs, there was a highly consistent pattern of "three crests," that is, the Labor Day holiday (May 1), the National Day holiday (October 1), and the summer vacation.

During long holidays, overcrowding was the norm in the Forbidden City, which forced us to implement one-way tours in the Imperial Garden. Sometimes it took five minutes to pass through one palace gate. The Palace Museum was experiencing an unrestricted increase in visitor quantity. As a world cultural heritage, cultural relics and ancient buildings would suffer greatly, and the comfort of a tour would be much less. Sometimes, visitors got lost in the crowd, and more seriously, there was a great risk of stampede. In January 2015, after failing to limit the number of visitors several times, we proposed another attempt to limit it, setting upper limit as 80,000. At the time, we held a special press conference to solicit opinions. I explained that the goal was not only to relieve pressure, but to guarantee a better tour experience because if there were over 80,000, 90,000 or 100,000 visitors at a time, it would be overcrowded, and the main exhibit would be the back of each other's head.

Some journalists once questioned me why not try to increase the ticket price. Honestly, this never crossed my mind because there is only one Forbidden City in the world, whose cultural volume is enormous and cultural resources are abundant. The current fare is RMB 40 per person in the off-season and 60 in the peak season. Raising it to 100 will not effectively limit the visitor number because most people will not find it expensive. But this change prevents low-income citizens from visiting the Forbidden City, which we never want to happen. Once, while I was conducting a research at the Gansu Museum, I noticed a group of college students carefully copying the commentary. During our chat, I learned that they are junior students majoring in tourism. They entered the museum for the first time while there was an event that did not charge the RMB 35 fare. I believe there must be many more visitors like them, and we shall never raise the fare and keep them out of the Palace Museum.

Therefore, controlling the total number of visitors in a single day is our best option.

On June 13, 2015, the tenth Cultural Heritage Day in China, the Palace Museum began to trial to limit the visitor volume to 80,000, a rigid measure to ensure the safety of the Palace Museum, including the safety of the visitors, of the ancient architecture, and of cultural relics collections. Meanwhile, it implemented the real-name system for ticket sales. Travel agencies were required to book tickets online for their group customers as it canceled on-site ticket sales for them, and visitors were encouraged to book tickets online, as well. Gradually, the proportion of online pre-sale went up.

The Palace Museum's 80,000 visitors limit measure never aimed to prevent them from visiting, but to guarantee the safety, order, and comfort of the visits.

Through this measure, visitors can tour around in an orderly manner and enjoy better experience museum service, which was also the purpose and significance of the refined management of the Palace Museum. The success of the 80,000-visitor limit and the online ticket sales is not only the first achievement of the refined management, but laid the foundation for further the advancement of the refined management in the future.

The Palace Museum limited the visitor number 32 times in 2015 and 48 times in 2016. In 2017, during the summer vacation and other public long holidays, the limit of 80,000 visitors was implemented. Although fewer visitors visited the Palace Museum during peak seasons and holidays due to the limit, the total number of visitors throughout the year kept increasing year by year. It exceeded 16 million for the first time in 2016. It reached 16.7 million in 2017, 17.54 million in 2018, and 19.33 million in 2019. However, the number of visitors received in a single day throughout the year has been basically controlled. There was an effective "flattening the curve." Through the visitor number limit, the order of visits has witnessed significant improvement, and so has the tour environment. During the peak season the Palace Museum is not crowded, and during the off-season not deserted. And the safety of visitors, ancient buildings and cultural relics collections have been further guaranteed to meet the expectations as well.

While limiting the number of visitors, we strive to promote "shunting," which aims to shunt the visitors to different time slots of the day or year. Specifically, shunting tries to guide a great number of visitors on a certain day and a certain period of the peak season to the off-season, and those at a certain hour on a certain day to different time periods.

We hold the exhibitions just as well in the off-season. There are a series of free visits, such as free day for teachers, free day for medical staff, free day for sanitation workers, and free day for bus drivers. People have gradually realized that it is not bad to visit the Palace Museum in the off-season, and more and more of them choose the off-season to come.

January to March is the off-season for the Palace Museum. In the past, it used to receive only 20,000 to 30,000 visitors a day. From January to March 2019, we held

🖻 The Palace Museum realized total online ticket sales (October 8, 2017).

🖻 Forbidden City QR code verification system (September 1, 2014).

the *Lunar New Year—Celebration in the Forbidden City* exhibition, which attracted up to 80,000 visitors every day. Particularly exciting is that 50% of the visitors were young people. I am gratified that the younger generation is showing great interest in the ancient Forbidden City, in the Palace Museum that has been open for nearly a century. Many young visitors checked in the Palace Museum early in the morning, enjoyed the various exhibitions, and participated in interesting activities. It was not until the closing hour that they reluctantly left. I believe that is the cultural ambience that a museum should have.

The development of digitization and network technology strongly supports visitor flow shunting and limiting. On September 25, 2011, the Palace Museum began to pre-sell tickets online, and only 287 tickets were booked online that day. From 2011 to 2014, the annual online ticket sales lingered around 2% of the total. In June 2015, the trial of 80,000 visitors limit and real-name system began. In 2015, online ticket sales accounted for 17.33% of total sales. In 2016, the number increased to 41.14%. Since July 2017, the Palace Museum has comprehensively promoted online ticket sales, opening online sales of same-day tickets and on-site code scanning to purchase tickets. During the National Day holiday (the week of October 1) in 2017, it realized total online ticket sales for the first time. Thereafter, the Palace Museum has officially entered the era of "100% online ticket sales." In order to effectively implement the total online ticket sales plan, the Palace Museum upgraded the supporting systems and facilities during preparations, developed multiple ticket purchase channels, and guided the on-site visitors to purchase tickets several months in advance, thus gradually transforming from offline ticket purchase to online ticket purchase. Meanwhile, it has also developed an on-site ticketing solution. Tourists can scan the QR code with their smart phones to purchase tickets on the spot, and obtain ticketing assistance through the on-site ticketing service information desk and comprehensive service window.

At presents, the Forbidden City implements online reservations for all tourists, bidding goodbye to traditional on-site ticket sales. The daily quota is 80,000. If the quota is filled on a certain day, visitors have to choose other dates. This controls the peak and shunt those visitors who fail to make a reservation to the off-season or the days with relatively fewer visitors. At the same time, on the reservation interface, people can choose to visit in the morning or the afternoon, which divides the more concentrated flow of visitors on a certain day. Since the implementation of online ticket sales and the daily quota of 80,000 visitors, there are no longer huge crowds of visitors and long queues on holidays.

In the future, the Palace Museum will continue to improve the reservation system. A more refined visitor shunting scheme is going to be implemented, like part-of-a-day ticket sales. At that time, visitors can choose a specific time slot to enter the Palace Museum. This not only shunts tourists visiting the Forbidden City, but creates a better cultural space and visiting experience for them.

"Toilet Revolution" under Big Data

As science and technology advance, our service management is heading towards refinement, which is epitomized by the "toilet revolution."

For a long time, we received wide complaints that there were not enough toilets in the Palace Museum. Especially during the Golden Week and minor vacations, there were long queues at the toilets. This problem was not only constantly reported by visitors, but mentioned by some celebrities, experts, and scholars.

Allow me to share a story. On December 15, 2018, I was honored to win Cultural Figure of the Year in Influence China, People of the Year Awards. Mr. Huang Yongyu bestowed the award upon me. On stage, he asked me a special question. According to his recollection, he was a frequent visitor to the Forbidden City in the 1950s, when its toilets were called "River of Sand." In the blink of an eye, 60 years have passed. Recently, he often read about the new changes in the Palace Museum in magazines and newspapers, or heard them from friends, who described them as "major." Now that he is too old to visit it in person, he still wonders: "How are the toilets in the Forbidden City?"

This was a challenge for the Forbidden City staff. In recent years, we have noted that the problem of insufficient toilets was indeed serious, which wasted the precious time of the visitors and affected their mood. Especially female visitors had to queue for long times. There was a time when there were signs at the toilets that wrote "Ladies, please line up." But I have observed that some men were doing no better. They were taking care of the children while waiting.

Therefore, the work team of the Palace Museum conducted research and reached the conclusion that the number of toilets for women should be 2.6 times that of men.

To this end, we have added and adjusted the toilets of the museum. There was a serious shortage of toilets in the End Door Square, so we expanded the toilets there, and transformed a staff canteen into toilets for the visitors. In peak season, the toilets on the west side are exclusively for women, the toilets on the east side are half for men and half for women, and the toilets on both sides are 50 meters away. At present, there are 35 women's toilets in the Palace Museum. We ran a trial and it turned out to be successful. Even in the peak season, there are no longer long queues at the toilets. With the refined management concept, some old and tricky problems are readily solved. The "toilet revolution" in the Palace Museum is still going on. I believe that there are many visitors who are as concerned about the changes of the Palace Museum as Mr. Huang Yongyu is. And we invite all to "visit" out new Palace Museum toilets.

On this basis, we started to set up baby care rooms last year. It is inconvenient that mothers have to hide in corners to change diapers for their children and breastfeed them. Since there are maternity rooms at airports and train stations, why not set up them in the museums? We have set up a baby care room at the best location on the west side of the Gate of Heavenly Purity Square, so that mothers who come with their children to the Palace Museum can also enjoy the tour without embarrassment. From this, we have gained a deep understanding that all services must not be based solely on the convenience of the operators, but give priority to the convenience of the visitors. Targeted at this goal, there will be more solutions than problems.

In addition, 90% of the visitors to the Palace Museum are from outside of Beijing. After entering the Palace Museum, they often get disoriented. There are few and inconspicuous signs to guide the way. And the signs are not standardized and the instructions not helpful enough. Therefore, we have comprehensively upgraded all the signs in the Palace Museum, and unified their design to a style in harmony with the ancient architecture. In the first year, 512 signs were set up at three-way intersections, intersections, places with toilets, and places with exhibitions. As the open area expanded, the number of the signs continues to grow so that visitors know where they are and where are heading to all the time. With the advancement of digital technology, we have added electronic signs, which inform them of the latest information every day.

Serving visitors with special needs (May 17, 2015).

Baby care room (July 16, 2016).

◨ Forbidden City wall.

At the same time, visitors also listen to explanations as they walk, so we have upgraded the automatic explainers. At present, the automatic explainers of the Palace Museum are perhaps the most language-rich automatic explainers in the world. There are a total of 40 languages, including foreign languages, the languages of some ethnic groups, and local dialects, such as Cantonese and Hokkien. There is also expert version, children's version, and dialogue version. People can choose whichever they prefer. In addition, the way people receive information today keeps improving, so the Palace Museum has expanded the coverage of free Wi-Fi, so that visitors can use their mobile phones to independently obtain more information that they need. In short, the efforts to better serve them will never end. For example, with 5G in use, we will continue to explore how to use new technologies to better serve our visitors.

In March 2019, the Palace Museum and Huawei signed a strategic cooperation agreement to jointly build a 5G Palace Museum. There are two key objectives: to monitor the protection status of immovable cultural relics and movable cultural relics in all-dimensions and all-time, and to provide better service to the visitors. I hope that soon, when the visitors walk into the Palace Museum, they can find out how many exhibitions there are, what the content of each exhibition is, and where the exhibitions they want to see are, and how many people are in the exhibition hall on their smart phones. With one click, they can see the location of the nearest toilets, and their vacancy. Should they feel like sipping some tea, they can check on their mobile phones how many tea houses are open, what kind of tea is being served, and what new books are available. If they want to buy cultural and creative products of the Forbidden City, their phones enable them to know where the cultural and creative products are and how much they are in stock. In short, the Palace Museum has been trying to provide more accurate services to the visitors.

Today, before a Palace Museum tour, visitors can consult some visiting matters at the service center, receive a free map of the Palace Museum, watch its introductory video, and design their own visit routes on a touch screen, such as the routes to visit exhibitions or the routes to visit ancient architecture. The Service Center also provides wheelchairs for the elderly and the handicapped and strollers for the infants free of charge.

Everything we do is to give the visitors a better tour experience, so that they can fully enjoy the architecture, the exhibitions, and the culture and creativity of the Forbidden City . . .

No Entry for Foreign Guests' Cars, Either

―――

Before the implementation of the online reservation system, many people shared the impression that it was difficult to get into the Palace Museum. Especially in the peak season, it took half an hour or even longer to buy a ticket. When a ticket was purchased, there were more procedures to go through, such as ticket inspection, security check, and luggage storage. When all of these were complete, visitors were exhausted before the tour of the Palace Museum began. Having tried the experience myself as an ordinary visitor, I had to admit they did not exaggerate the fact. This situation had to change.

So, we made major adjustment of the ticketing process. The ticket price for the Forbidden City has remained unchanged for 20 years. It is RMB 40 in off-season, RMB 60 in peak season, half-price for those over 70 years old, and RMB 20 for students. There is no bank note with the denominations of RMB 40 and RMB 60. When visitors paid in cash, there was often change to give back, which slowed down ticket sales. At that time, the Palace Museum was not ready to implement total online ticket sales, so the solution was to open more windows for manual ticket sales. The added ticket windows were located in the Gate of Correct Deportment Square. Many people remember that the square used to be occupied by petty street merchants. Having taken over the square, the Palace Museum conducted a thorough clean up and used the building on the west side of the square as ticket windows, so that the number of ticket windows rose from 16 to 30, and to 32 on the busiest days. So, we could finally promise to the public: 95% of the visitors of the Palace Museum will be able to buy tickets within three minutes, and the waiting shall never exceed 15 minutes, even during the busiest holidays. I have repeatedly observed the situation on-site, and this

Visitors seats in the Forbidden City.

promise has indeed been kept. When there is less time spent on buying tickets, there is more time and energy to visit the exhibitions of the Palace Museum. This is not only an improvement of the visiting experience, but also encouragement and affirmation to those who have worked hard to organize the exhibition. It greatly benefits both the Palace Museum and the visitors.

Next, there was the lack of resting facilities. Since there was no resting place in the End Gate Square, visitors had to sit on the ground when they were tired. The huge square was filled with visitors sitting on the ground. This not only affected the environment, but also created obstacles for those who tried to move forward. More importantly, sitting on the ground was not a good way to rest. After observation, we found that their favorite place to sit was the tree wells. In order to enable everyone to rest with comfort, we have made 200 benches, each of which could hold three people. In total, 600 visitors could sit. In this way, nobody sat in the tree wells. We immediately filled the tree wells and made 56 sets of tree benches for the 56 trees on

🖻 Gate of Divine Prowess of the Forbidden City after the rain.

both sides of the road, allowing another 600 people to sit. Consequently, there are more places for the visitors to rest.

Inside the Palace Museum, it was equally difficult to have a rest. For example, there used to be plenty of iron railings and stone corridors in the Imperial Garden. When tired, visitors sat on the iron railings and squatted on the ground. Now a great number of iron railings have been removed, effectively expanding the viewing space, and dozens of seats have been added. To solve the problem of insufficient resting space in the Palace Museum, we have specially developed seats and tree benches suitable for the large visitor flow and in harmony with the historical environment of the Palace Museum. In the first year, 1,400 seats were customized. With the expansion of the open area, the number of seats continues to grow. People can rest with grace and comfort. Currently, 11,000 visitors can sit and rest at the same time at various locations. When well-rested, everyone will naturally have the strength and the mood to better immerse themselves in the culture of the Forbidden City.

After the Gate of Correct Deportment was improved, we began to improve the Meridian Gate Square. The entrance to the Palace Museum is the Meridian Gate. There are three gates on the front of the Meridian Gate, but common visitors in the past could only pass through the small gates on both sides, queueing for security checks and ticket checks. The middle gate was reserved as a courtesy for distinguished guests. As a result, there used to be long queues at the small gates on both sides. Visitors could only stare at the middle gate. They complained. I recalled that Buckingham Palace, Versailles, and the Tokyo Imperial Palace are also open to the public, except the motorcade of the VIPs could not directly drive in. It is a matter of visitor rights and cultural dignity. Therefore, the Palace Museum issued an announcement that no motor vehicle shall enter the Meridian Gate.

On April 26, 2013, then French President François Hollande and his entourage visited the Forbidden City. He was the first foreign head of state to get out of the car in front of the Meridian Gate. I approached and told him the story of the Meridian Gate. He gazed up at the majestic Meridian Gate ancient architecture complex, content to feel the splendor of the Forbidden City before entering it. Then, he walked with his girlfriend through the long gate into the Palace Museum, an experience that he will never forget. I always believe that the most important benefit of the Forbidden City tour is a rare cultural experience. When the distinguished guests get out of the car in front of the Meridian Gate, the first thing they see is the majestic Meridian Gate Tower, and the long walk into the Forbidden City through the Meridian Gate is mysterious because there is the common expectation for the greater spectacle that lies ahead. As they step out of the Meridian Gate and the Gate of Supreme Harmony Square meets their eye, the expectation is met. In the past, foreign heads of state who visited the Palace Museum entered it by car, missing part of the visiting experience. Having discussed with relevant departments, we canceled the practice of VIP motorcade driving into Meridian Gate. Today, the three gates on the front of the Meridian Gate are open to the public, greatly improving the reception capacity, and people no longer need to queue to enter the Palace Museum.

⬛ Hosting French President François Hollande (April 16, 2013).

⬛ Resting on the seats with the Irish Ambassador to China (March 1, 2017).

There are improvements in tickets and security checks, too. In the past, regarding ticket checks, the ticket checker inside the iron railing checked the tickets in the hands of the visitors outside the iron railings. Regarding security check, the security check machine was installed inside the Meridian Gate, which blocked half of the gate. Therefore, there was queueing for both the ticket and security checks. In the peak season, crowds filled the Meridian Gate. It was total chaos. In order to change this situation, both the ticket check railings and the security check machine were removed and relocated to the east and west sides of the Meridian Gate Square, therefore freeing up 12 times more space at the gate. As a result, there are never again overcrowded visitors at the Meridian Gate.

In short, after optimizing ticket sales, ticket checks, security checks, and adjusting the reception for foreign guests, the environment of the square in front of the Palace Museum has been significantly improved. In the past, in the less spacious Meridian Gate Square of the Forbidden City, people crowded together to buy tickets, go through ticket and security checks, and store their bags. At the time, loudspeakers used to broadcast: Mr. X, your child is waiting for you at spot X. For every visitor, before entering the Palace Museum, when their child is lost, they are definitely in no mood to visit it. Today, it only takes 8–10 minutes to enter the Palace Museum with a good mood and sufficient strength.

With the gradual expansion of the open area of the Palace Museum, the visiting hours have been prolonged. And it is necessary to provide more and better rest areas for the visitors. Back then, during the visit of the Palace Museum, visitors had to eat outdoors, which was neither graceful nor hygienic. For example, before the opening of the western part of the Forbidden City, the corridor of Gate of Thriving Imperial Clan used to be a fast food restaurant. It was unsanitary for people to dine there, and it was cold in winter and hot in summer. When the western area of the Forbidden City was opened, we canceled that fast food restaurant. However, a new dining area had to be re-selected nearby because about one-third of all visitors come to Palace of Compassion and Tranquility, Palace and Longevity and Health, and Garden of Palace of Compassion and Tranquility in the western area every day.

Under the circumstances that we can neither build temporary buildings nor make unreasonable use of cultural relics, after careful research we chose the ice cellar building complex of the Forbidden City. There are four ancient buildings behind a row of red parapets on the west side of the Gate of the Thriving Imperial Clan. They have no wooden structures, but the rare masonry structure in the Forbidden City. There used to be the imperial ice cellar. In the past, every winter, ice in the moat was extracted, cut into cubes of 1.5 by 1.5 *chi* (about 14 inches), and carried to the ice cellars for storage. Each ice cellar could store 5,000 cubes of ice, and four ice cellars 20,000 ice cubes. The walls of the ice cellar were two meters thick. When ice was moved in, the cellar was sealed. Ice was taken out in the summer for the royals to refrigerate food and adjust the room temperature. But in the past century, the ice cellar stored no ice, but served as a general warehouse.

During field investigation, we noticed that the building materials such as wooden boards, gasoline barrels, and cement stacked in the ice cellar had not been scientifically protected and utilized properly. Therefore, we repaired and conserved the ice cellar building complex and set up the Ice Cellar Service Center, where there is a reading corner, a tea house, a café, and a fast food restaurant to render high-quality services to the visitors. The Ice Cellar Service Center is less than 500 meters away from Hall of Supreme Harmony, and can accommodate up to 300 customers for meals and rest. Thanks to the fast food service, it can receive a group of visitors in an average of half an hour. During lunch hour, it can cater to thousands of visitors. When people dine and rest with comfort, they can also appreciate the charm of this complex of ancient architecture.

Following the same concept, the color steel rooms used as shops in Gate of Good Fortune were demolished, too. And the snack booths in the Imperial Garden were evicted. While eliminating fire hazards and increasing the space for visitor activities, the historical appearance of the ancient architecture was restored. In particular, a group of cultural and creative halls in harmony with the cultural ambience of the Forbidden City have been built in the East Changfang area. As the "last exhibition hall" of the Palace Museum trip, they realize the visitors' wish to "take the museum culture home."

Interior of the ice cellar restaurant.

Dishes at the ice cellar restaurant.

We have also set up cultural service area of the Forbidden City on the east and west sides of the Gate of Divine Prowess, integrating food culture, book culture, and tea culture in the Forbidden City. It charges no entry fee, and is not subject to the closing hours of the Palace Museum, thus more convenient for the visitors to feel the Forbidden City culture at a close distance.

The Palace Museum, as a public cultural facility, should be kept clean and tidy. Frankly, for the enormous Forbidden City, it is indeed challenging for it to be totally "weed-free" and "garbage-free," but when every corner of the Forbidden City is clean and tidy, visitors will consciously maintain it and stop littering at will, and the environmental quality is greatly improved. It is under this stringent or even impossible standard that the Palace Museum addressed the above-mentioned issues in a relatively short period of time. Practice has taught us that the environment can affect people.

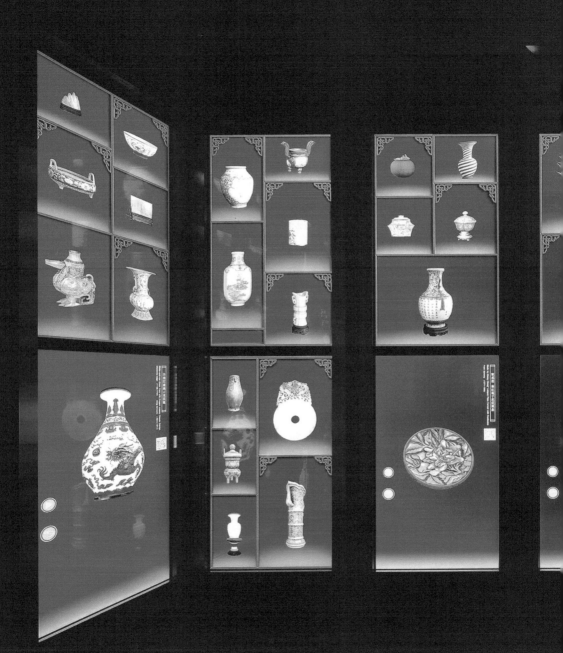

CHAPTER 6

Hundreds of Millions of Visitors

Some netizens sum up the official Weibo account of the Palace Museum as: when there is proper business, it issues a formal announcement; when there isn't, it posts pictures of itself. When there is, for example, an exhibition to be promoted or an event to be held, the Palace Museum's Weibo account announces it, but during ordinary days, it is busy with sharing pictures of itself. The series of beautiful pictures on its Weibo account, with strong and poetic expressions of the Palace Museum elements, presents to the public a living museum.

What the public wants to see, we show. A group of photos of the first snow in the Forbidden City in 2016 was posted attracted 14.25 million clicks. In 2017, before the snow fell, a red moon rose. At the time, on a business trip in Suzhou, I called, suggesting to take a group of photos of the Forbidden City in the red moon and post them on Weibo. They were viewed over 20 million times the next day.

After six years of hard work, we have developed 10 kinds of apps, each of which is an award winner. We therefore have received a fair evaluation from the media, "What the Forbidden City presents must be excellent."

Always Trending on Social Media

As the Palace Museum expands its influence, the number of visitors has soared, reaching an all-time high in 2019, exceeding 19 million for the first time. But we are aware that the annual visitors of the Palace Museum are a tiny fraction of the global population. Therefore, it is necessary to spread the culture of the Forbidden City wider through more ways.

Since 2011, social media platforms such as Weibo and WeChat have witnessed a boom. With the astounding advances of Internet technology and the development of new media, the Palace Museum has opened its official Weibo account and WeChat accounts. In 2011, as soon as the Palace Museum Weibo account was activated, it attracted millions of followers. In 2014, the Palace Museum opened the WeChat account Micro Palace Museum. Micro Palace Museum, in the micro language with the characteristic of the Palace Museum, organizes micro topics, holds micro exhibitions, and provides comprehensive, three-dimensional and convenient service for the visitors to see the ancient architecture, cultural relics collections, special exhibitions, etc. These social media accounts not only facilitate the public to visit the Palace Museum, but also spread its culture and the concept of cultural relics protection. And the public speaks highly of them. I was once informed that whatever the Palace Museum Weibo account posts will be trending. And Micro Palace Museum has indeed become a platform for many fans to learn about the Palace Museum.

We have noted that new media has become a good channel for the Palace Museum to communicate with a sea of visitors, and that the relationship between the two has evolved from one-way output to two-way communication. Every post receives millions of clicks, and thousands of comments and reposts. We are able to directly hear feedback from the visitors, understand their expectations, operate new media through research and visitor voting, develop a series of apps and cultural and creative products of the Forbidden City, and continue to improve the services.

The Palace Museum's Weibo has hash tagged the posts "four seasons in the Forbidden City" and "falling in love with the Forbidden City," made the kitten Strong the "spokescat" of polite visits, and published the widely popular comics "Cats in the Forbidden City." Every "security" cat of the Palace Museum has a name. Photographers took vivid photos of them and made them into postcards. And visitors vote on which cat gets to be on the cover.

When coloring games were the talk of the town, the Palace Museum selected some of the collected dresses and ancient architecture to be the subjects of line drawings, and visitors colored them. Next, a vote was organized on Weibo to let the public choose the best three colored works. The Forbidden City Publishing House, having noticed that the attempt was a success, designed and released a coloring book series *Coloring the Forbidden City*, which sold rather well.

In 2015, the series of photos *Phenology of the Forbidden City* with the theme *Twenty Four Solar Terms* were posted on the Palace Museum's Weibo and WeChat accounts. They presented a living historical site to the public and received millions of "likes."

Also, aware that the public wants to see the beautiful scenery of the Forbidden City more often, we often post pictures of the Forbidden City via the Weibo account. In 2016, a group of photos *First Snow in the Forbidden City* attracted 14.25 million

🖾 First snow in the Forbidden City.

clicks. In 2017, before the snow fell, a red moon rose. At the time, on a business trip in Suzhou, I called, suggesting to take a group of photos of the Forbidden City in the red moon and post them on Weibo. They were viewed over 20 million times the next day.

Of course, there is also the popular *Mysterious Palace Puzzle Book*. The book is not only the first creative interactive puzzle book by The Forbidden City Publishing House, but filled a gap in the Chinese puzzle book market. With ancient texts, it integrates the puzzle-solving content of Chinese style with the historical knowledge and culture of the Forbidden City, thus innovating the dissemination of its culture and knowledge. The uniqueness and innovation put the book in the spotlight before it was released. On October 24, 2018, the Palace Museum's Weibo post that the Palace Museum had published a mysterious ancient book quickly attracted five million views. By November 12, the number of views exceeded 19 million. And it received 22,000 likes. This is the cultural power of the Palace Museum fans!

Some netizens sum up the official Weibo account of the Palace Museum as: when there is proper business, it issues a formal announcement; when there isn't, it posts pictures of itself. When there is, for example, an exhibition to be promoted or an event to be held, the Palace Museum's Weibo account announces it, but during ordinary days, it is busy sharing pictures of itself. There is also a funny remark from a Weibo user: the Taobao account sells cultural and creative products to make a buck; the Weibo account keeps a reserved manner to make an impression. The series of beautiful pictures on its Weibo account, with strong and poetic expressions of the Palace Museum elements, present the public a living museum.

These many comments on the Forbidden City are a positive interaction between the Palace Museum and the netizens, as well as the general public. The public no longer sees the Palace Museum as a rigid teacher with a sullen face, but a close friend. Therefore, they are more than willing to give advice to the Palace Museum. Inevitably, there will be sometimes harsh criticisms, but it is these criticisms and suggestions that help the Palace Museum do better.

Our unsung heroes—the lovely new media team deserves a compliment. They are dedicated to studying the changes in visitor groups and updating the way of traditional culture dissemination. They have accurately grasped the interests of young people through flexible online and offline interaction methods such as updating official websites, making official Weibo posts, opening WeChat accounts, and marketing cultural and creative products. And they are promoting and spreading the broad and profound Chinese civilization in the form of rich connotation and fun. As a result, they have gained massive popularity among the young netizens, becoming a successful practice of the network dissemination of Chinese civilization. This series of practices shows that regarding the cultural communication of museums, as long as the psychological characteristics and interest preferences of online audiences are thoroughly studied, and flexible and diverse communication ways are figured out, we can turn caviar to the general to what is approachable.

Certainly, we will continue to do more. After the success of the official Weibo account and Micro Palace Museum, we continue to apply Internet technology to provide a variety of cultural services and experiences. The *Adept at Forbidden City* mini program co-developed with Tencent Map uses a "new method" to connect the "new public."

The *Adept at Forbidden City* mini program connects the scene-based service according to the map location with the real Forbidden City. It vividly displays the whole picture of the Forbidden City with a lively hand-painted panoramic map, and objectively restores the real architecture and various service facilities to the mobile phone map, thus fully meeting visitor needs when they visit the Palace Museum. Through the scene-based service based on geographic data, according to the changes of the crowd and the environment, the route can be intelligently customized. Combined with the easy use feature of the mini program, without complicated operations, it effectively innovates the museum's service mode, and comprehensively enhances visit experience.

🖻 Drizzling and blossoms in the Forbidden City.

In the *Adept at the Forbidden City* mini program, visitors can not only obtain important information regarding the opening hours and exhibition of the Forbidden City in advance, but also comprehensively understand the Palace Museum through accurate map services such as a general introduction and location search. And the "point search" plans routes for visiting points and service facilities such as buildings, exhibitions, restaurants, shops, entrances, and exits, so that visitors can quickly reach the desired destination during the trip, thus visiting more within less time.

In addition to the customized panoramic tour, quick tour, and detailed tour, which help the visitors save time and enrich the visiting experience, the mini program has specially launched the function of "checking in" for important buildings, which allows visitors to record their footprints and create their own "routes." For example, in the special route of "Looking for good luck in the Forbidden City," visitors can collect "lucky beasts" cards by clicking "checking in" at the marked locations and learn about their stories, or share the route to friends, or post the experience. When tired, they can chat with "the Minister," an artificial intelligence robot. There are 670 fun quizzes from *The Collection of Notes on Daily Life in the Qing Dynasty* and *Records of Qing Dynasty*, waiting for visitors to explore. The humor of "the Minister" may resolve some small troubles in the daily life of the visitors.

Popular Apps

The Palace Museum apps—what could be better? This is the evaluation from countless netizens.

On May 18, 2017, *Palace Museum Community*, our ninth app, was released. It aims to combine the rich cultural heritage resources of the Palace Museum with modern scientific and technological means through the exploratory construction of the museum's new digital ecological community, so as to provide the public with a more open and interesting interactive experience, and to create a Palace-Museum-style online living space.

As the ninth of the "Palace Museum" app series, *Palace Museum Community* is a brand-new museum app. Integrating more than 10 categories of cultural resources and service forms of the Palace Museum, including basic information, tour guides, architecture, collections, exhibitions, academics, and cultural creativity, it explores innovative models of digital cultural services.

In this app, users can build their own "house," their own "Forbidden City," become the "master," and create their own digital life online. The *Palace Museum Community* envisages improving the interactivity and fun of the user-generated content platform by gradually building a complete user growth system: experience points are earned by publishing articles, reading or liking other users' articles, and completing tasks; they are used to upgrade users' "exclusive mansion" as the display and communication space of personal creation. Through an online virtual city recreated based on traditional architectural elements, users are encouraged to experience the life with most classical features in a modern way. It is believed that enthusiastic users will learn more and more cultural knowledge of the Forbidden City through their continuous participation in the digital *Palace Museum Community* activities.

In the future, the *Palace Museum Community* will also be endowed with more creative space and interesting gameplay, revitalize the Forbidden City culture in this organic ecosystem, and continue to absorb more value.

In fact, this app is only one example of the many Palace Museum apps. It is widely acknowledged that the Palace Museum apps continuously go viral. In 2018, the new downloads of the Palace Museum apps exceeded one million, a year-on-year increase of 22%.

Before the *Palace Museum Community*, the Palace Museum released eight apps, which received wide praise. *Twelve Beauties* and *The Night Revels of Han Xizai* are some of the best apps of the year in Apple Store; children adore *Emperor's Day* and *Forbidden City Auspiciousness*; *Daily Forbidden City* allows users to appreciate one piece (set) of cultural relics collections every day; *Forbidden City Exhibition* enables users to watch the exhibition without leaving home. These apps, with their own characteristics, have won the hearts of the public.

The earliest released app, *Twelve Beauties*, won Asia's Most Influential Excellent Design Award at the DFA Awards. It was praised as "sophisticated and well-made." *The Night Revels of Han Xizai* app extensively adopts scientific and technological means to present a total of 100 content annotation points, 18 expert audio and video guides and one postscript. Also, it includes the performance of Han-Tang Yuefu Music Ensemble from Taipei that interprets the paintings with Nankuan, a style of Chinese classical music from the southeastern province of Fujian and an intangible cultural heritage, thus providing the users with a fresh and fashionable interactive experience.

All the rich knowledge contained in the app *Emperor's Day*, which was developed for children, is input after careful and in-depth research. Such academic research findings ensure a rich and forward-looking culture carried and disseminated by the cultural creativity of the Palace Museum. They embody the Forbidden City culture and the flavor of traditional Chinese culture.

Forbidden City Auspiciousness was first released in 2014. The combination of imperial culture and a fresh hand-painted style has won the hearts of the users. In June, when it was released, it was labeled best of the month and listed as editor's choice. It was also selected as one of the best apps of 2014. In 2018, *Forbidden City Auspiciousness* was upgraded to *Forbidden City Auspiciousness PRO*. Compared with the old version, *Forbidden City Auspiciousness PRO* has the following outstanding features: First, the content is richer. There is a stronger lineup of auspicious elements such as the dragon, phoenix, kylin (a legendary hooved chimerical creature that appears in Chinese mythology), turtle, lion, gourd, flowers (wintersweet, chrysanthemum, peony), chicken, magpie, pomegranate, Spring Festival, peach, crane, elephant, fish, mandarin duck, etc.; it creates the concept of an "auspicious island," which layer by layer goes deeper, and displays a total of more than 170 cultural relics of the Palace Museum. The second is the interaction with the cultural relics. Illustrated cultural relics are easier to understand. For example, when some cultural relics are enlarged for the first time, hidden knowledge points will appear on them, which are more visual than simple text descriptions; the "playing method" tailored for the cultural relics makes them more interesting. For example, there is the hanging heart aroma. Users can extract the structure of the "hanging heart," and see why no matter how it rolls, the center can always remain horizontal. Small surprises like this are hidden everywhere in the app, waiting for users to discover. Third, there is encyclopedic reading so that users can deeply feel the "beauty." There is cross-border combination of cultural relics and literature that enables multi-dimensional expression of artistic conception. For example, through the Song Dynasty painting *Group of Fish Playing with Algae*, the joy of fish that Zhuangzi sensed when watching them in Haoliang is depicted; "Beautiful and natural. Nature is biased when making them" perfectly depicts the purple and yellow peonies in Shen Kui's painting *Wealthy and Everlasting*; the incense burner giving off fragrance is described as "curls of smoke, ethereal; as they ascend, spreads a delightful smell." Sometimes the artistic conception of classical literature can better express how cultural relics make people feel. *Forbidden City Auspiciousness PRO* tries to

The Night Revels of Han Xizai app launch conference (January 12, 2015).

give users a deeper understanding of "beauty" through the beauty of cultural relics and writings, and to cultivate their ability to appreciate the artistic conception of works of art through aesthetic experiences.

As soon as the popular app *Daily Forbidden City* was upgraded to version 2.0, the number of downloads exceeded one million.

In 2016, at the Fourth International Forum on Cultural Heritage Protection and Digitization, *Forbidden City Series app + V Forbidden City* won the highest award in the first Digital Heritage Best Practice Case Competition—Best Practice Award. This probably attests to the public evaluation: what the Forbidden City presents must be excellent.

Website Redesign and Digital Showroom

The Palace Museum holds 1.86 million pieces of in its collection, and around 30,000 pieces are displayed through exhibitions every year. We provide visitors with a sumptuous feast for the eyes: there are exhibitions in the original forms, showing the historically realistic view by restoring the original state of the interior of the architecture; there are also thematic exhibition halls for cultural relics that display a single type of cultural relics, or multiple types of cultural relics under one specific theme. Of course, we understand deeply that it is impossible to exhibit everything in one day. Visitors must pay more visits, and this may be difficult for some visitors. Can we make it easier for them to visit?

In order to allow more people to fully understand the cultural heritage resources of the Palace Museum, in addition to Weibo, WeChat, and the series of apps it has developed, we have also upgraded the official website of the Palace Museum: making the English website more powerful, and the youth website more lively. In addition, we hold online exhibitions and open digital showrooms, so that people can attend the exhibitions of the Palace Museum remotely.

The official website of the Palace Museum underwent an upgrade in 2017. The flat page design combined tradition and fashion. It took the unique red walls, yellow tiles, red gates, and brass nails as the basic elements, and traditional patterns as ornaments, adding a classical artistic taste to the pages and forming the unique "Palace Museum aesthetics." The content structure was optimized and divided into sections such as tours, exhibitions, education, exploration, academics, and cultural creativity, making it easier and faster for visitors to find the information they want.

The Gate of Correct Deportment Digital Showroom and *Along the River during the Qingming Festival 3.0* are relatively representative digital showrooms. As new digital exhibition halls are built in traditional architecture, both of them allow visitors to enjoy more novel, more comprehensive, and deeper exhibitions.

The Gate of Correct Deportment Digital Showroom is located at Gate of Correct Deportment on the north side of Tiananmen Square and on the south side of the Meridian Gate. The Gate of Correct Deportment used to be an important royal building in the past. Together with the Forbidden City, the Imperial Ancestral Temple, and the Imperial Divine Temple, it was part of the "complete Forbidden City." After we set Meridian Gate as the only entrance, for many visitors, the Gate of Correct Deportment is the first stop of their Palace Museum tour. It is also the first business card that the Palace Museum hands over to the visitors.

The Gate of Correct Deportment Digital Showroom is a brand-new digital exhibition hall built in traditional buildings. It is different from but closely related to the physical exhibition hall. It fully highlights the technological advantages of the information age in the form of "digital architecture" and "digital cultural relics." In the digital form, it presents the fragile cultural relics that are difficult to be displayed among all precious cultural relics in the Palace Museum, or the content that is difficult to be expressed in physical exhibitions to the visitors. Also, it adopts new media interactive means to meet the range of needs of traditional culture, while ensuring the safety of the cultural relics. More importantly, it can stimulate the public interest in physical cultural relics.

In digital showrooms, the "digital sand table" is based on the high-precision panoramic three-dimensional model of the buildings. Through the dynamic demonstration and interactive control of the sand table, the digital tour is carried out with a vivid "three-dimensional digital map." The "Virtual Reality Theater" activates a highly immersive and interactive mode to help the visitors feel the charm of the Forbidden City and of traditional culture in astounding audio-visual effects. In 2015, to celebrate the 90th anniversary of the Palace Museum, we held the first digital exhibition with the theme "The Forbidden City is a Museum," which included three major sections,

⊡ Digital Belvedere of Treasures.

⊡ Digital Hall of Mental Cultivation.

"From the Forbidden City to the Palace Museum," "The Forbidden City Treasures, the Palace Museum Collections," and "Forbidden City—The Emperor's Palace." Through a complete streamlined visit, it introduced what the Palace Museum is, has, and presents from three aspects of its history, collections, and architecture. And we received enthusiastic responses towards the event. Although there is no physical cultural relics collection in the digital museum, the cultural heritage resources of the Palace Museum are vividly presented through digital technology.

On October 10, 2017, the exhibition "Discovering the Hall of Mental Cultivation: A Digital Experience," the second phase of the themed digital experience exhibition in *The Gate of Correct Deportment Digital Showroom* was officially opened to the public. It continues to uphold the innovative concept of "Internet +." The exhibition relies on the academic achievements of the special research on the Hall of Mental Cultivation, and adopts virtual reality, artificial intelligence, and human-computer interaction to make up for the pity that the Hall of Mental Cultivation was temporarily unable to receive visitors, as it was under research, restoration, and protection. Here, visitors can play the role of ancient craftsmen to paint on the purlin or vase, or the role of a high-ranking minister to discuss national affairs. In short, they can experience "One Day in Hall of Mental Cultivation" that condenses "government affairs, culture, and—daily life." At the same time, "Discovering the Hall of Mental Cultivation: A Digital Experience" was also designed both online and offline in combination with the Palace Museum's research resources, visitor preferences and technical advantages, especially the digital achievements over the years.

"Discovering the Hall of Mental Cultivation: A Digital Experience" was divided into four parts: introduction, interaction, experience, and review. The introduction gives the visitors a macro understanding of the history, structure and function of Hall of Mental Cultivation through the HD video of the digital sand table. Interaction included six programs: "summon the minister" simulated the scene where the emperor summoned the ministers and met the officials in Hall of Mental Cultivation. Visitors could conduct real-time Q&A with the "minister" through mobile phones; "review the memorials to the throne" simulated the scene where the emperor reviewed the memorials to the throne. Visitors could unlock the original copy of the memorials as they reviewed them; "appreciate the treasures" selected 90 pieces of collections and placed them in Belvedere of Treasures, and 49 of them were designed to be in-depth interactive activities; "Into the Hall of Sages" showed the Hall of Sages in the original form thereof. Visitors could move some collections in Belvedere of Treasures to the Hall of Sages or "pick up" the collections in the Hall of Sages for close appreciation; "cook imperial meals" enabled visitors to learn about the how an imperial meal was prepared and matching tableware was selected; "dress Qing clothes" gave visitors the chance to put together an imperial outfit of the Qing Dynasty, or "try it on"; in the "experience zone," they could put on VR glasses and walk into the virtual main hall and back bedroom of Hall of Mental Cultivation to have a highly immersive visual experience; "review zone" was the virtual reality theater, where visitors were played the video of the Hall of Mental Cultivation. Following the guide's introduction, they would see many rare details of the building, like the structure inside its roof.

Through various means, *Exhibition Discovering the Hall of Mental Cultivation: A Digital Experience* invited the visitors to enter Hall of Mental Cultivation to converse with history, experience it, and look back on it. When virtual reality meets the real Forbidden City, traditional culture and new technological elements collide and merge, igniting a dazzling spark. At last, *Exhibition Discovering the Hall of Mental Cultivation: A Digital Experience* won the Gold Award of the 2018 International Cultural Heritage Audio-Visual and Multimedia Art Festival and the Technical Innovation Award of the 2nd International Digital Heritage Case Competition.

In 2018, visitors who visited the north side of the Arrow Pavilion of the Palace Museum must have noticed a temporary shed there. In fact, this was "Along the River during the Qingming Festival 3.0," a high-tech interactive art exhibition, which we co-held with Phoenix Satellite TV.

In 2017, the Palace Museum exhibited *A Thousand Li of Rivers and Mountains*. In addition to the original work, visitors were amazed by the 3D picture scroll produced by Phoenix Satellite TV that served as the backdrop for the main exhibition hall. Inspired by this, the Palace Museum and Phoenix Satellite TV selected a legendary long scroll in

勤政親賢

一心裏而記為君止矣
仁二典傳

家法勤民三
公何私親四序偷時月
天及勤民三無凜然奉大

用其要以備身五事惟效
熙緒在祖六府賴

時省家慎私欲治八
備省惟愛人七情

珍育幸廿念彼紀倫
九歌政戒御彛倫

陳十聯書屏彞式聽
維以明直體

係譯綜持叙叙明直
乾隆慇懃面念至御

當為天下奉一人

惟以一人治天下

朱批奏折
MEMORIALS WITH
EMPEROR'S INSCRIPTIONS

◭ Review the memorials to the throne.

◭ Put together an imperial outfit of the Qing Dynasty.

the collections of the Palace Museum—*Along the River during the Qingming Festival* by Zhang Zeduan of Northern Song Dynasty for research and development. As one of the most famous national treasures, it is irreplaceable, and the most recognizable ancient Chinese painting in the world. This long scroll magnificently and delicately depicts the urban style of the Song Dynasty. It is truly one of a kind. From expansive land, babbling rivers, boats, bridges, shops and landscapes, to rivets on boats, merchandise from dealers, words on billboards, the painting has it all. The connected teahouses, the taverns and restaurants all over the city, the busy Bian River, the outings in spring and the crowds running around the city, and the foreign camel caravans full of goods altogether demonstrate the stunning prosperity at the time. Around 960 AD, GDP per capita of the Northern Song Dynasty exceeded that of Europe by about 30%. The capital city of Bianjing (present-day Kaifeng) held a population of over one million. It was the most populous city in the world at that time. Its economy, technology, and culture were best in the world. And *Along the River during the Qingming Festival* vividly depicts the wisdom of the Chinese nation. It is the epitome of prosperous urban life in the Northern Song Dynasty.

Faced with such a painting and cultural relic with extremely high artistic and academic value, how to balance the relationship between the original work, technology and art has made high requirements for the research and development team. This was the first time for China to re-research and re-create upon a national treasure painting through the integration of culture, art, and technology. It was a tremendous challenge. Around this priceless cultural relic, professionals from the Palace Museum Research Office, Data and Information Department, The Forbidden City Publishing House, Phoenix Satellite TV Linker Culture, and Phoenix Digital Technology have devoted themselves to the research, development and creation. And China's best artists, cultural experts, and high-tech development teams gathered and formed a special team to ensure that the exhibition presents the unique historical and cultural value of *Along the River during the Qingming Festival.*

The Palace Museum Research Office, as the general academic guide, participated in every step of the project research and development. Wang Lianqi, a research librarian of the Palace Museum and member of the National Cultural Relics Appraisal Committee, had multiple discussions about the form of the exhibition with the team members, and made necessary revisions to ensure the academic accuracy of the exhibition, so that the exhibition can best present the connotation and charm of the painting to the visitors. And the Data and Information Department of the Palace Museum applied its rich experience in digitizing and informatizing the Palace Museum collections to help the special team to combine high technology with art.

After a year and a half of trial and error, *Along the River during the Qingming Festival 3.0* was able to offer an immersive experience for the visitors by excavating the artistic charm, cultural connotation, and historical features of the original work, and integrating 8K ultra-HD digital interactive technology, and 4D dynamic images.

The exhibition hall occupied about 1,600 square meters. There were three exhibition rooms, including the huge interactive scroll of *Along the River during the Qingming Festival,* the Immersive Theater, and the Dome Cinema, in addition to a Northern Song Dynasty Humanities Space, which maximized the immersion and interaction of viewing the exhibition from various aspects and creatively presented the humanistic life of the Northern Song Dynasty. In the series of music chapters, the visitors could experience the various forms of life in Bianjing, the capital of the Northern Song Dynasty, from a first-person perspective. They could become characters in the long scroll, cross the Bian River where there were busy ships, and awaken the cultural memory in the humanity and elegance of the Song Dynasty. These historical information and artistic essences, which are difficult to perceive directly due to their long history, have become within reach in the multimedia exhibition hall of *Along the River during the Qingming Festival 3.0.*

Also, the visitors could study the exquisite structure of boats and buildings through the HD dynamic long scroll, observe the subtle expressions of the Song citizens, feel the advanced and developed Bianjing at that time; the Immersive Theater for the first time simulated and restored the customs, life, and music of the Northern Song Dynasty in a 360-degree holographic three-dimensional space. Outside the windows, the chatting and singing of the Song citizens echo in the air; after "strolling" in the lane full of surprises in spring drizzles, the visitors can also "board" on a big boat in the 4D dynamic Dome Theater to feel the river under their feet and the willow dance in the breeze, and admire the prosperity of the Bianhe River and the beauty of both banks. For foreign visitors, how *Along the River during the Qingming Festival 3.0* was presented enabled them to overcome language barriers and unfamiliarity with Chinese history and culture, and directly enjoy the immersive experience and the charm of Chinese civilization.

The high-tech art interactive exhibition of *Along the River during the Qingming Festival* has made the visitors realize that cultural relics can be imaginative and vibrant. We truly hope that when people talk about *Along the River during the Qingming Festival* in the future, they will think of not only the precious painting by Zhang Zeduan of the Northern Song Dynasty, but the high-tech art interactive exhibition jointly organized by the Palace Museum and Phoenix Satellite TV. When the high-tech art interactive exhibition *Along the River during the Qingming Festival 3.0* started, it indeed attracted public attention to the culture of the Palace Museum and cultural heritage, and once again refreshed the understanding of the Palace Museum from all walks of life.

Diversification of Digital Applications

The Digital Palace Museum is our new brand. The Palace Museum integrates excellent digital resources, adopts a variety of technological means, and continues to build the digital Palace Museum brand. It not only prepares a cultural feast for the visitors who enter the Palace Museum but also offers a new channel for those who cannot be present.

After three and a half years of hard work, we have built the Digital Palace Museum Community, which I believe is the most powerful digital information platform in the museum industry at present. It has a rich variety of functions of public education, cultural display, guided tour, consultation and communication, leisure and entertainment, socialization, academic exchange, and e-commerce. Moreover, new functions are under continuous development and improvement, and there will be stronger interactive functions, too.

Adopting cutting-edge digital technology, we have also developed our original digital museum, and made digital cultural products by digging deeply into the cultural information of the Palace Museum collections. Through the "digital map," visitors can learn the information of the 1,200 ancient buildings in the Forbidden City, browse the details of the 1,500 Forbidden City carpets, and make an imitation copy of the calligraphy works in the Forbidden City online.

VR (Virtual Reality) has played a key role in constructing the Digital Palace Museum. With this technology, the Palace Museum Cultural Assets Digital Application Research Institute has completed six VR works based on the theater environment: *The Forbidden City: the Emperor's Palace,* the *Three Halls,* the *Hall of Mental Cultivation,* the *Studio of Exhaustion from Diligent Service,* the *Spirit Pool,* and the *Corner Towers*;

two interactive experience projects based on virtual reality helmet equipment: the *Hall of Mental Cultivation* and the *Imperial Garden*; three webpage-based online interactive experience projects: the *Hall of Mental Cultivation,* the *Spirit Pool,* and the *Studio of Exhaustion from Diligent Service*. The Digital Palace Museum, by constantly trying new and innovative means of digitalization, shows the ancient buildings, cultural relics collections of the Palace Museum, and the historical and cultural knowledge behind them to the public.

At the end of 2018, the Imperial Garden, the seventh VR work of the *Forbidden City—Emperor's Palace* series under our *Palace Museum VR* project made its debut. For the first time, it adopted the best 3D engine in the industry to color the light and shadow of the Imperial Garden in the Forbidden City in real time, and created the 3D special effects to creatively present the whole picture of the Imperial Garden, thus fully demonstrating the different charms of the Imperial Garden at different hours of a day.

The *Imperial Garden VR* not only presents the true architectural style of the Imperial Garden in a visual way, but combines historical data to realistically restore the ecosystem of various vegetation, animals, pools, and rockeries in the Imperial Garden, such as the deer, fish, and begonia trees that were once raised there. While visually showing the historical appearance of the Imperial Garden, it also created a lively garden space. In the virtual world, a vibrant imperial garden was built. Even in the freezing winter, the virtual Imperial Garden embraces the visitors with the warmth of spring. In this innovative work, the interactive viewing method of simultaneous images on both large-screens and small-screens was adopted for the

▣ Into the Hall of Sages.

▣ Special opening event of the Gate of Correct Deportment Digital Showroom (December 18, 2015).

first time, revealing richer hidden knowledge to the visitors and offering them a more personalized in-depth experience.

In addition, we have also applied digital immersion technology in the popular *Lunar New Year—Celebration in the Forbidden City* exhibition at the beginning of 2019. It was held in the east room of the Palace of Heavenly Purity. Focused on the rich traditional Lunar New Year culture of the Forbidden City, it adopted digital technology, virtual images, and motion capture to implement innovative forms. Supplemented by interactive experience areas and cultural and a creative product matrix, it presented an open platform with multiple ends. The exhibition was divided into six parts: Ice Skating Paradise, Blessing of God of Doors, Blossoms of the Spring Festival, Opera and Paintings, Lanterns and Fireworks, and Happiness and the Auspiciousness. This exhibition practically implemented rich interactive display forms, and demonstrated the expressive power of visual interaction under traditional cultural context by adopting scientific and technological means. The auspiciousness and expectations contained in painting, calligraphy, and utensils were made visible in the immersive experience of the visitors. It was an innovative holographic visual experience of Lunar New Year in the Palace Museum.

For a long time, we only regarded whoever walked into the museum as the visitors, but the present "super-connected museum," through Internet technology and digital technology, has widened the scope to those who cannot physically enter the museum. As the new loyal museum visitors, they enjoy the museum culture. The Palace Museum will keep pace with the times, continue to carry out cultural and creative research and development according to how the public prefers to receive information and what the young generation needs culturally, and built a "Smart Palace Museum" at the end of 2020. In this way, the volume of visitors the Palace Museum can serve is expected to expand from tens of millions to hundreds of millions.

CHAPTER 7

Out of the Palace Museum

Today, the international influence of the Palace Museum continues to expand. Both UNESCO and the International Council of Museums have praised the Palace Museum as one of the "Five Museums in the World," a well-deserved title. What are the other four museums? They are the British Museum in the UK, the Louvre in France, the Metropolitan Museum of Art in the USA, and the State Hermitage Museum in Russia. What do these five museums have in Common? There are five permanent member states at the United Nations: China, the UK, France, the US, and Russia. There is one great museum for each state, which implies that unless you have a great museum, you have no chance to become a permanent member state of the United Nations.

In 2018, when asked what I expected from the cultural exploration program *National Treasure*, I joked about outperforming Dong Qing's program, *Reader*. Both *Reader* and *National Treasure* have become widely beloved cultural TV programs, which jointly spread the fascinating traditional Chinese culture. But I believe there is a difference between their audiences. *Reader* has achieved excellent TV rating, while *National Treasure* received a considerable number of views on online platforms.

More Approachable

———

Besides going to the exhibitions in the Palace Museum, is there any other equally effective way to let people learn about the Palace Museum and Chinese culture? Absolutely yes. In recent years, the Palace Museum has become more approachable through a series of TV programs and documentaries. It has truly reached every ordinary family.

At the end of 2017, a TV program called *National Treasure* broadcast by China Central TV went viral all over China. In this program, cultural relics "came alive" and museums got "closer" to the people. It made the Palace Museum, the cultural relics, and Chinese culture the talk of the town.

In fact, as early as the beginning of 2017, when the *National Treasure* shooting crew first came to the Palace Museum, the chief producer, Yu Lei, explained me the idea of this program. At first, I was very curious, because the creativity and concept of this show were never before seen in any previous domestic shows. This curiosity ignited everyone's passion. Nine Chinese museums (academies), headed by the Palace Museum, have joined forces to make this idea come true.

After the official release of the first season of *National Treasure*, both the enthusiasm of the audience and the social sensation have exceeded my expectations. Nine major museums, including the Palace Museum, Shanghai Museum, Nanjing Museum, Hunan Provincial Museum, Henan Museum, Shaanxi History Museum, Hubei Provincial Museum, Zhejiang Provincial Museum, and Liaoning Provincial Museum presented a total of 27 pieces of precious cultural relics and invited dozens of celebrities for better publicity. They worked hard to combine traditional culture with contemporary culture, to realize the modern transformation of traditional culture, and to narrate well the history of these cultural relics.

In the two months when the program aired, the "museum craze" expanded from the TV screen to the Internet, and extended to real life. The show soon attracted 800 million TV audience. On Bilibili.com, it received over 20 million views and was reposted in large numbers. Related fan-made videos on Weibo were viewed almost 400 million times. And it was rated 9.5/10 on Douban.com (a database like IMDB). After the program was broadcast, the number of visitors to the nine major museums (academies) increased by an average of 50%. Compared with the same period in 2017, their number of visitors increased by 13% during the Spring Festival in 2018. And since the program was broadcast in early December 2017, searches for domestic tourism products through "museums" have gone up by 50%. "Treasure hunt" has become the first choice for parents to arrange parent-child trips and learning trips. And the silver-haired are keener on cultural trips to museums.

When asked what I expected from the cultural exploration program *National Treasure*, I joked about outperforming Dong Qing's program, *Reader*. Both *Reader* and *National Treasure* have become widely beloved cultural TV programs, which jointly spread the fascinating traditional Chinese culture. But I believe there is a difference between their audiences. *Reader* has achieved excellent TV rating, while *National Treasure* received a considerable number of views on online platforms. In a way, behind the *National Treasure* sensation is the alliance of top Chinese cultural institutions. The cooperation between the museums and the television industry hopes to display and

At the recording of *Reader* on CCTV (November 1, 2017).

At the recording of *National Treasure—The Palace Museum* episode (November 1, 2017).

interpret traditional culture in a way that the audience is comfortable with, to interact with the expectations of the audience, to wake up the sleeping cultural relics, to give voice to the culture, the history, and the cultural relics, and to satisfy the cultural needs of the general public. And truly, *National Treasure* well kept the promise in the opening subtitle of each episode: bring the national treasures to life.

At first, I said to the *National Treasure* production team, "This show will run at least five seasons." They laughed in disbelief. Today, if I give them the same statement, they will not believe it, either. They must think, "only five?" In October 2018, the shooting of the second season of *National Treasure* started. One year ago, when the Palace Museum decided to cooperate with the *National Treasure* program, most of the eight museums that were also invited called to ask: Is it true that the Palace Museum is going to participate in a variety show? They would only join the program if the answer were positive. During the preparation the second season of *National Treasure*, none of the eight museums invited called the Palace Museum again, which we were a tad disappointed at. On the contrary, many museums uninvited to join the program called to ask when would be their chance to appear on *National Treasure*.

National Treasure is a cultural event. Behind the 27 cultural relics displayed in the first season are the outstanding traditional Chinese culture and Chinese spirit that have been passed down. I always believe that cultural relics have their dignity. To dignify them in physical space such as appearance, collection, and exhibition is the responsibility of we "gatekeepers" and "guardians," and their spiritual dignity requires mutual efforts. The program has attracted the audience to turn on their TVs and feel the Chinese charm behind these cultural relics, let more parents and children understand the spiritual origin of Chinese culture, and encouraged more people to walk into museums and immerse themselves in the five thousand years of Chinese culture.

In addition to *National Treasure*, there are some other TV programs with high ratings and wide public attention. For example, in 2018, we cooperated with Beijing Radio & Television Station and jointly produced a full-length cultural season program *Update—The Forbidden City*. It was a reality show where developers of new cultural and creative products and celebrity guests followed the Palace Museum cultural relics experts into the Forbidden City to explore the historical secrets of the precious collections of the Palace Museum, and to decipher their cultural codes. The program not only demonstrated the strong cultural vitality of the Palace Museum, but injected new cultural vigor to it by collaborating with well-known designers and design-major students in college to explore the best creativity. From a young perspective and with the carrier of cultural creativity, it integrated creative curiosity and imagination, and explored the Forbidden City in every person's mind. Every episode of the show made a series of cultural and creative derivatives popular, bridging a new connection between the public and the Forbidden City culture. Consequently, more young people get to take the Forbidden City culture home.

In fact, *Update—The Forbidden City* can be seen as the "pilot show" of the documentary, *The Forbidden City*.

The Forbidden City was produced to commemorate the 600th anniversary of the Forbidden City and the 95th anniversary of the Palace Museum. It was broadcast in September 2020. This full-length documentary supports the cultural succession of the Forbidden City, reaffirms the sense of mission of innovation of the times, and deeply explores the hidden corners of the imperial palace. It comprehensively presents a sea of precious cultural relics and documents, thus showing the profound history and great vitality of the 600-year-old Forbidden City. More people therefore get to understand the Forbidden City, the largest cultural relic, and its rich history and culture of over six centuries. The Forbidden City is a whole, one that embodies the Chinese cosmology, philosophy, and art. Only by interpreting it as a whole can we understand it more deeply and comprehensively. This documentary also provides a coordinate system for the public to understand every part of the Forbidden City. Otherwise, their understanding of it will be fragmented and unsystematic. In the past years, there have been some TV series or documentaries that depicted some palaces and courtyards in the Forbidden City. They have succeeded in attracting more young visitors to come to the Palace Museum and check out where their beloved characters in the series used to live. But some fragments are never better than the whole. We were looking forward to the release of this full-length documentary.

That the two programs of two forms and two temperaments present the same Forbidden City implies that the traditional theme of the Forbidden City holds inexhaustible cultural resources and sufficient space for various new expression. In addition to these two shows, the Palace Museum will further explore to show the Forbidden City in various artistic forms such as opera, drama, film, and TV series, so that its cultural charm is made seen in an all-round and three-dimensional manners. More importantly, it reflects the continuously growing power of the times while showing that the Forbidden City culture and the Chinese culture keep up with the times and that it holds a profound cultural and historical heritage.

It deserves a special introduction that there is a drama club called the Begonia Club in the Forbidden City, and the play *Begonia Still* dedicated to the Forbidden City. The founding of the drama club was inspired by the play *Begonia Still*, which was produced between the end of 2012 to the beginning of 2013 by the young Palace Museum employees. The play, based on the true story of the Palace Museum employees guarding the national treasures during the southward and westward relocation of the Palace Museum's collections from 1933 to 1948, depicts the devotion of the older generation of Palace Museum employees to protecting the national treasures. In 2013, *Begonia Still* was performed five times in the Palace Museum and received rave reviews. In October 2015, to celebrate the 90th anniversary of the Palace Museum, the play was performed live in front of Hall of Embodied Treasures of the Forbidden City. Thereafter, it was performed in Nanjing Museum and Gulangyu Concert Hall in Xiamen. In September 2017, the play was brought to the stage of Poly Theater of Beijing as a charity show to share this little-known history of the Palace Museum to more audiences.

Today, we are delighted to see that museum culture has become a part of popular culture. In the past, when tourists visited the Palace Museum, 80% would go straight along the central axis, enjoying the landscape without going to the exhibitions, but today the percentage is reversed when 80% of the visitors attend the exhibitions. Both the exhibition hall at the Sparrow Wing Towers of the Meridian Gate and at the Gate of Divine Prowess receive over 10,000 visitors every day, and sometimes 20,000 to

30,000. There are visitors from all over the world attending dozens of exhibitions in the Palace Museum held at the same time. With unremitting efforts, the Forbidden City has completed the transition to the popular Palace Museum.

For museums, what ultimately attracts and is conveyed to the visitors must be the stories behind the collection of precious cultural relics, the touching elements in their stories, and the spiritual wealth of the entire Chinese nation. It is necessary to help the public realize that these cultural relics are all just around them. All kinds of people are related to them. They are people's jobs, the hobbies, and lives. Some guard them with their lives, and some explore and study them throughout their lifetime. Some dedicated their lives to making them seen. They donate their private collections of cultural relics to museums, so that more people get to see them, and know what our ancestors have left behind.

Steps All over China

In addition to remote exhibitions in various channels and forms, the Palace Museum has also been working hard on physical exhibitions and on-site exhibitions in recent years to make its culture more accessible to the public in a variety of ways.

It is a common experience that every holiday, whether it is the minor vacation like the Labor Day and Mid-Autumn Festival, or the long vacation such as the Spring Festival, the National Day Golden Week (October 1), or the summer vacation, the Palace Museum is overcrowded. It is often reported in the news that the Palace Museum is in the top three among the most crowded scenic spots in China. But the crowding is inevitable, because the magnificent Forbidden City is permanently located in Beijing, and visitors have to come to the capital to see it. The architecture of the Forbidden City are immovable cultural relics, but the 1.86 million pieces (sets) of cultural relics collected in the Palace Museum are movable to certain degrees. In order to enable people all over the country to see and experience the Forbidden City, the Palace Museum has held a great number and variety of exhibitions in various regions of China in recent years.

For example, in 2014, *Precious Collections of the Palace Museum—Exhibition of Empress Dowager Cixi's Porcelains* was held in Xiamen Municipal Museum, *Evergreen—Exhibition of Emperor Qianlong's Secret Garden* in the Capital Museum, and *Jade Buddhist Statues—Exhibition of Buddhist Statues in the Northern, Sui and Tang Dynasties, Unearthed in Quyang* in the Shenzhen Museum. In 2015, there was *Exhibition of 99 Palace Museum Ruyi Collections* at Hebei Museum, and *Exhibition of Western Science and Technology in the Eyes of the Emperor* at Shandong Provincial Museum. In 2016, we held *Walk into Hall of Mental Cultivation* at the Capital Museum, and *Once in Mukden—Special Exhibition of Cultural Relics Relocated to the South of the Imperial Palace in Shenyang* at the Shenyang Imperial Palace. In 2017, we organized *Walk into the Hall of Mental Cultivation—Exhibition of the Strength of the Qing Dynasty* at the Nanjing Museum, and *Wise Emperor and Ministers—Special Exhibition of Paintings and Calligraphy by the Emperor Qianlong* and *Father and Sons of the Dong Family* in the Gongwang Art Gallery of Hangzhou. In 2018, we cooperated with Taiyuan Museum to hold *Imperial Charm—2018 Taiyuan—Palace Museum Cultural Relics Exhibition*, and participated in *Hometown Blooms——Exhibition of Qi Baishi's Works Returning Home* in Xiangtan Museum, and held *Fair and Merciful—Walk into Hall of Mental Cultivation* in Shandong Museum. These exhibitions have received strong support from local governments and museums, and were rather successful. In this way, the Palace Museum culture has entered the lives of more people.

It is noted that among the many temporary exhibitions in various places, several were related to the Hall of Mental Cultivation. In a way, we might as well call it the Hall of Mental Cultivation Tour across the country. As is well-known to all, being an important part of the overall maintenance and preservation project of the ancient architectures of the Forbidden City, the Hall of Mental Cultivation has been fully closed since 2016. The Palace Museum has formulated a five-year maintenance and preservation plan for it. Aimed at research-oriented conservation, the Palace Museum conducts related academic studies around the Hall of Mental Cultivation area. It strives to preserve the historical information of Hall of Mental Cultivation, to keep the original state of its ancient architecture and cultural relics, and to combine the display of original forms with thematic exhibitions to improve the exhibition effect of the Hall of Mental Cultivation area. Meanwhile, as the Hall of Mental Cultivation was under repair, the cultural relics in it were selected for exhibitions with distinct themes, thus the temporary exhibitions in various museums. For the first time, the cultural relics in the Hall of Mental Cultivation went out of the Forbidden City, and more people could have a deep understanding of the history behind it and appreciate its fine cultural relics.

In a way, this type of exhibition not only makes up for the inaccessibility to the Hall of Mental Cultivation area during the research-oriented conservation, but helps the public understand its value, protection, and management, and attract their attention to and stimulate their interest in cultural heritage. Certainly, this type of exhibition was a success. In the future, it will continue to be used.

Recently, in order to promote the cultural dissemination of the Palace Museum, the Palace Museum has actively sought cooperation with diverse partners. While promoting our colorful exhibitions across the country, we have also "taken root" in some provinces, autonomous regions, and municipalities. For example, the Palace Museum and Xiamen City co-built the Gallery of Foreign Cultural Artifacts from the Palace Museum Collection.

In 2014, the Palace Museum and Xiamen Municipal Government officially launched a joint construction project on Gulangyu Island. After over two years of intensive preparations, the Gulangyu Gallery of Foreign Artifacts from the Palace Museum Collection opened on May 13, 2017. Located in the old site Salvation Hospital and Nursing School on Gulangyu Island in Xiamen, it covers a floor area of 11,000 square meters and a building area of 5,180 square meters. This was the first time that the Palace Museum set up a locally themed branch.

Why built a gallery of foreign cultural relics? China is an ancient civilization that has never in history looted nor stolen cultural relics from other countries. Meanwhile, under economic limitation in history, Chinese museums were unable to collect large numbers of cultural relics from other countries. Therefore, Chinese museums have only collected and displayed Chinese cultural relics, and rarely foreign pieces from all over the world for a long time. But the Palace Museum is an exception in this regard. As the Imperial Palace of the Ming and Qing Dynasties, the Forbidden City used to receive foreign diplomatic corps, and there were Western craftsmen and artists working for the royal family, so it hoarded a great quantity of exotic handicrafts and daily necessities. Collected in the Palace Museum, they are the witness of the past exchanges between China and foreign countries.

⬥ An exclusive interview with CCTV's *Face to Face* at Gallery of Foreign Artifacts of the Palace Museum on Gulangyu Island (May 13, 2017).

⬥ The opening ceremony of Gulangyu Gallery of Foreign Artifacts from the Palace Museum Collection (May 13, 2017).

Gulangyu Island has always enjoyed the reputation of "world architecture exposition." There are exotic architectural relics that reflect the humanistic environment of modern China and the world intermingling on the island. The establishment of Gallery of Foreign Cultural Artifacts from the Palace Museum Collection there gives people the chance to appreciate world culture and understand the history of Sino-foreign exchanges. It is also the Palace Museum's contribution to the Belt-and-Road Initiative.

In 2017, the first exhibition of the Gulangyu Gallery of Foreign Artifacts from the Palace Museum Collection presented a total of 219 pieces (sets) of cultural relics. These exhibits covered various categories such as lacquerware, pottery, porcelain, glassware, enamelware, metalware, embroidery, painting, book, sculpture, furniture, clocks and watches, and technological instruments from the UK, France, Germany, Switzerland, Russia, Italy, Austria, the U.S., Bulgaria, Japan, and North Korea, etc. Most of them used to be the imperial possessions of the Qing Dynasty, and some were collected from the public or donated by individuals. Their history spanned from the 16th century to the early 20th, and most were from the 18th and 19th centuries.

One organ displayed at this exhibition is the best preserved among the pipe organs collected in the Palace Museum. It had never been exhibited before. It was chosen because Gulangyu Island is known as the Island of Music. The instrument has an elegant shape and a complete internal structure. Its front is decorated with golden floral patterns. The readable text on the organ says that it was produced by the Limonaire Brothers, located at 166 Daumesnil Street in Paris. Rumor has it that when strings are blown with the tremolo, the air is sealed in the bellows, where there are a wooden whistle, metal whistle, and trumpet set up on the bellows. Under the impact of the air flow, they make sounds. It is able to play nine pieces of music. And a man figurine and a woman figurine standing on the columns together strike the bells.

In addition to cultural relics from Europe, Gulangyu Gallery of Foreign Artifacts from the Palace Museum Collection exhibited shippō from the neighboring country of Japan for the first time. Japanese shippō and Chinese cloisonné are in fact the same type of object that has over a hundred years of history. They share a common name—enamel. There are several exquisite pieces of shippō shipped from the Palace Museum this time, such as the beige bamboo-chicken-patterned shippō, fired in Japan at the end of the 19ᵗʰ century. It has a copper body, a flat bottom, a gray floor, and vivid patterns of sparse bamboo in which hens take care of chicks. And the blue flower-patterned shippō bottle's whole body is painted blue and patterned with flowers.

Among the Western clocks and watches exhibits, there is a ship-shaped barometer. This industrial model barometer can tell temperature and humidity. It has the most popular shape for instruments in France at the end of the 19ᵗʰ century. It was produced in France and distributed in China by the Swiss Ullmann trading company. It is shaped like a ship, with the hull placed on a marble base. There are two cylinders on the deck. A single two-handed clock is embedded in the front cylinder, a barometer in the back, a thermometer in between, and a compass on the top. What's more unique is that when it works, the cylinder rotates clockwise, as does the propeller at the stern.

In addition to Gulangyu Gallery of Foreign Artifacts from the Palace Museum Collection on Gulangyu Island in Xiamen, the Palace Museum has also set up the Hong Kong Palace Museum in West Kowloon, Hong Kong. In recent years, there have been more frequent exchanges between the Palace Museum and cultural and educational institutions of Hong Kong. For example, from July to October 2013, it held the exhibition titled *Imperial Dresses of the Qing Dynasty* in the Hong Kong Museum of History exhibition; from June to September 2014, it attended the exhibition *Extraordinary: Travel through Time and Space to See the World* in Hong Kong Cultural Museum; from June to September 2015, it held *Western Implement—Science and Technology Exhibition of the Qing Dynasty* at Hong Kong Science Museum; in November 2016, it attended the opening ceremony of *Imperial Wedding—Qing's Emperor's Wedding Celebration* at Hong Kong Heritage Museum, which lasted until February 2017; in 2017, during the 20ᵗʰ anniversary of the establishment of the Hong Kong Special Administrative Region, *Residence of Eight Emperors—Exhibition of Cultural Relics of Hall of Mental Cultivation,* and the exhibition named *Long Live the Imperial Family—Birthday Celebrations of Emperors and Empresses of the Qing Dynasty* were held in Hong Kong, attracting hundreds of thousands of local citizens and tourists. Hong Kong citizens have showed their strong interest in traditional Chinese culture.

📷 Opening Ceremony of the Western Implements—Science and Technology Exhibition of the Qing Dynasty at Hong Kong Science Museum (June 25, 2015).

Based on the long-term close cooperation between the Palace Museum and the Hong Kong museums, both the Palace Museum and the Hong Kong SAR Government hope to take advantage of each other's strengths to further bolster cooperation in the fields of exhibition, research, and education. In September 2015, I discussed with the then Chief Secretary for Administration of the Hong Kong SAR Government, Carrie Lam Cheng Yuet-ngor, about the feasibility of building a museum in Hong Kong to permanently display the Forbidden City culture and traditional Chinese culture. Next, both parties conducted a feasibility analysis on the proposal.

On June 29, 2017, President Xi Jinping attended the signing ceremony of the Cooperation Agreement for the Construction of the Hong Kong Palace Museum in the West Kowloon Cultural District of Hong Kong, marking the official launch of this significant project. The West Kowloon Cultural District is the largest cultural investment in Hong Kong's history. Following the signing of the cooperation agreement, the detailed design of the Hong Kong Palace Museum commenced and construction started in 2018 with completion scheduled for 2022.

As per the Cooperation Agreement on the Construction of the Hong Kong Palace Museum, the cultural relics exhibited by the Palace Museum in the Hong Kong Palace Museum are divided into permanent long-term exhibitions and special temporary exhibitions. The exhibition period of permanent exhibitions is usually one year. Appropriate extension may be applied as per the exhibition needs and national regulations. There will be no less than 600 pieces (sets) of cultural relics in these permanent exhibitions. The cultural relics exhibits at the Hong Kong Palace Museum will receive proper repair and maintenance, so that they are displayed to Hong Kong citizens in a healthy state. Where maintenance is required during the exhibitions, the Palace Museum will send "doctors" from the Palace Museum Cultural Relics Hospital to Hong Kong.

In addition, the Palace Museum will also develop an app that explains the details and cultural connotations of the collections, so that Hong Kong citizens can attend the exhibition through their mobile phones. Based on the characteristics of Hong Kong and the content of the exhibitions, a series of cultural and creative products will be designed, so that visitors can "take the Forbidden City culture home" after the exhibitions. In the meantime, the completed Hong Kong Palace Museum will make full use of high technologies to present a three-dimensional museum culture to the public. It will continue to expand the functions, including opening lectures regarding the Palace Museum knowledge to all teenagers, organizing forums regarding the Forbidden City culture for the public, and offering newly published books with the theme of Forbidden City culture and newly developed cultural and creative products of the Palace Museum, etc. Through public education, cultural exhibitions, tour guides, consultation and communication, leisure and entertainment, and e-commerce, Hong Kong Palace Museum has evolved into a cultural space with comprehensive and diverse culture, an exhibition space of the Forbidden City culture with unique traditional Chinese cultural characteristics.

Lately, there have been a growing number of museums in China, but few of them can attract visitors to attend exhibitions. Some museums are deserted. High-quality museums and high-quality exhibitions are concentrated in certain cities, and there is still imbalance in cultural supply between eastern China and western China and between urban areas and rural areas. Stronger cooperation between museums can lead to positive outcomes such as resource sharing, complementary advantages, personnel exchanges, and the healthy development of Chinese museums.

The Palace Museum has been taking advantage of its rich collection of cultural relics to help other Chinese museums hold exhibitions by lending them exhibits. We have not only helped provinces, autonomous regions, and municipalities directly under the central government hold exhibitions by lending them exhibits, but offering them experience. We have shared our experience in ancient architecture protection, cultural relic restoration, collection exhibition, digital display, cultural relics, and museum publicity, talent training, and cultural and creative product development with museums and cultural heritage protection departments around the country. For example, in terms of cultural creativity, the Palace Museum has established the Huizhou traditional handicraft workstation in Huangshan City, Anhui Province, to promote the inheritance and innovation of Huizhou traditional handicrafts, and to enhance their brand. There is another example that in March 2018, the Palace Museum Cultural and Creative R&D and Exchange Center was founded in Pingyao, Shanxi Province. Together with the local government, it aims to turn Pingyao into a "new highland" for the Chinese cultural and creative industry.

◉ Carrie Lam Cheng Yuet-ngor, Chief Executive of the Hong Kong SAR Government, visits students from Hong Kong and Guangdong at the Palace Museum Youth Internship Program (August 6, 2017).

◉ Hong Kong Phoenix Satellite TV interviewed me at the exhibition *Long Live the Imperial Family—Birthday Celebrations of Emperors and Empresses of the Qing Dynasty* (June 30, 2017).

"Standard Configuration" for Permanent Member States of the UN Security Council

Today, the international influence of the Palace Museum continues to expand. Both UNESCO and the International Council of Museums have praised the Palace Museum as one of the "Five Museums in the World," a well-deserved title. What are the other four museums? They are the British Museum in the UK, the Louvre in France, the Metropolitan Museum of Art in the USA, and the State Hermitage Museum in Russia. What do these five museums have in Common? There are five permanent member states at the United Nations: China, the UK, France, the U.S., and Russia. There is one great museum for each state, which implies that unless you have a great museum, you have no chance to become a permanent member state of the United Nations.

As a world-class museum, it should continue to take a variety of exhibitions around the world, and to bring excellent exhibitions from museums around the world into the Palace Museum.

Since Exhibition of Cultural Relics Unearthed in the PRC to the 40th anniversary of reform and opening up, the Palace Museum has organized over 200 major cultural relics exhibition and exchange projects, leaving footprint in over 30 countries across five continents. It received more than 100 million viewers. Wherever the Palace Museum cultural relics exhibition goes, there is a cultural sensation. The exhibitions become talk of the town. There has been: *National Treasures—Exhibition of the Best Cultural Relics of the Palace Museum* held in Japan in January 2012, *Heavenly Gems—Jade Civilization Exhibition* held in Mexico in March 2012, *Imperial Glamour—Exhibition of Imperial Life Art of Qing Dynasty* held in Germany in October 2012, *Exhibition of Famous Ancient Chinese Paintings* held in the UK in October 2013, *Imperial Treasures—*

Exhibition of Ming and Qing Court Life Cultural Relics held in Canada in March 2014, *The Forbidden City—Exhibition of Imperial Treasures in the Palace Museum* held in the U.S. in October 2014, *Exhibition of the Prosperous Qianlong Years* held in Australia in March 2015, *The Prosperous Age—Exhibition of Imperial Art of the Qing Dynasty* held in Chile in September 2016, *Evergreen—Exhibition of the Glory of the Qing Dynasty* held in Finland in April 2017, *Pen and Sword—Exhibition of the National Strength under Different Emperors of the Qing Dynasty* held in Morocco in July 2017, and *Glorious Days—Exhibition of Cultural Relics of Palace of Double Magnificence Its Original Form* held in Greece in September 2018, etc.

Meanwhile, we have also cooperated with many countries and regions around the world to introduce their exhibitions to the Palace Museum, so that Chinese can appreciate civilizations from all over the world without leaving the country. Especially, when the enormous exhibition hall of Sparrow Wing Towers at the Meridian Gate was completed, there is a better environment for the exhibitions from foreign museums.

For example, in 2016, the Palace Museum and the National Museum of India well-orchestrated *Brahma and East Earth: A Sino-Indian Sculpture Art Exhibition from 400 to 700 AD*, which displayed sculpture cultural relics from nine Indian museums and 17 Chinese museums in China in the exhibition hall of Sparrow Wing Tower of the Meridian Gate. It was the first time that China has conducted comparative display of ancient Chinese and Indian sculpture arts of the same period. The exhibition makes an important part of cultural exchanges between China and India. After the exhibition in the Palace Museum ended, it toured in museums in Fujian, Zhejiang, and Sichuan along the Silk Road and the Maritime Silk Road to further promote and spread the cultures of China and India.

For another example, in 2017, the Palace Museum introduced the exhibition *Born of Fire—Exhibition of Treasures from the National Museum of Afghanistan*. Following the main thread of four archaeological discovery sites, it presented the history of Afghanistan from the 3rd century BC to the 1st century AD to the public through 231 Bactrian treasures saved by Afghan cultural relic experts. They witnessed the early days of the Silk Road. This was the first exhibition of cultural relics of Afghanistan held in

🖼 *Born of Fire—Exhibition of Treasures from the National Museum of Afghanistan*, held in the Palace Museum in 2017.

China. It not only showed the checkered history of the Afghans in protecting precious cultural relics, but symbolized the recovery and progress of Afghanistan. The exhibits of different periods of the Silk Road also presented the history of friendly exchanges between China and Afghanistan to the Chinese people, thus encouraging them to think deeply of cultural heritage protection. Since 2017, the exhibition toured around Chinese museums in Beijing, Dunhuang, Chengdu, Zhengzhou, Shenzhen, etc.

Recently, the number of exhibitions from all over the world held in the Palace Museum has been going up year by year. For example, there was *Glamour—Exhibition of Treasures from the 18th Century* held in 2017, *Princess Sissi and Hungary: The Life of Hungarian Nobles in the 17th and 19th Centuries, The Rarest—Al Thani Collection Exhibition of Qatar* held in 2018, *Nobleness—Exhibition of the Grimaldi Dynasty of Monaco, Relics of the Aegean—Exhibition of Underwater Archaeological Relics of*

Antikythera, Greece, and *Flowing Colors—Exhibition of Ukrainian Museum Cultural Relics*, etc. These exhibitions covered a wide range of themes and presented rich content. Every time a foreign exhibition is introduced, wide social attention will be attracted. Visitors flocked in the Palace Museum to check out the exoticness. The Palace Museum has therefore become a window for international cultural exchanges.

We have also established strategic partnerships with important international cultural relics museums, research departments, and government agencies, and signed memorandums of forgiveness and cooperation framework agreements. We planned to bridge extensive cooperation of various forms in exhibitions, cultural relics protection, restoration, and research, archaeology, education, training, digitization, cultural and creative product research and development, etc. In fact, we have built close partnerships with the British Museum, the Metropolitan Museum of Art in New York, the State Hermitage Museum in Russia, the Kremlin Museum in Russia, the Louvre in France, Dresden State Art Collection in Germany, National Gallery of Victoria in Australia, Royal Ontario Museum in Canada, the Tokyo National Museum in Japan, the National Museum of Korea, the National Museum of Iran, the National Museum of India, and the National Museum of Indonesia. Simultaneously, the Palace Museum has also strengthened exchanges with all parties by regularly holding the Forbidden City Forum and Forum on Protecting the World's Ancient Civilizations, where it shares the achievements of ancient civilization protection.

Moreover, the Palace Museum also holds quite a few major foreign events every year, where foreign guests get to experience Chinese culture during their tour of the Palace Museum. In recent years, it has actively hosted major activities with wide influence, which has resulted in the deeper understanding of museum peers from more and more countries and regions about the Palace Museum. Since 2015, it has repeatedly become an important venue for Party and state leaders such as President Xi Jinping and Premier Li Keqiang to receive foreign guests and host international events. From 2015 to 2017, it received nearly 200 groups of over 3,000 state guests, including French Prime Minister Manuel Valls, German President Joachim Gauck, Canadian Prime Minister Justin Trudeau, and Prince William of England.

Memorandum of Forgiveness signed with the British Museum (October 15, 2012).

故宫博物院

新卫城博物馆
The Acropolis Museum

Closing ceremony of Taihe Forum on Protecting the World's Ancient Civilizations (September 21, 2017).

On May 15, 2017, Peng Liyuan, the First Lady of China, invited the spouses of the foreign delegation leaders who attended Belt and Road Forum for International Cooperation to visit the Palace Museum. The guests took a group photo in front of the Hall of Supreme Harmony, and attended the exhibition of Belt and Road-themed cultural relics collected in the Palace Museum. In the Imperial Garden, the guests visited the exhibition area of the Intangible Cultural Heritage in Beijing, enjoyed dance, the guqin, tai chi, a cappella chorus, and Peking Opera performances, and experienced the time-honored Chinese culture together as well as the people-to-people exchanges between China and the countries along the Belt Road Initiative route for thousands of years.

Trump Visited the Palace Museum

On November 8, 2017, U.S. President Donald J. Trump visited the Palace Museum.

That day, President Trump and his wife Melania, who were visiting China for the first time, arrived in Beijing. After the plane landed, they were chauffeured straight to the Forbidden City and visited the Palace Museum in the company of President Xi Jinping and first lady Peng Liyuan. The Forbidden City witnessed the historic meeting between the heads of China and the U.S.

Throughout history, the Forbidden City, having received American presidents and dignitaries many times, is of special significance in Sino-US relations. In July 1971, Henry Kissinger, then U.S. National Security Adviser, paid a secret visit to China. Of his 48-hour stay in China, he arranged four hours to visit the Forbidden City, which was his only outing during the trip. In February 1972, when then U.S. President Nixon visited China, he also visited the Forbidden City. In 1998, then-U.S. President Bill Clinton visited the Forbidden City with his family during his trip to China, and called it spectacular. In November 2009, then-U.S. President Barack Obama made his first visit to China after taking office and entered the Forbidden City as well. The *Associated Press* commented on Obama's visit to the Forbidden City that visiting the places of interest in China showed the leader's respect for the Chinese culture.

Former U.S. President Donald Trump received high standards during his state visit. Trump and First Lady Melania visited the Forbidden City, attended exhibitions, enjoyed Peking Opera, and sipped tea with President Xi Jinping and the First Lady of China in the Baoyun Building. They "repaired cultural relics" together. It was a peaceful and friendly moment. Traditional Chinese culture became the bridge and bond of two great powers on both sides of the Pacific.

President Xi Jinping is not only familiar with all aspects of traditional Chinese culture, profoundly knowledgeable, and skillful, but has a deep understanding of the Forbidden City culture and the current situation of the Palace Museum, which impressed me greatly. Whether it is the historical figures and events, cultural resources and space of the Forbidden City, the ancient architecture, the cultural relics collections, the historical environment, or the future development of the Palace Museum, President Xi was able to explain to President Trump, who exclaimed: "This is great!" and was in awe of Chinese history and culture.

I noticed that Trump showed great interest in several sites. The first was the area of the Hall of Supreme Harmony, the Hall of Central Harmony, and the Hall of Preserving Harmony. From the Gate of Supreme Harmony to the Hall of Supreme Harmony, he was astonished by the grandeur of the Forbidden City complex. The second was the Cultural Relics Hospital, where he witnessed the professionalism and fantastic skills of the Palace Museum craftsmen. He was deeply impressed to see the "revival" of the severely damaged cultural relics. The third was the Belvedere of Pleasant Sound stage. The environment of Chinese traditional culture and the wonderful performance of the Peking Opera, the quintessence of China, dazzled the Trumps.

Afterwards, he tweeted to thank President Xi and First Lady Peng for the unforgettable visit to the Forbidden City in Beijing, and for their kind invitation for them to visit China. He also changed the background of his Twitter homepage into a photo of the four of them in front of the Belvedere of Pleasant Sound. In the photo, they are smiling and standing in the middle with the Peking Opera performers around. It was a lovely moment. Certainly, this trip has brought Trump joy and left him a deep impression.

President Trump's visit to the Forbidden City is unprecedented in four aspects: the highest standards, the longest time, the largest scope, and the most content.

The Palace Museum was able to undertake this reception because through unremitting efforts, it has become a dignified and respectable cultural space that strives to display the unique charm of Chinese culture in various ways.

⬛ President Trump and the First Lady visited the Palace Museum Cultural Relics Hospital.

In the Cultural Relics Hospital of the Palace Museum, the two heads of state and their spouses watched how paintings and calligraphy, furniture, woodenware, ceramics, textiles, metalware, and other cultural relics were restored, tried the restoration of paintings and calligraphy themselves, and attended the exhibition of the restored cultural relics in the Palace Museum. In particular, the restorers showed them several clocks and watches that had been fully restored, such as the copper-and-gold-gilded stone-inlaid tower clock, copper-and gold-gilded gourd-bottle-shaped flower clock, copper-and-gold-gilded music water clock, and activated their musical functions to put on a wonderful audio-visual performance for the guests. Meanwhile, they introduced them the repairing techniques of the Forbidden City's western clocks, taking the copper-and-gold-gilded wooden tower triangular clock and the copper-and-gold-gilded music box clock with double-horse base under repair as examples.

In the embroidery cultural relic restoration studio, the two heads of state and their spouses stopped in front of an 18th-century bright yellow kesi imperial robe, which was the dress of Emperor Qianlong's favorite empress in the Qing Dynasty. She mainly wore it during major celebrations and rituals. It contains the most exquisite craftsmanship, and is very precious.

In the paintings and calligraphy restoration studio, they together experienced an important step of the national intangible cultural heritage—restoration of the mounting of ancient paintings and calligraphy. There is an old Chinese saying that the beauty of a painting lies 30% in the painting itself and 70% in the mounting thereof. In high spirits, the American guests had great fun trying to repair a painting themselves.

In the *Exhibition of Finest Cultural Relics Collected in the Palace Museum*, there was the golden tower Emperor Qianlong ordered the craftsmen to customize for his mother Empress Dowager Chongqing, a set of golden bells with Chinese dragon patterns, the golden celestial globe made by the Imperial Workshop of Qing Dynasty, the gorgeous chalice of eternal stability, the Qianlong pastel bottle painted with nine peaches that is shaped like a celestial body, the Lang-kiln red-glazed Guanyin statue, the intricately carved rectangular lacquer case painted with landscape and figures, and the 3,000-year-old bronze ritual utensils, etc.

There was also a magnificent scroll on display—the Silk Road Map. It was painted in the late 16th century, 30.12 meters in length and 0.59 meters in width. The map depicts the vast area from Jiayuguan in Gansu Province, China to Tianfang City, which is known as the holy city of Mecca in Saudi Arabia today. It covers nine contemporary countries, and with precious geographic information along the ancient Silk Road, it has high artistic and important historical value.

The Palace Museum undertakes a great many diplomatic receptions every year. When heads of state and delegations from various countries visit the Palace Museum, we will introduce traditional Chinese culture displayed in the Palace Museum, such as the red walls, the yellow tiles, and the blue sky. The three primary colors can create any color in the world. Our world must be colorful, not monochromatic. Every nation has a proud history and a future to look forward to. Today, when leaders of various countries, foreign delegations, and Chinese and foreign visitors walk in the Palace

◢ With First Lady Michelle Obama (March 21, 2014).

Museum, seeing the well-repaired ancient architectures of the Palace Museum that appear so magnificent, so healthy, and so dignified, they will inevitably be moved by China's active efforts and contributions to the protection of world cultural heritage.

In fact, in addition to receiving heads of state, the Palace Museum has also held various cultural activities in recent years, like Ambassadors to China in the Palace Museum, to spread Chinese traditional culture to foreigners, strengthen communication and contact with embassies of various countries in China, and promote its international exchanges and cooperation. In 2012, the Palace Museum hosted the first Ambassadors to China in the Palace Museum event. The ambassadors from Australia, Egypt, Italy, Turkey and other countries and their spouses visited the Palace Museum and experienced its cultural charm. In 2013, the Ambassadors to China in the Palace Museum event invited representatives and officials from various United Nations organizations in China, including: the United Nations Development Programme, the

United Nations World Food Programme, the International Labor Organization, the United Nations Children's Fund, the International Monetary Fund, the World Health Organization, the United Nations Environment Programme, UNESCO, the United Nations Asia-Pacific Agricultural Engineering and Machinery Center, the United Nations High Commissioner for Refugees, etc.

The Palace Museum attaches great importance to communication and exchanges with embassies in China and international organizations and institutions in Beijing. In 2014 and 2015, Ambassadors to China in the Palace Museum was a special event for the Russian Embassy in China and the U.S. Embassy in China. In 2016, the Palace Museum cooperated with the Foreign Affairs Committee of the National People's Congress to host Ambassadors to China in the Palace Museum. Ambassadors or ministers from 15 countries visited the Palace Museum. In the same year, it cooperated with the Foreign Affairs Bureau of the Ministry of Culture to hold Consuls to China in the Palace Museum, and consuls from consulates of 11 countries in China attended the event. In 2017, 16 embassies in China, 12 ambassadors to China and 48 diplomatic officials to China were invited and visited the Palace Museum.

In 2018, Ambassadors to China in the Palace Museum invited ambassadors from 38 countries including Spain, Cameroon, Samoa, Tajikistan, Chile, Jamaica, and more, as well as 110 high-level diplomats and their families from the U.S., the UK, Japan, and South Korea to visit the Palace Museum. During the visit, they appreciated the grandeur and magnificence of the Palace Museum, and the rich connotation of traditional Chinese culture, and experienced the new charm of the modern digital technology applied in the Palace Museum.

In traditional Chinese culture, the central hall is the most important place of a house as it is a concentrated display of the host's cultural accomplishment. The Palace Museum is to China, what the central hall is to the house. Able to represent the national image and display Chinese civilization, it plays the role of a "national parlor" in China's foreign exchanges. It has become a business card and bridge for Sino-foreign exchanges. Foreign political heavyweights who come to China can easily learn about the cultural roots of the country by walking into this "national parlor."

Today, the Palace Museum is becoming a window for the world to understand China. We hope that people from all over the world can have a deeper understanding of Chinese culture through the Palace Museum. Meanwhile, we respect and cherish the cultures of all countries in the world. When advocating "respecting difference" and building a "community with a shared future," the Palace Museum is willing to serve as a "cultural parlor" to promote cultures from all over the world, and be a better platform for cultural exchanges between China and foreign countries.

CHAPTER 8

More Fun in the Palace Museum

Today we realize that it is best that cultural products are creative. Cultural and creative products must be practical, preferably fun, and able to enrich people's cultural life.

The cultural creativity of the Palace Museum is one of the most discussed and concerned topics among the media and the public. Representing an approachable Palace Museum, it is widely popular among young people thanks to spreading rapidly on the Internet.

Both the Cultural and Creative Experience Center and the Cultural and Creative Shop have opened outside the Palace Museum, so the public, without entering it, can check out and purchase its cultural and creative products. The Forbidden City culture gets closer to the public as visitors can sip coffee in its ice cellar café and shop for cultural and creative products outside its walls.

The Fantastic Cultural and Creative Products

———

Recently, the cultural and creative industry of Chinese museums has been blooming. The Palace Museum has developed a total of over 10,000 kinds of cultural and creative products, forming a diversified series of cultural and creative products. And they have won dozens of awards in related fields. There are many people who have had a new understanding of the Palace Museum through these products, and fell in love with it.

In 2010, the online store Treasures of the Palace Museum opened, which sells the Palace Museum's self-developed cultural and creative products. At the beginning, those products severely lacked originality. They were mostly imitations of other cultural products. Although there were a dozen series of them, in general, they performed poorly on practicality, fun, and interaction. In the past, more than 80% of the cultural products sold in the Palace Museum stores were supplied from third parties. And it was impossible for museums to sell whatever was popular, because what visitors expected to bring home were souvenirs related to the museum culture. Then, we adjusted our business thinking, added creative designs to the cultural products of the Palace Museum, and integrated the cultural resources of the Palace Museum into people's lives. Our development of cultural products is purely based on the cultural expectation of the public. By exploiting these cultural resources for the development, popular cultural and creative products come into being.

We have developed quite a few hot products. For example, as smart phones are widely used, the Palace Museum has continued to design unique phone cases; there are also the phone chargers called Upright and Righteous, flash drives, and earphones called Court Beads, which are popular among young people; we are offering the enameled teapot set based on the enameled teapots in the five colors of red, yellow, green, purple, and black that were once used by the five emperors of the Qing Dynasty. The set is called Five & Five; we have designed building blocks with Palace Museum elements for children and purses with Palace Museum elements for women; there are handbags and business card holders with the sea and cliff patterns from the imperial robes; there are handkerchiefs and shawls of various colors with phoenix and wintersweet patterns from ancient dresses; there are ties and fruit forks with the white horse pattern from the painting *The Qianlong Emperor in Ceremonial Armor on Horseback*; there are teapots and water cups in the shape of the four-sheep lei (wine vessel), which can be both a domestic ornament and an useful utensil to serve tea to house guests; the caisson in Hall of Supreme Harmony is famous. In order to let people take the caisson culture home, we have designed the caisson umbrellas; the gates in the Palace Museum usually leave the public a deep impression. Therefore, bags painted with the gates in the Palace Museum are made available; Emperor Yongzheng's painting *Twelve Beauties* is popular, so we customized *Twelve Beauties* outfits and *Twelve Beauties* umbrellas for the four seasons of spring, summer, autumn and winter; the cultural and creative products with the theme of Five Oxen are suitable ornaments in the vestibule; inspired by the exquisite C-shaped jade dragon of the Hongshan Culture donated by Fu Xinian's father, Fu Zhongmo, we have designed incense holders and imperial incense; the ornamental beasts on the eaves of Hall of Supreme Harmony inspired us to make checkers and clothes clips; based on two cute little pottery figurines, we developed unique toothpick-holders.

⬚ Tie.   ⬚ Embroidery.

In the autumn of 2017, the Palace Museum held the annual exhibition *A Thousand Li of Rivers and Mountains—Special Exhibition of Landscape Paintings of Past Dynasties* in the exhibition hall of the Sparrow Wings Tower at the Meridian Gate. While planning it, the Palace Museum had already commenced the research and development of related cultural and creative products. It designed and developed over 20 categories and over 150 kinds of cultural and creative products with the theme of *A Thousand Li of Rivers and Mountains*, such as the *A Thousand Li of Rivers and Mountains* fans, whose silk surface shows part of the painting. The fan uses traditional Song Dynasty brocade on the edge, a mahogany handle, and with a sandalwood carving as the frame. It has appeared multiple times at the reception of state guests, conveying the long history, elegance, and solemnity of traditional Chinese culture to international guests. And the small fan is easily affordable, priced only RMB 85. Within a year, it sold a total of 40,000 in the physical and online stores of the Palace Museum. It is one of the most popular products among this series of cultural and creative products. In addition, there are slightly more expensive folding fans, which are priced at RMB 258. The cultural and creative products with high, medium, and low prices better cater to the cultural needs of different customers.

After six years of hard work, by the end of 2018, the Palace Museum had developed a total of 10,500 cultural and creative products. With both online and offline sales, it achieved annual sales that exceeded RMB 1 billion. Through the cultural and creative products, we are transforming the traditional culture contained in the cultural symbol of the Palace Museum into popular culture that is more acceptable and more in line with current aesthetics.

◾ Five Oxen.   ◾ Fruit Forks.

To summarize the reasons for the success of the cultural creativity of the Palace Museum, I believe they are: "four principles," "five categories," "multiple channels," and "three tricks."

The Palace Museum's cultural and creative product development follows four principles, which were summarized from practical experience and key to its success. These four principles are: oriented to the needs of the public, based on the research findings of the collections, supported by the research and development of cultural creativity, and premised on the fine quality of cultural products. Under the guidance of these four principles, the cultural and creative products of the Palace Museum have gradually built their distinctive features and styles.

The Palace Museum, committed to making full use of its rich cultural resources, combines independent research and development and cooperative research and development, and humbly receives public help to design and develop cultural and creative products. Meanwhile, according to different social needs and audience, there are distinctions in the categories of the cultural and creative products.

First, there are state gifts. Among the cultural and creative products of the Palace Museum, there are many state gifts that represent the image of China, like the hand-embroidered shawl with phoenix patterns inspired by the Vair (fur of squirrels) Outer Garment with Moonlight White Kesi (a kind of silk), and Phoenix and Plum Blossom Patterns, one of the many collections of the Palace Museum. The main patterns are the Chinese character 寿 (*shou*, longevity), a phoenix, and plum blossom around. They are classic traditional Chinese patterns. The beautiful shawl is made of silk and hand-embroidered. It is given as a state gift to foreign heads of state.

The second is educational products. Books published by The Forbidden City Publishing House are also an important part of the cultural and creative products of the Palace Museum. And they cover three topics: imperial culture, cultural relics and art, and Ming and Qing history. There have been several series of publications such as the *Palace Museum Collections*, the *Palace Museum Classics*, and the *Palace Museum Books*. They play an important role in demonstrating the research findings of the Palace Museum, and promoting the culture of the Forbidden City with the help of exhibitions. And they are well received and praised among the majority of readers.

The third is the quality life series. For example, there is the popular "sea waves and cliffs" series, including table flags, placemats, tissue boxes, candy boxes, laptop bags, wallets, passport holders, business card holders, and handbags. Their exterior is made of brocade with the patterns of golden sea waves and cliffs, while their interior uses leather or silk, a perfect combination of royal vibes and modern fashion.

The fourth is the fashion series. For example, elements of the gates in the Palace Museum, including doornails and golden knockers are seen on the "Palace Museum Gate" suitcases. Made of super fiber leather, they take the red of the Palace Museum walls as the main color, and have functional layers inside, which are rather practical. The Heavenly Blessings series of pottery tea sets have the elements of ruyi and auspicious clouds of the Palace Museum. Glazed blue or black, they look simple and elegant, reflecting modern aesthetics and traditional redesign concepts.

Next, there is the mass trend series. People have been calling our cultural and creative products "cute." For example, there is the widely popular "imperial doll family." As soon as they were launched, they won the hearts of teenagers. They are cute dolls with the identities of the imperial family, including the "little emperor," the "little empress," the "little prince," the "little princess," the "little imperial guard," the "little eight-banner dolls," the "number one scholar," etc. These dolls are all designed to be cute. They are made into bobblehead dolls, car dolls, phone holders, tableside dolls, seasoning jars, piggy banks, bonsai basins, creative ornaments, note clips, refrigerator magnets, key chains, jewelry boxes, etc. However, the "cute" products are not the mainstream cultural and creative products of the Palace Museum. They merely account for 5% of the total Palace Museum products.

Also, the Palace Museum has opened up various channels to display and disseminate cultural creativity.

The first channel is the physical store. A variety of channels have been opened up to make it easy for the public to purchase the various cultural and creative products of the Palace Museum. As per the commodity categories and visitor distribution, the marketing network of the Palace Museum has been re-planned, the environment and service facilities upgraded, and the display and dissemination of cultural creativity incorporated into the overall development of the Palace Museum to render the visitors high-quality services.

In September 2015, the Cultural and Creative Experience Center started operations in the East Long Rooms of the Palace Museum. As the "last exhibition hall" of the Palace Museum, the Cultural and Creative Experience Center is committed to displaying and selling the various cultural and creative products developed by the Palace Museum. It aims to make sure each product is a fine product that integrates history, knowledge, art, fun, fashion and practicality through innovative design on the basis of mining the cultural resources of the Palace Museum. At present, the Cultural and Creative Experience Center is divided into eight distinctive exhibition halls, including the Silk Hall, the Garment Hall, the Royal Kiln Hall, the Video Hall, the Wood Art Hall, the Copper Art Hall, the Ceramic Art Hall and the Palace Museum Academy. They exhibit totally different cultural and creative products, thus are able to meet the various needs of different customers. The Cultural and Creative Experience Center has made extra efforts in many aspects such as product display, cultural ambience, and thematic design. In addition to concentrated display and sales of various cultural and creative products developed by the Palace Museum, it creates an elegant, vivid and rich traditional cultural ambience, where the visitors can have an immersive experience of the Forbidden City culture.

In addition, the Palace Museum stores in the Gate of Correct Deportment West Rooms have earned a fine reputation for their beautiful interior design, exquisite layout, various themes, and distinctive features. Moreover, the east and west sides outside the Gate of Divine Prowess have been redesigned into two rows of cultural corridors of the Palace Museum to display and sell the fine books and cultural and creative products of the Palace Museum, thus better spreading the Forbidden City culture and facilitating the visitors' purchase.

Both the Cultural and Creative Experience Center and the Cultural and Creative Shop are open outside the Palace Museum, so the public, without entering it, can check out and purchase its cultural and creative products. The Forbidden City culture gets closer to the public as visitors can sip coffee in its ice cellar café and shop for cultural and creative products outside its walls.

The second channel is new media promotion. Besides physical stores, the Internet and new media are equally important channels for the display and dissemination of the Palace Museum's cultural creativity. In addition to the official flagship store of Treasures of the Palace Museum mentioned above, the Palace Museum Wechat Store was opened in December 2015. It aims to sell exquisite life products to promote an elegant life style. The store can be accessed to from the official WeChat account of the Palace Museum. The merchandises available there are not only exquisitely designed, but have profound historical and cultural charm. At present, the Palace Museum WeChat store sells six themed cultural and creative products, including paintings, ceramics, stationery, writings, clothing, and other products.

The third channel is other forms of promotion. The form and content of the dissemination of the Forbidden City culture are becoming increasingly vivid, lively, and diverse. For example, in June 2016, the Palace Museum held *The Grand View of Famous Paintings—the Night Revels of Han Xizai* Digital Art Exhibition, where the antique garden landscape of *Misty Rain in Suzhou* was restored, as well as the life scenes of ancient literati, including the ancient Nanyin music, operatic dances, flower ceremony, tea ceremony, incense ceremony, etc. The life aesthetics of the Forbidden City were gracefully extended through time and space there. Also, cultural and creative products of the Palace Museum are available on the Royal Caribbean cruise ship, spreading the Forbidden City culture. Subsequently, the Palace Museum cooperated with Alibaba and Tencent. It opened the Official Flagship Store of the Palace Museum that sells tickets, cultural and creative products, and publications on Flypig and Tmall of Alibaba to maximize the diversification of functional requirements. The cooperation with Tencent started with taking the NEXTIDEA Tencent Innovation Competition as the platform to explore the exploitation of traditional cultural IPs, which could cut in from emoji design and video game design. These actions have widened the path for Palace Museum's Culture +.

The Palace Museum is exploring ways to lead the public lifestyle, too. It does not only develop cultural and creative products that can be integrated into daily life, but has opened the Palace Museum Academy, its cultural experience center that intends to spread life aesthetics for the first time outside its walls in the Yantian District of the southern China city of Shenzhen. With the mission to enable the public to "take the Forbidden City culture home," the Palace Museum Academy, themed with "books, paintings and calligraphy, study, and elegant lifestyle," uses contemporary design and creativity to build a contemporary cultural space with a traditional literary vibe. At present, branches of the Palace Museum have been opened in the cities of Jingdezhen, Zhuhai, Fuzhou, Wuyishan (Fujian Province), and Qingdao. In the future, there will be more all over China to realize the multi-layer and diversified dissemination and promotion of the Forbidden City culture.

In 2017, the cultural and creative products and brands of the Palace Museum attempted international promotions. Internationally, they have attended events such as International Stationery and Office Supplies Exhibition in Frankfurt, Venice Art Biennale Exhibition—Past and Present, and the International Brand Licensing Expo in Las Vegas. Domestically, they have participated in China's Intangible Cultural Heritage of Traditional Techniques Exhibition, the Cultural and Creative Industry Expo in Hangzhou, the International Cultural Relics Protection Equipment Expo, the Cross-Straits (Xiamen) Cultural Industry Expo and Trade Fair, etc. As a result, the cultural and creative products of the Palace Museum are appearing in museums around the world.

Moreover, in May 2018, the Palace Museum held a special exhibition in Japan—*Bring Cultural Relics to Life—Palace Museum Cultural and Creative Products*. It intensively displayed part of the four series of bronze, lacquerware, porcelain, and wood products. The creation of all these cultural and creative products was inspired by the

⛰ Cats and the Forbidden City series.

⬛ Gates in the Palace Museum and Themed Backpacks.

cultural relics of the Palace Museum. By digging deep into traditional craftsmanship, we handcrafted them. As the finest of the Palace Museum's cultural and creative products, they realize the inheritance of intangible cultural heritage.

The most important thing for the Palace Museum is to create our own cultural Intellectual Property. At last, on performing well on cultural creativity, we have three tips to share: deep research, careful observation and analysis, and effective use of creativity. The more people like the products, the more necessary it is to improve their quality, the more effective brand building. Today, as the public demand for a better life is increasing, the requirements for cultural and creative products are higher. They must have not only rich cultural content, but good quality, such as environmental-friendliness and strong practicability.

In this way, I believe great cultural creativity is bound to happen.

The Palace Museum Brand

I believe that the public has noticed the stronger influence of the Palace Museum's cultural creativity. However, we are deeply aware that cultural creativity alone is not enough. More importance must be attached to openness, meaning that traditional culture should interact with the Internet to form cultural spaces open to the public, and that people's rights to know, to participate, to supervise and to benefit from the status quo of cultural relics protection must be guaranteed. As a result, cultural relics protection can become a practice open to everyone, and museums a second classroom for students. The Palace Museum is determined to become a true well-known cultural brand.

In addition to continuing the traditional public education service projects, the Palace Museum has built a brand in social education. Annually, it organizes 25,000 public education activities of various types, receiving 200,000 participants. And the representative brands of public education service projects are the public education platforms such as the Palace Museum Forum and the Palace Museum Classroom.

The Palace Museum Forum is a thematic lecture for adults. Both the elderly over 60 and the youth in their 20s are loyal fans of this brand. The lecture experts are mostly famous scholars from the Palace Museum and young and younger core experts. The lecture content revolves closely around the Forbidden City culture that covers ancient architecture, research and appreciation of cultural relics, history of Ming and Qing Dynasties, scientific and technological protection of the cultural relics, protection of intangible cultural heritage, etc. The lectures of some popular experts were so desirable

📷 The 100th Lecture of Palace Museum Forum (February 12, 2017).

that all seats were taken and some audiences had to stand throughout. In 2017, Palace Museum Forum won the award Beloved Brand of Lifelong Learning.

The Palace Museum Classroom was launched in 2006. Oriented at teenagers, it was more relaxing, more lively and more participatory, thus widely praised by teenagers and their parents. Tens of thousands of teenagers took part in the activities of the Palace Museum Classroom, gaining knowledge while having fun.

In addition, there is also the brand Palace Museum Academy, which offers professional talent training. Established in 2013, it was mainly engaged in training staff of the Palace Museum, training Chinese museums and related industries, public education, and international training. The training content covers the fields of imperial history and culture, identification, restoration, and protection of cultural relics, preservation of ancient architecture, museum management, etc. It gave consideration to both knowledge and skills, and theories and practice. The Palace Museum Academy serves the Palace Museum, and radiates its services to museums and related industries at home and abroad. It has gradually become an important talent training base in museology.

Palace Museum Services is another equally well-known brand. In recent years, the Palace Museum has been creating conditions to expand the open area, so that the public can visit more and more ancient architecture of different styles. The overall renovation and preservation project of the ancient architecture of the Palace Museum and the Safe Palace Museum project secure the safety of the visitors and the Palace Museum, thus laying a solid foundation for its future development; total demolition of the color steel rooms and temporary buildings, removal of the iron railings that extended thousands of meters, restoration of the traditional masonry flooring, flattening of the manhole covers, installation of lanterns, and planting more trees and flowers create a clean and pleasant visiting environment; the reform in service management has been intensified: online ticket sales, daily visitor quantity limit, additional seats, optimized proportion of toilets, and baby care rooms together offer more complete services to the visitors. They build the concept and cultural brand of Palace Museum Services.

In 2017, the Beijing Municipal Commission of Tourism Development and the Palace Museum co-published *Palace Museum Services*. This book comprehensively demonstrates a series of practices of the Palace Museum in improving public services for the visitors in recent years. It sets the example for domestic and foreign museums and tourist destinations. I once used the eight words, "sincere," "worry-free," "safe," "original," "satisfying," "pleasing," "comfortable," and "passionate" to summarize the service of the Palace Museum to the visitors. Essentially, it implements a humanized and people-oriented service concept with the purpose of having the cultural resources of the Palace Museum enter people's daily lives. This is a management revolution, whose core is that all daily work is centered on the convenience of the visitors. Different service concepts will definitely have different effects. In the future, the Palace Museum staff will earnestly fulfill our mission and responsibilities, and build the better and stronger concept and cultural brand of Palace Museum Services.

At present, there are 38 departments (divisions) in the Palace Museum. Among them, four teams take charge of its cultural and creative product research and development: Operational Management Department, Cultural Relics Service Center, Palace Museum Publishing, and the Data Center. Among them, Palace Museum Publishing has become a famous cultural brand.

The Palace Museum founded Palace Museum Publishing in 1983, publishing books related to Forbidden City culture. There is a Palace Museum Culture Communication Company affiliated to it, which is responsible for the promotion and marketing of cultural and creative products and publications. Palace Museum Publishing makes the Forbidden City culture "alive on paper" through their books, magazines, postcards, and so on. All cultural relics selected in the *Compendium of Collections in the Palace Museum* are rare world treasures, and most of them are shown to the public for the first time. The book holds an extremely high academic and cultural value. *The Complete Collection of Ming and Qing Furniture Collections in the Palace Museum* incorporates nearly 2,000 pieces of furniture collected in the Palace Museum, covering almost all types of furniture in Ming and Qing Dynasties, especially imperial-style pieces. The *Mysterious Palace Puzzle Book* innovatively designs this unique physical book + online puzzle-solving, allowing readers to experience a new artistic conception and new fun with the Forbidden City culture.

Among the many publications, the more well-known is the *Palace Museum Calendar*. In 2009, it was reprinted and published on the basis of the 1937 edition. The *Palace Museum Calendar* is popular reading material that introduces the collections of the Palace Museum and spreads traditional culture. It carries the history and culture of the Forbidden City. The content, text, and pictures, on each page is carefully selected so that the essence of traditional Chinese culture is demonstrated in the rich cultural relics collection of the Palace Museum and the profound cultural connotation. As soon as the *Palace Museum Calendar* came out, it went viral in the cultural and creative circles. And a bilingual version in Chinese and English and customized versions were later launched. It became one of the representatives of the cultural and creative products of the Palace Museum.

Now, the Palace Museum brand has started cultural dissemination; in the future, we will continue to make it bigger and stronger, so that the Forbidden City culture reaches hundreds of millions of people and leaves footprints all over the world.

The Power of Culture

I grew up in a quadrangle dwellings, and I have never imagined myself working in "the world's largest quadrangle dwellings," where the four seasons of spring, summer, autumn and winter are distinct. There, we get down-to-earth, and we look forward to the future.

In fact, long before I became Director of the Palace Museum, I had been deeply fascinated with every inch of the Forbidden City. In 1989, my son was five years old and my wife was studying abroad. Usually, my parents-in-law took care of the boy, except the Sundays. He asked me where I would take him for fun on Sunday. I told him that we would go to see where the emperor lived. Our destination was the Palace Museum. The next Sunday, we went there again. On the third Sunday, he showed obvious unwillingness to go. For five consecutive Sundays, I took my son to work. I photographed many details of the Forbidden City and studied them carefully. I wanted to read the magnificent imperial ancient architecture as a book instead of a mere tourist attraction.

Since my "gatekeeping" days at the Palace Museum, every morning at 8:00 a.m., I would patrol around it clockwise. The media reports wrote that I was "the first to walk through the 9,371 ancient architectures of the Forbidden City," and "the first to accurately measure the number of collections in the Palace Museum to single digits." I believe that is simply the duty of a "gatekeeper." One news agency noticed that I always wear cloth shoes, and asked if it is easy to get them. I answered that I just ordered 20 pairs online. Soon, the story of me wearing out 20 pairs of shoes within five months of taking office came out. In fact, during the years of my "gatekeeping" the Palace Museum, there were more than 20 pairs of shoes worn out. Walking in the Forbidden City in the cloth shoes, when the dawn broke, when the sun set, when the moon rose, I felt the happiness of quietly guarding the Forbidden City from the bottom of my heart.

The 600-year-old Forbidden City has carried a long history with rich memories, and has witnessed the changes of the times. At present, whether museums, or the related academia, cultural relics circle, and the media all ready to reform, or already going through it. For a long time, museums have been worried and complained that despite the long history and rich culture in the precious cultural relics exhibited, many people would rather go shopping than visit a museum. When the public think of museums, they show little interest. Cold and boring are used to describe the cultural relics in the showcases. Many visitors merely take a few pictures and quickly leave. Hardly do they gain any knowledge. How to bring the cultural heritage resources of the Palace Museum to life is an important topic that it should think about, study and practice.

In my opinion, cultural relics themselves are alive. Time does not pass them quietly without leaving a trace. We simply have to discover it; the value of cultural relics does not come from us but themselves. Even without historical knowledge, we should stay curious and approach them, so that they get the dignity they deserve. I believe that in the future, we will look at them differently—culture far above the artifacts.

Today, the construction and development of the Palace Museum have received support from all walks of life. The Palace Museum is going to repay the society by holding better exhibitions and more colorful activities. In 2019, it received a notice that Beijing requested to light up the city's central axis. At the time, the employees of the Palace Museum had already started their vacations. On the third day of the Spring Festival holiday, we called back the relevant personnel to start preparations. After four days of research and development and eight days of installation, the Palace Museum was opened to the public for the first time on the 15th day of the first lunar month as scheduled at night. It was the first massive night illumination in the Forbidden City.

People climbed the city walls of the Forbidden City and attended a series of connected exhibition halls, including the *Lunar New Year—Celebration in the Forbidden City* in the Sparrow Wing Towers of the Meridian Gate, *The Architectural Art Exhibition of the Forbidden City* in East Prosperity Gate, and *Relics of the Aegean—Exhibition of Underwater Archaeological Relics of Antikythera, Greece* in Gate of Divine Prowess. Also, in the exhibition halls, they could enjoy the artists' performances. Along the city walls, visitors could see the splendid illuminated Forbidden City, and the magnificent full projections of *Along the River during the Qingming Festival* and *A Thousand Li of Rivers and Mountains* on the roof of the ancient architectures. They could watch a Peking Opera from the artists in the Belvedere of Pleasant Sound, watch a video clip in the Corner Tower, and walk down the city walls to read the Lantern Festival verses projected on the red walls. For two consecutive nights, the Palace Museum hosted model workers from Beijing and Beijing citizens who had made appointment in advance. Meanwhile, ambassadors and diplomats from 125 countries attended the event, too. The Palace Museum at night was a cultural experience that they have never had before. Hundreds of domestic and foreign media have widely shared to the world the fascinating night color of the Forbidden City, one that embraces modern urban life, one that unremittingly strives to meet the cultural needs of the public, one that presents itself with a new image.

The installation of sky lanterns and longevity lanterns in the Ming and Qing Dynasties was one of the most important imperial activities, but since the Opium War in 1840, the Qing Dynasty weakened. It was no longer able to install sky lanterns and longevity lanterns in front of Palace of Heavenly Purity. In 2019, the 70th anniversary of the PRC, the Palace Museum re-installed a pair of 11-meter-high longevity lanterns, and a pair of 14-meter-high sky lanterns in front of the Palace of Heavenly Purity. Many visitors came to witness this installation, and a group photo was taken of ambassadors from 80 countries in front of the lanterns.

The three-month *Lunar New Year—Celebration in the Forbidden City* exhibition ended. But the longevity lanterns, sky lanterns and palace lanterns that we worked hard to develop should not go to waste but remain in the city. Therefore, the Palace Museum held a public charitable auction, whose total proceeds were donated to the national-level poverty-stricken counties. The auction received wide public support. In the end, the longevity lanterns, sky lanterns and palace lanterns sold for more than RMB 20 million, and every penny was donated to four poverty-stricken counties in Guangxi Province and the Inner Mongolia Autonomous Region. Despite the modest donation amount, we were very proud. Usually, museums receive donations from the public. Today, the Palace Museum can donate to the public. Poverty alleviation is the most important task of the times in China, and the Palace Museum is honored to be a part of it and contribute to building a moderately prosperous society in an all-round way.

The Palace Museum's practice has proved that effective cultural heritage protection is that, instead of locking cultural heritage resources in warehouses, cultural heritage is brought back into social life, because cultural heritage originally comes from the ordinary people in the society. Today, efforts should be made to make cultural heritage work their unique charm in the public's life again. Only in this way will the public care about them; only when cared about, can they be dignified; only when dignified, can they promote social development. When the abundant cultural heritage resources of China becomes a positive force for social development after systematic sorting and scientific protection, more people are benefited and more people are encouraged to be part of cultural heritage protection. This is what effective cultural heritage protection should be, and this is how a virtuous circle of cultural heritage protection comes into being.

今年春色胜常全

此夜风光最可怜

鳷鹊楼前新月满

凤凰台上宝灯燃

The Palace Museum's practice has also demonstrated what makes a good museum. A good museum is not defined by an enormous premise, a rich collection of cultural relics, or a growing number of visitors. A good museum performs an in-depth study of people's actual needs and an in-depth excavation of its cultural resources. It generates strong cultural energy, constantly launches fascinating exhibitions, and constantly holds colorful activities, so that people can feel its presence in their life. They are willing to visit it during their spare time, feel reluctant to leave it, and are eager to return to visit it again.

It is necessary to systematically sort out traditional cultural resources, so that the cultural relics stored in the Forbidden City, the heritage displayed on the vast land, and the words written in the ancient books come back to life. It is precisely because the Palace Museum unswervingly implements the concept of "bring the cultural relics to life" that through arduous efforts, it can now fulfill the solemn promise of "Hand the magnificent Forbidden City over intact to the next 600 years."

At Metropolitan Museum of Art, China: Through the Looking Glass, exhibition press conference.

With Alessandro Nova, Director of the German Studies Center in Florence, Italy.

With Mr. Geng Baochang.

Receiving Professor Wu Liangyong's visit to the Palace Museum.

Representatives of Taihe Forum on Protecting the World's Ancient Civilizations visited the Palace Museum Cultural Relics Hospital.

The on-site meeting on the maintenance and protection of the ancient architecture of the Palace of Mental Cultivation in the Palace Museum.

⬛ Service Team during the National Day.

⬛ Enthusiastic listeners of the themed report.

⊡ A corner of *Lunar New Year—Celebration in the Forbidden City* exhibition at the Sparrow Wing Towers of the Meridian Gate.

Index

A

Aftermath Committee of Royal Family of
Qing, 2, 3, 16
Alibaba, 282
Along the River during the Qingming Festival,
49, 70, 83, 85, 106, 230, 233, 235, 236,
237, 295
Anhui, 54, 59, 75, 156, 259
Area of Six Western Palaces, 9, 151
Associated Press, 267
Australia, 114, 262, 264, 271

B

bamboo, wood, ivory, and rhino horn
carvings, 49, 60
Beijing, 4, 5, 10, 15, 29, 31, 34, 39, 55,
100, 103, 108, 109, 115, 119, 133, 134,
139, 169, 177–79, 195, 203, 247, 249,
251, 263, 266–68, 272, 289, 294, 295
Beiyang government, 2
Belvedere of Literary Profundity, 74
Belvedere of Pleasant Sounds, 74
Bite of China, A, 163

Board of Great Benevolence, 65
bonsai, 31, 32, 64, 153, 280
British Museum, 18, 261, 264, 265
bronze, 3, 5, 8–10, 49, 51–53, 63, 68,
70, 71, 98, 114, 132, 152, 162, 165,
168–71, 173, 270, 283
Bronzeware, 49, 52, 53, 68, 132, 152, 162,
165, 168–70, 173

C

Caisson of Hall of Supreme Harmony, 40
Canada, 262, 264
Carrie Lam Cheng Yuet-ngor, 257, 260
Castiglione, Giuseppe, 68
Central Academy of Fine Arts, 13
central axis, 7, 9, 33, 93, 134, 145, 189,
249, 294
ceramics, 47, 49, 68, 74, 75, 94, 98, 99,
121–22, 124, 132–33, 162, 269, 282
Ceramics Gallery, 74, 98
China Central TV (CCTV), 104, 162, 244,
246, 254
Chinese Academy of Social Sciences, 13

Chu Shi Song, 66, 70
Clinton, Bill, 267
Cloisonné, 57
Corner Towers, 7, 138, 139, 141, 192, 238, 295

D
Donghuamen, 29
Dong Qing, 245
Douban, 163, 245
Dresden State Art Collection, 264
Dunhuang, 263

E
East China Bureau of the CPC, 5
Eight Banners, 62, 110, 111
embroidery, 28, 39, 49, 53, 54, 71, 155, 165, 172, 175, 255, 269
Emperor Daoguang, 193
Emperor Huizong, 8, 87
Emperor Kangxi, 50, 59, 114, 145, 162, 177
Emperor Qianlong, 47, 49, 50, 52, 59, 71, 151, 155, 190, 193, 251, 252, 270
Emperor Xuantong, 192
Emperor Yongle, 35, 82, 143, 192
Emperor Yongzheng, 59, 151–52, 175, 277
Empress Dowager Chongqing, 190, 270
enamels, 49
enamelware, 56, 58, 255
Engravings, 51

F
Fifth Session of the 12th CPPCC National Committee, 128
Five Oxen, 49, 70, 277, 279
Forbidden City, 2–12, 14–16, 18–25, 29–39, 41, 44, 45, 47, 51–56, 58, 59, 60, 62, 64–65, 67, 68, 70–71, 73–76, 82–84, 92, 95, 110, 117, 120–21, 124, 127–29, 133–35, 138–40, 142–51, 153–58, 160–67, 172, 175, 177, 179, 184, 189, 190, 192, 193, 195–97, 199–202, 205–10, 212, 213, 215, 218–28, 230, 232, 233, 238, 239, 241, 247–53, 257, 258, 262, 264, 267, 268, 269, 280–84, 287, 290, 291, 293–95, 299
Forbidden City Classical Flower Center, 34
Forbidden City Publishing House, The, 117, 134, 219, 220, 235, 280
Foreign Affairs Bureau of the Ministry of Culture, 272
Foreign Affairs Committee of the National People's Congress, 272
Furniture Gallery, 74
Fuzhou, 82, 283

G
Gallery of Clocks, 74, 92, 98
Gallery of Historical Architecture, 74
Gallery of Painting and Calligraphy, 74, 98
Gansu Province, 270
Gate of Correct Deportment, 207, 210, 230, 232, 240, 281
Gate of Divine Prowess, 11, 38, 82, 93, 127, 141, 145, 156, 209, 215, 249, 281, 295
Gate of Good Fortune, 33, 213
Gate of Heavenly Purity, 33, 203
Gate of Supreme Harmony, 33, 86, 99, 108, 111, 141, 145, 210, 268
Gate of Thriving Imperial Clan, 190, 212
Gauck, Joachim, 264
Germany, 64, 178, 255, 261, 264
Gugong Studies, 15, 19, 120–21, 124

Gulangyu, 249, 253–56
Guo Moruo, 5
guqin, 64, 266

H
Hall of All Peace, 74
Hall of Antiquities, 3, 4
Hall of Central Harmony, 9, 41, 139, 140, 268
Hall of Imperial Peace, 61
Hall of Imperial Supremacy, 7, 52, 74
Hall of Martial Valor, 47, 73, 82–85, 90, 91, 93, 192
Hall of Preserving Harmony, 9, 41, 139, 140, 268
Hall of Supreme Harmony, 9, 40, 41, 110, 138–40, 143, 145, 191, 213, 266, 268, 277
Hall of Union, 9, 41
Han Buddhism, 61
Henan Province, 52, 147, 173, 174
Hong Kong Heritage Museum, 256
Hong Kong Palace Museum, 256–258
Hong Kong SAR Government, 257, 260
Hong Kong Science Museum, 256–57

I
Imperial Garden, 31, 33, 129, 140, 154, 196, 209, 213, 239, 266
Imperial Garden VR, 239
Imperial Household Department, 34–35
Imperial Palace, 49, 50, 52, 56, 117, 120, 148, 210, 248, 252–53
inkstone, 54
Inner Golden Water River, 31, 35, 139
inscriptions, 5, 47, 49, 51–53, 131, 146, 173

Institute of Museum Legal Affairs, 124, 129
Institute of Palace Gardens, 124, 129
intangible cultural heritage, 14, 94, 114, 150, 156, 165, 169, 178, 226, 266, 270, 283, 286, 287
International Council of Museums, 261
International Labor Organization, 272
International Monetary Fund, 272

J
jade, 49, 59, 60, 64, 68, 71, 75, 124, 132, 152, 153, 155, 251, 261, 277
Japan, 4, 64, 178, 255, 256, 261, 264, 272, 283
Jiayuguan, 270
Jilin University, 13
Jingdezhen, 283

K
Kissinger, Henry, 267
Kuomintang, 5, 50

L
lacquerware, 49, 58, 64, 68, 70, 162, 165, 177, 255, 283
Land Silk Road, 125
Las Vegas, 283
Liaoning Provincial Museum, 244
Li Keqiang, 179, 264
Limonaire Brothers, 255
Louvre Museum, 18
Lunar New Year—Celebration in the Forbidden City, 75, 183, 200, 241, 295, 296, 302

M
Ma Heng, 3, 4, 5, 44

mahogany, 55, 278

Marco Polo Bridge Incident, 4

Maritime Silk Road, 75, 76, 82, 125, 262

Masters in the Forbidden City, 138, 162–65, 175, 177, 178

Mecca, 270

Melania, 267

Meridian Gate, 7, 33, 35, 38, 82, 86, 90, 93, 140, 145, 190, 210, 212, 230, 249, 262, 278, 295

Metropolitan Museum, 18, 261, 264, 300

Ming Dynasty, 35, 56, 68, 71, 82, 93, 131, 143, 151, 157, 190, 192

Ministry of Culture, 6, 14, 144, 272

Ministry of Housing and Urban-Rural Development, 143, 144

model calligraphy, 49–51, 68, 70

Moscow Kremlin Museums, 18

Mukden Incident, 4

N

Nanjing Museum, 244, 249, 252

National Committee of the Chinese People's Political Consultative Conference, 150

National Cultural Heritage Administration, 35, 50

National Day, 92, 93, 99, 145, 184, 196, 200, 251

National Museum of Afghanistan, 80, 262, 263

National Museum of Brazil, 24

National Treasure, 104, 244–45, 247, 261

New York, 264

Night Revels of Han Xizai, 70, 226, 282

Northern Song Dynasty, 70, 86, 87, 235, 236, 237

Notre Dame de Paris, 24

O

Obama, Barack, 267

Opium War, 295

P

Palace Museum, 2–21, 23–24, 27, 29–39, 44–52, 54–56, 58, 59, 61, 62, 64–68, 73–75, 81–88, 90, 91, 93–95, 97–117, 118, 119–35, 138–40, 142–44, 148–50, 152, 155, 157, 160–65, 167–69, 173, 175–79, 184–93, 195–203, 205–10, 212–13, 215, 218–23, 225–27, 229, 230, 232–33, 235–39, 241, 243, 244, 247–64, 266–73, 276–83, 285–91, 293–97, 299, 300

Palace Museum Cultural Relics Hospital, 105, 107, 108, 123, 258, 269

Palace of Accumulated Purity, 7, 141

Palace of Earthly Tranquility, 9, 61

Palace of Great Benevolence, 7, 65, 141

Palace of Heavenly Purity, 9, 41, 151, 241, 295

Palace of Longevity and Health, 74, 92, 190, 191

Palace of Tranquil Longevity, 52, 102, 154

Paris, 24, 255

Peking Opera, 266–68, 295

Peking University, 3, 13

Peng Liyuan, 266–67

People's Liberation Army, 6

Picture of Ten Poems, A, 66

porcelain, 58, 64, 68, 70, 75, 82, 93, 110, 133, 152, 165, 251, 255, 283

PRC, 34, 44, 49–52, 131, 139, 261, 295

pre-Ming, 64

pre-Qin, 52, 53, 173

President Nixon, 267

Prince William of England, 264

Q

Qi Baishi, 75, 252
Qingdao, 283

R

Reader, 245
red sandalwood, 28, 55
reform and opening up, 6, 261
Renmin University, 13
Royal Ontario Museum, 264
rubbings, 5, 51, 69, 114
ruyi, 64, 110, 114, 251, 280

S

Saudi Arabia, 270
Sculpture Gallery, 74, 92
seals, 49, 53, 71, 110
Shaanxi History Museum, 244
Shamanism, 61
Shang Dynasty, 8, 47, 51–53, 131
Shanghai, 4, 10, 14, 244
Shanghai Museum, 14
Shenzhen, 251, 263, 283
Sichuan, 125, 175, 262
Silk Road Landscape Map, 66
southeast Corner Towers, 7, 141
Sparrow Wing Towers, 7, 33, 35, 86, 91, 93,
   141, 190, 192, 249, 262, 295
Spring and Autumn Period, 52, 169, 173
State Council, 7, 11, 14, 25, 47, 150
State Hermitage Museum in Russia, 261,
   264
stationery, 49, 54, 55, 282
stone drums, 4, 51

T

tai chi, 266
Taipei, 15, 18, 50, 127, 128, 226
Taiwan, 5, 18, 50, 52
tanggu, 62
Taoism, 61
Taoist, 61, 157
Tencent, 129, 222, 282, 283
thangkas, 62, 71, 165, 175
Thousand Li of Rivers and Mountains, A, 49,
   75, 83, 86, 87, 90–93, 103, 233, 278,
   295
three back halls, 7
three front halls, 7
Tibetan Buddhism, 61, 71
Tokyo National Museum, 264
Tools of War Gallery, 74
Treasure Gallery, 74, 92, 98
Trudeau, Justin, 264
Trump, Donald, 267, 268, 269
Twelve Beauties, 226, 277

U

UNESCO, 114, 261, 272
UNESCO Intangible Cultural Heritage
   Lists, 114
United Nations Asia-Pacific Agricultural
   Engineering and Machinery Center, 272
United Nations Children's Fund, 272
United Nations Development Programme,
   271
United Nations Environment Programme,
   272
United Nations High Commissioner for
   Refugee, 272
United Nations World Food Programme,
   272

U.S. Embassy, 272

V

Valls, Manuel, 264
Vatican Museum, 81
Venice Art Biennale Exhibition, 283
volunteers, 85, 98–105, 107–9, 111, 115

W

War of Liberation, 4, 5, 173
War of Resistance, 4, 5, 12
Warring States, 51, 52, 58
WeChat, 105, 218–219, 222, 229, 282
Weibo, 105, 218–222, 229, 245
World Health Organization, 272
Wuyishan, 283

X

Xia Dynasty, 52
Xiamen, 249, 251, 253, 256, 283

Xiamen Municipal Museum, 251
Xi Jinping, 257, 264, 267–268

Y

Yi Peiji, 2, 4
Yongle period, 68
Yuan Dynasty, 56, 68, 70, 71, 86
yueqin, 62

Z

Zhang Zhongpei, 11, 12, 17, 22, 122
Zhejiang, 59, 262
Zhejiang Provincial Museum, 244
Zheng Xinmiao, 14, 17, 22, 45, 120, 122,
    131, 189
Zhengzhou, 263
Zhou Dynasty, 52, 53, 132, 147
Zhuhai, 283
Zhu Jiajin, 120, 132

ABOUT THE AUTHOR

Shan Jixiang, a native of Jiangning, Jiangsu Province, has a doctorate in engineering, is a research librarian, a senior architect, and a registered urban planner. He was formerly the Director of the Beijing Municipal Commission of Planning and Natural Resources, the Director of the National Cultural Heritage Administration, and the Director of the Palace Museum. He is currently a Researcher at the China Central Institute for Culture and History, the President of the Chinese Society of Cultural Relics, and the Director of the Academic Committee of the Palace Museum.